DOWNSTAIRS AT THE WHITE HOUSE

DONALD M. STINSON

Edited by Karin Kohlmeier, Ph.D.

DOWNSTAIRS AT THE WHITE HOUSE

Published by Eastern Harbor Press, LLC • Boca Raton, Florida
www.easternharborpress.com

Represented by Donaldson + Califf, LLP • Beverly Hills, California
www.donaldsoncallif.com

Published in the United States of America

ISBN-10: 0-692-95253-5
ISBN-13: 978-0-692-95253-5

Library of Congress Control Number: 2017915241

Edited by Karin Kohlmeier, Ph.D.
kkohlmeier@gmail.com

Cover design by R.J. Matson
rjmatsoncartoons@gmail.com

Citations available at www.downstairsatthewhitehouse.com

For Mom and Dad.

"In an emergency, the cows will be evacuated before you are."

— A White House veteran on the author's
importance to the nation.

ABOUT THE AUTHOR

 Don Stinson is a graduate of American University and a former newspaper executive. A truly insignificant member of the White House staff during the Watergate scandal, he frequently loitered outside of the Oval Office.

After the collapse of the Soviet Union, he worked with newspapers in Russia, Slovakia, and Poland to establish a free and independent press. His accomplishments included being held hostage in a smelting plant, sleeping in an insane asylum guarded by sheep herders, and fighting a goat defending a lavatory door on Russian airliner Aeroflot.

The goat won.

He (the author, not the goat) lives in Miami, Florida.

CONTENTS

ACKNOWLEDGEMENTS

My thanks and deep appreciation go to Elizabeth Stinson Ray, Esq., Christopher Stinson, Deb Jones, Karin Kohlmeier, Ph.D., Mark Adelman, M.D., Dean Cheley, Esq., Melissa Morse, Camellia Webb, the Richard Nixon Presidential Library, the Gerald R. Ford Presidential Library, the White House Historical Association, Emily Jones, Lucy Jones, Adam Howells, and David Frantz, Esq. for their help, support, and suggestions. Some of these folks read so many drafts that they could likely spit out every sentence from memory.

The debt of gratitude I owe to my late parents, Huey and Henrietta Stinson, is much larger than I can ever possibly repay. My Mom wanted the first copy of this book, an understandable request since she was still telling everyone she met that I had worked in the White House forty years after I'd turned in my security pass. It left some folks wondering if I had been unemployed since the '70s. I love and miss you guys every day.

Last, but far from least, I would dearly love to hand a copy to one of my former bosses, the late John Seigenthaler, then chairman and publisher of *The Tennessean*, Nashville's morning newspaper and one of the finest people anyone could ever hope to meet. John read an early version of the manuscript and cheered me on. His encouragement meant more to me than he could have ever known.

There's a funny story about the first time John and I met that oddly fits here.

One of America's most distinguished journalists, John served as assistant to U.S. Attorney General Robert F. Kennedy and a member of Kennedy's innermost circle during his bid for the Presidency in 1968. He was the founder of the First Amendment Center at Vanderbilt University and, among other endeavors, was chairman emeritus of the John F. Kennedy Library Foundation's Profiles in Courage Award and chairman of the Robert F. Kennedy Book Award.

As a Kennedy partisan, of course, Seigenthaler and Nixon weren't exactly close.

When John interviewed me for the top advertising sales job at *The Tennessean* and then-*Nashville Banner* in 1991, I had no more than seated myself in his office when he told me that we had something in common.

"You worked for Nixon," he said. "I was on Nixon's enemies list."

He laughed warmly almost as quickly as the words came out of his mouth, a good thing because in that split second I developed an urgent need to restart my heart. Thankfully, everything turned out just fine. I didn't need a cardiac defibrillator to finish the interview and I got the job.

Thanks, John. Godspeed.

PRINCIPAL CAST OF CHARACTERS

Mark Adelman
George Washington University student

Giulio Andreotti
41st Prime Minister of Italy

Spiro Agnew
40th Vice President of the United States of America

Judy Agnew
Second Lady of the United States of America

Eugene Allen
Maître d' hotel, The White House

Jim Brown
American Actor, NFL Hall of Fame (Class of 1971)

John Connally
61st U.S. Secretary of the Treasury, 39th Governor of Texas

Peter Flanigan
Assistant to the President, The White House

Gerald Ford
38th President of the United States of America

Barry Goldwater
United States Senator, 1964 Republican Presidential nominee

Alexander Haig, Jr.
White House Chief of Staff

Charlton Heston
American Actor

Clint Hill
Deputy Director, United States Secret Service

Bob Hope
American Comedian, Actor

Fred Jefferson
Social Aide and Butler, The White House

George McGovern
United States Senator, 1972 Democratic Presidential nominee

Richard Nixon
37th President of the United States of America

Patricia Nixon
First Lady of the United States

Frank Sinatra
American Singer and Actor

Helen McCain Smith
Press Secretary to the First Lady, The White House

Jean Spencer, Ph. D.
Assistant to the Vice President for Research, The White House

Glen Stafford
Administrator, Council on International Policy,
The White House

Don Stinson
American University student, White House staff

Norwood Williams
Butler, The White House

INTRODUCTION

If you bought *Downstairs at the White House* because you wanted to know where the government hides space aliens or read a tale about a dashing, young White House aide, you're going to be disappointed.

This book is about a much, much younger me, a guy I sometimes remember and laugh about, who frequently got himself into trouble because everything around him was so damn interesting.

Often, it was for loitering around the Oval Office.

At the age of 17, I accidentally landed a job at 1600 Pennsylvania Avenue during the height of Watergate, so far the worst political scandal in American history. Within only 18 months of cashing my first paycheck, the scandal ripened into a national nightmare, the President and the Vice President of the United States resigned, and a little-known Michigan Congressman became the nation's first unelected Chief Executive. It was a tragedy, a political and constitutional crisis of epic proportions, and a circus. And somehow, I ended up with a ringside seat.

Before I tell you my story, though, I'd like to set some things straight.

First, to be perfectly clear, as President Nixon used to say, I was not an intern. Most people who have heard these stories have assumed that, probably because of the publicity surrounding a young White House intern some 20 years ago. In the White

House I worked in, internships were generally earmarked for the sons and daughters of large campaign contributors. Not only did my family lack political connections, I doubt that my parents ever even voted for Richard Nixon.

Second, I was woefully short in the dashing department. As a perpetually broke student at American University, the coolest things I owned were a Ford Pinto, a bottle of Hai Karate cologne, and an oyster-colored poplin suit that carried a slight hot dog aroma. Try as I might to make myself as presentable as possible, I was far away from the spit-shined, well-pressed, impeccably groomed White House types Hollywood often portrays. I had at least one polyester dress shirt with little wagon wheels on it that had clearly been hit with an ugly stick and several others that were close runners-up. It was the '70s after all.

Third, I was just a teenager who did the same kind of hare-brained things that most kids without a fully connected frontal lobe do. The only difference was that I did them on a much bigger stage and with a Top-Secret security clearance. One morning, I devised a shortcut across the north lawn of the White House that tripped countless alarms and summoned an agitated band of uniformed Secret Service officers. I spilled ice water on Frank Sinatra's left sock. I did a lot of other things that were worse. On the other hand, I worked hard, developed at least passing acquaintances with learned, fascinating, and sometimes famous people, and learned a lot about a lot of things that ended up serving me well as the years passed.

Last, but not least, more than a few people over the years have rather bluntly asked me if my stories are true. That question may occur to you as well, and I want to tell you that the answer is unequivocally "pretty much." While I can assure you that the events in this story occurred, it doesn't mean that all of the details are perfectly accurate. My memories are now almost 45 years old and some are understandably sharper than others. In some cases, however, I purposely altered details or made composite characters to protect identities or avoid disclosing information that is not publicly available.

Accuracy, however, is not a question in a section of the book that purports the existence of something utterly extraordinary, a claim that some people may find both controversial and somewhat unbelievable at the same time. In this case, my recollections are clear as a bell. I know what I saw and what I held in my hands.

Leave it to say that the matter should send chills down the spine of anyone even remotely interested in American history.

Donald M. Stinson

Miami, Florida
August 2017

Chapter One

"YOU'RE THE GUY?"

Odd as it may seem, it's not entirely unusual for celebrities, particularly the few who qualify as living legends, to come across people who are shy and reluctant to approach them.

That may have been why Bob Hope was sitting alone in the midst of crumpled napkins and empty lunch dishes one particular day in Palm Springs, California.

In 1989 I was an executive with *The Desert Sun*, the daily newspaper that served the Coachella Valley, a stretch of desert 100 miles east of Los Angeles that includes Palm Springs and other renowned communities such as Palm Desert, Indian Wells, and Rancho Mirage. Populated by people who like dry heat and endless sunshine and don't mind using oven mitts to open their car doors in summer, the area has a rich assortment of famous faces that regular folks come upon in places as unexpected as the antacid aisle at the drug store.

Living there was an experience I wouldn't have wanted to miss. Sonny Bono was the mayor and promoted tourism with the slogan "I've Got You, Babe, in Palm Springs, California." In a single evening in Palm Desert I overheard James Earl Jones record a voiceover in his commanding baritone and chatted away with Broadway superstar Sarah Brightman without realizing who she was. And on yet another fortunate evening a few months later, an elderly gentleman ambled into my office during an open house at the newspaper. He turned out to be Gene Autry. A genuine living legend with five stars on the Hollywood Walk of Fame, Autry was not only a movie star, a broadcasting tycoon, and the owner of the California Angels but the original singing voice of *Rudolph the Red-Nosed Reindeer, Frosty the Snowman,* and *(Here Comes) Peter Cottontail.* He was also a class act, a gentleman who asked if he'd be disturbing me if he sat down for a few minutes. I was so stunned that I could barely get a "please, by all means" out of my mouth. Gene Autry was cowboys, baseball, Christmas, and Easter all rolled up in one and, as far as I was concerned, it just didn't get any better than that.

That morning, my boss, Ed Manassah, had asked me to join him for a luncheon honoring Bob Hope and his wife, Dolores. Not surprisingly, the room was packed to overflowing, noisy with the incessant pings of glass, silverware, and china bumping into one another, but nonetheless spectacular. No one spoke in a sleep-inducing monotone, and the ends of the speeches were sensibly close to their beginnings for a midday crowd. Even at 86 years old, Hope was exceptionally funny, as sharp as a tack, and brought the audience to its feet more than once for standing ovations. When the event was over and the room had all but emptied out, I happened to glance at the head table which was on a raised platform. By that time, the table should have been unoccupied. To my great surprise, there he sat.

Having rarely ever been shy, I walked up to Hope and introduced myself. Not unexpectedly, he was very warm and friendly. As we talked, I casually mentioned that we had met in Washington at one of the parties celebrating President Nixon's second

Inauguration in 1973. I also thanked him for the kindnesses he and Charlton Heston had shown to my date, a sweet 18-year-old with lush black hair, violet eyes, and a porcelain complexion whom I had secretly dubbed Snow White.

Hope's eyes sprang wide open.

"You're the guy?" he asked.

I was stunned.

"Yes, sir, I am," I replied. "I'm absolutely amazed that you remember."

"Remember?" he responded with evident amusement. "Son, we've been laughing about you for years."

The event for which I had apparently become infamous had occurred almost 18 years earlier.

Thanks to an early admissions program that allowed me to skip my senior year of high school, I joined the freshman class at American University in Washington about six weeks before the 1972 elections. Friends persuaded me to volunteer for President Nixon's campaign, and, after spending a few days in the Committee to Re-Elect the President's headquarters on Pennsylvania Avenue, I became an official Nixon supporter. It wasn't because of his record or policies, however. I was 17, loaded with testosterone, and my political opinions were dictated by the number of attractive young women per square foot. Frankly, my cup had runneth over at the Nixon office.

Thanks to the contacts I made during my stint at the Committee to Re-Elect the President, which, true to the laws of unintended consequences, was later branded CREEP as the Watergate scandal unfolded, new opportunities to work for free or for something I perceived as cool started to emerge. The next recipient of my limited talents was the Inaugural Committee where the Inaugural

Parade from the Capitol to the White House, the Inaugural Balls, and other events were planned. In fact, my best friend, Mark Adelman, a freshman at George Washington University and a high school classmate, and I worked there together. Running errands, making copies, and stocking supplies didn't bother us in the least, particularly if an assignment even remotely involved the daughter of a U.S. Senator who was hot enough to melt iron. Through a blend of awkward charm and almost certain clerical errors on somebody's part, we came up with four free tickets to an awesome assortment of events. They included a reception for Vice President and Mrs. Agnew at the Smithsonian and a Salute to the States concert at the Kennedy Center on Thursday, January 18, a special Youth Concert at the Kennedy Center on Friday, and the swearing-in, parade and Youth Inaugural Ball on Saturday, January 20.

Considering that my acne had acne and I was as thin as a rake, it wasn't easy for me to get a date. Mark, who looked like a young version of Sylvester Stallone, had a date to every event before we even knew there were events to go to. I, on the other hand, had the benefit of being able to practice my selling skills on a bevy of innocent young women from one end of campus to the other. Despite my best efforts, it unfortunately became clear that J. Edgar Hoover had a better chance with the ladies than I did. And he was dead.

Call me crazy, but if somebody had invited me to attend a concert at the Kennedy Center, rub elbows with celebrities, and eat and drink for free, I'd have said "yes" before they finished the sentence. Unfortunately, most young women I spoke with on campus didn't share that sentiment, even when I mentioned the incredible, unbelievable fact that James Brown, "The Godfather of Soul" himself, was on the bill.

I also learned that asking a girl to a Nixon event could even be dangerous.

American University has a well-deserved reputation for having some of the nation's most politically active students. It was no different in 1972 which, on top of continued demonstrations for civil rights and women's liberation and against the war in Vietnam, brought the first presidential election since the voting age had been lowered to 18. Popular opinion held that the new, younger voters who would show up at the polls that year would favor the Democratic nominee for President, Senator George McGovern, who advocated an immediate U.S. withdrawal from Vietnam. On our campus, at least, an overwhelming number of students were loudly and enthusiastically on the McGovern bandwagon. If one thing was clear, it was that President Nixon didn't get much, if any, credit from my fellow students for his accomplishments. It wasn't that opening relations with China and Russia, ending the draft, increasing employment, lowering the voting age to 18, starting the Environmental Protection Agency, ending gender discrimination in the funding of school sports and other activities, starting a war on cancer, and removing hundreds of thousands of troops from Vietnam were bad things: it just wasn't popular to say that they were good things.

With that as the backdrop, supporting President Nixon for re-election could get you anything from a funny look to a rock in the back of the head. Even though Nixon won the election by a landslide, the responses I got to my inauguration invitations were regularly both nostril-flaring turndowns and angry, finger-poking tirades about everything from Vietnam to the state of the egg salad in the cafeteria. Just as my chances of landing a date with a member of my own species were looking increasingly dim, one seemingly nice young lady said "yes." I was overjoyed; that was until she told me that she "really, really" wanted to go because she "really, really" wanted to throw something at Nixon's head. Seeing the words "Federal Prison" stamped in big black letters all over both of our futures, I withdrew my offer as diplomatically as possible, suggesting that she might prefer a relaxing evening at a double-feature of *Psycho* and *The Last House on the Left*.

She told me that I was the first guy who ever understood her. That made me worry about both of us.

A day or two later, I was walking at breakneck speed through the crowd in Mary Graydon Center, the campus hub. Burning the rubber off the heels of my Dingo boots for some long-forgotten reason, I made such a fast, sharp left turn at the end of one corridor that I came around at a 45-degree angle to the wall. Like a slow-motion scene in a movie, I saw a flash of dark hair from the corner of my eye as my left shoulder hit somebody full throttle, the collision having more than enough wallop to send him or her soaring into innocent passersby and me headlong into wobbly stacks of newspapers. As I was getting off my chest and onto my knees, red-faced with embarrassment, the person I crashed into was already standing. I looked up to see a long leg, clad in bell-bottom jeans decorated with butterflies. I couldn't believe my eyes when I saw that the jeans were being worn by a teenage version of Elizabeth Taylor. With her hand outstretched to help me up, she was either exceptionally polite or intent on crushing every speck of male chauvinist pig out of me. Within an hour after we met, she had invited me to take her to the Kennedy Center, and I had happily accepted.

How a guy like me got a chance to spend time with Snow White incarnate is a perfect example of why it's sometimes better to be lucky than good. To my astonishment, I managed not to spray saliva, sneeze, or spill anything on this spectacular beauty even once, a miracle considering that I turned into a trembling, sweat-blotched, nose-dripping wreck whenever I came within ten feet of her. When the day of the concert arrived, I was dry, steady, and beside myself with excitement.

Less exciting, however, was finding out that my dry cleaner had lost the olive sport coat and brown plaid double-knit slacks I planned to wear that night. Worse than realizing that I'd be without the outfit that I was sure would brand me as a stone-cold stud was the terror that a hand-me-down from my dad, a conservative navy suit with more conservative narrow lapels and even more conservative straight-legged, cuffed trousers, had become my only option.

I prayed that no one would mistake me for a middle-aged proctologist.

Nevertheless, it appeared that a higher authority had intervened with the dry cleaner to save me from myself. Apparently, my enthusiasm for the olive and brown plaid combo suit wasn't universally shared. That became painfully evident after a well-meaning friend told me that I looked like a used sofa.

When we made our plans for the Thursday night concert, Mark and I told our dates that we would take them out to a nice dinner beforehand. Unfortunately, as we got closer to the day of the event, we realized that we were too broke to take them anywhere that was even modestly clean, much less pleasant, and decided that it would be safer for everybody to eat on their own.

We were proud of ourselves for having set a high bar for hygiene; in retrospect, however, we should have told the ladies about our change in plans before we picked them up.

The news did not go over well.

We apologized. We pled poverty. We admitted our stupidity. It fell on deaf ears.

Scrambling for a solution as the girls' anger peaked, it suddenly dawned on us that there might be a way out of the woods. First, we had time on our side. We had picked up our dates extra-extra early because we forgot that we weren't taking them to dinner. Second, we had access to free small foods. We had the tickets to the reception at the Smithsonian in the glove compartment of Mark's car.

We had forgotten all about it.

So, we asked the ladies if they'd like to have hors d'oeuvres with the Vice President of the United States.

By the time we arrived at the Smithsonian Museum of History and Technology, there was about an hour left in the reception. Much to Mark's and my amazement, we found that our hors d'oeuvre strategy worked pretty well; that was, however, until the four of us had literally eaten through the caterer's inventory of "little hot dogs." Running out of "little hot dogs," known in more cultured circles as "pigs in blankets," was one thing. The ladies' realization that Mark and I were responsible for 95% of the shortage was quite another: for every "little hot dog" they ate, we downed four or five or maybe six apiece. Despite our apologies, we quickly learned that "hell hath no fury like a woman scorned" even when it comes to finger foods.

The atmosphere inside the Smithsonian had all the bang of a high voltage wire. Particularly for teenagers who had been loitering outside of convenience stores only a few months earlier, the whole scene was larger than life, more like something you'd see in a movie than an event you'd ever imagine attending. Everyone and everything simply glittered. The reception was loud, crowded, and buzzing with excitement as one celebrity after the next passed by.

We slipped into what turned out to be a VIP room in search of more "little hot dogs." While doing my best to act like I belonged there, I nearly ran into a Hollywood starlet with a dress so tight that you could see the outline of her liver, barely missing the opportunity to soak her cleavage with my soft drink.

Wisely concluding that I was an accident waiting to happen, Snow White suggested that we simply sit down on two of what must have been a hundred folding chairs lining one of the walls and stargaze for a while. And that we did until she pointed excitedly to two men, no less than Bob Hope and Charlton Heston, Moses himself, engaged in conversation on the other side of the room. The rosy glow in her cheeks changed to a blush as she talked about how much she and her mother adored them.

"Well, let's get their autographs," I said while giving her hand a gentle tug to follow me.

"Oh, no!" she replied, her blush fading to a pallor. "I wouldn't even be able to walk over there!"

"All right then," I said. "I'll bring them to you."

Having absolutely no plan to accomplish this, I was regretting my big mouth more and more with each step I took across the room. The men's backs were turned slightly towards me as I approached, and I couldn't help overhearing Hope say that his just-completed 1972 USO Christmas Show was his last. The two legends looked like giants to me, both literally and figuratively, and particularly so with Heston whose towering 6'2" frame made my not-so-lofty 5'8" seem like I was fun-sized. I walked around them to position myself face-to-face, apologized for my interruption, and made my plea. I anxiously explained how big a fan my date was and what it would mean to her to have their autographs, even pointing her out to show them how stunning she was. Expecting to be blown off, I took a very deep breath to sturdy my weakening knees for the embarrassment ahead. To my utter disbelief, they smiled and suggested that I lead them, teasing me every step of the way about how much I was going to owe them.

My beautiful friend took it all in with wide-open eyes and a broad, pearly-white smile as I came towards her with Bob Hope and Charlton Heston in tow.

And fainted.

This was a problem for several reasons even beyond the obvious, including the fact that as she toppled over to her right, the long sleeve of her dress snagged on a portion of an adjacent folding chair. Bouncing a little as she tumbled to the floor, the sleeve stretched and tore but stayed partially attached to the chair, leaving her face-down with her right arm sticking up in the air. Even I knew that none of this portended well for the rest of the evening. Proving that there is a merciful God, she came to quickly with the aid of a drink of water only to look up into the faces of two of the biggest stars in the universe and nearly faint again. Being grand gentlemen, they stayed with us a little while and autographed everything they could for her that would take ink.

Bob Hope was curious about what had happened in the aftermath, and I wish I could have given him a happier report that day in Palm Springs. The truth is that I never saw Snow White again. By the time the Salute to the States concert ended, she was barely speaking to me and decided not to go to the Youth Concert with me the next evening. Frankly, I could hardly blame her. Despite having good intentions, my eagerness to impress her drew unwanted attention and even more unwelcome embarrassment.

I called her up the following Monday, profusely apologized again, and asked her out for the following Saturday night. She told me she couldn't go because her dog had hiccups. I asked if she could go if the hiccups stopped sometime in the next five days. She said that she was sure that they wouldn't.

Amazingly, this was not my only—or, in fact, even my first—embarrassing brush with celebrity since I'd arrived in Washington. On November 7, 1972, election night in America, I had found myself volunteering among 5,000 pixilated Nixon supporters celebrating the President's victory at the Shoreham Hotel in northwest Washington. Although I don't remember everything that I'd agreed to do that night, I know that it had something to do with the comfort of the guests and I had to give the Secret Service my Social Security number for a background check. Having apparently passed muster, I received a cool lapel pin with the number 72 set on a red-white-and-blue background to wear. Some guy said it was just like the pins Secret Service agents wore. Several people I passed in the teeming crowd took note of it, including a boozy middle-aged woman with a napkin-full of shrimp tails, cocktail sauce on her chin, and a Nixon pin the size of Nebraska. She marched up to me, grabbed my lapel with moist fingers, and asked me if I was a security agent. The mere idea that I looked old enough to be mistaken for one gave new life to my ego, so much, in fact, that I was giddy with power as I did my job, which turned out to be directing the high, the mighty, and the frequently staggering to awaiting toilets.

After several hours of this kind of demanding work and two very not cool plantar warts I had picked up in the dorm, my feet started to scream. I looked around the packed party area and finally found a place to sit on a set of rounded white marble stairs split in half by a gold handrail. After squeezing my way through the horde of people already parked on the stairs, I sat down and introduced myself to a somewhat familiar-looking gentleman next to me. Rather than letting him tell me his name, my razor-sharp mind preferred to start a guessing game.

"I know you from somewhere," I said, shaking my finger and rattling off possibilities that ranged from reasonable to ridiculous, all of which, of course, were wrong.

Feeling dumber and more embarrassed by the second, I threw a "Hail Mary" and asked if he was an athlete. He told me that he had played lacrosse and a little football when he was younger. The blank look on my face must have been something because he reached out to shake my hand and put me out of my misery.

"Nice to meet you, Don," he said with a broad smile. "I'm Jim Brown."

"Sure you are," I replied, rolling my eyes with a typical teenage attitude.

I wasn't about to be made a fool of. First, everybody knew that Jim Brown played football, not lacrosse. Besides that, movie stars whose busts were in the Pro Football Hall of Fame certainly didn't have to sit on stairs.

I was so angry about being lied to that I stood up and walked away. That would have been the end of it if I hadn't watched *The Dirty Dozen*, a 1967 movie starring Lee Marvin, Ernest Borgnine, and Jim Brown, not long afterward. Oddly, the Jim Brown on the screen sure looked a lot like the guy I met at the Shoreham. Years later, all I could do was drop my head into my hands as I read an article about Syracuse University athletics. Jim Brown was not only an All-American football player at Syracuse who became an NFL legend, but an All-American lacrosse player, too.

◆

Considering that most of my experience with celebrations either involved birthday cake and "pin the tail on the donkey" or a bottle of Boone's Farm Apple Wine, it's not surprising that I found The John F. Kennedy Center for the Performing Arts overwhelming. Not that I was easy, but the opulent red carpeting, shimmering chandeliers, and eight-foot bust of President Kennedy inside the 600-foot foyer pretty much had me at hello.

The Salute to the States concert turned out to be much more of everything than I could possibly have imagined. With black limousines stretching the length of the Kennedy Center's entrance, throngs of women wrapped in furs and glittering diamonds, and Mrs. Nixon, Vice President Agnew, Henry Kissinger, John Connally, and Ronald Reagan in the audience, I had to occasionally check to make sure my eyes were still in their sockets. Even Governor George Wallace, who was confined to a wheelchair following an assassination attempt during his own presidential campaign the previous May, was there.

Despite the absence of President Nixon, who was flying back to Washington from Florida, the event drew such a large crowd that it had to be presented in both the Concert Hall and the Opera House, separate but adjacent venues inside the Kennedy Center that could jointly seat about 4,500. Our seats in the rich red Opera House were phenomenal, situated under a dazzling

Lobmeyr crystal chandelier that to this day still looks like a giant snowflake and spans a spectacular 50 feet across the theater's ceiling. Curiously, the show ran on both stages and remarkably without many hitches considering that the co-hosts, Bob Hope and Frank Sinatra, and entertainers Wayne Newton, Pat Boone, Solomon Burke, my personal heartthrob, Joey Heatherton, and others had to run back and forth between theaters.

After the intermission, Sinatra overwhelmed the Opera House audience by sauntering to center stage and singing "Fly Me to the Moon". At the end of the song, the crowd was so awestruck that you could have heard a pin drop.

Although I'd heard Sinatra on radio and television time and again, I'd never actually listened. I certainly did that night. I don't want to sound like a blushing groupie, but I was over the moon about hearing him sing live. As I would learn at much closer range just a few months later, it didn't take much to understand why Frank Sinatra was Frank Sinatra. A few weeks later, I walked into a record store to buy the album *Sinatra, A Man and His Music* on 8-track. I only played it when my roommates weren't around and with the volume on low at that. In January 1973, Ol' Blue Eyes and Jethro Tull weren't meant to coexist in the same college dorm.

The next day, Friday, January 19, was the Youth Concert featuring the world-famous Mike Curb Congregation, The Mob, the explosive, R&B group out of Chicago, Tommy Roe, famous for hits like "Dizzy", "Hooray for Hazel", and "Sweet Pea", and The New Seekers, who had a huge hit with "We'd Like to Teach the World to Sing (in Perfect Harmony)", a full-length version of the song "I'd Like to Buy the World a Coke", which was originally composed for the popular 1971 Coca-Cola commercial that featured a multi-cultural group of young people singing on a hillside in Italy. It was a great show, but it was just as well that Snow White had decided to stay home. Even though James Brown had performed at Nixon's first inauguration in 1969, singing "Say It Loud–I'm Black and I'm Proud", he was a no-show that night. With that layered on top of the Hope-Heston incident, Snow White might have sliced me into seven dwarfs.

Snow White had plans to spend inauguration weekend in New York even before we met. Happily, through a friend of a friend, I had been incredibly lucky to find a fellow student who was beautiful inside and out, wanted to go to the swearing-in, the Inaugural Parade, and the Youth Inaugural Ball, and didn't want to hurt me or anyone else.

Inauguration Day, Saturday, January 20, was all about logistics. Even in the overgrown small-town atmosphere of the Nation's Capital in 1973, you had a better chance of removing your own appendix with a spoon than finding a good place to park on Inauguration Day. To park close enough to the reviewing stands to make a quick getaway once the parade was over, Mark picked us all up at a painfully early hour in his dark green 1964 VW Beetle, a car that had attained near mythic status during a Christmas road trip from Washington to Atlanta. After gassing up around 3:00 a.m. near Butner-Creedmoor, North Carolina, we realized that we got on the wrong ramp and were heading north instead of south on I-85. Less than thrilled about driving to the next exit to turn around, we took a long look at the highway median. It was deep, grassy, and shaped like a wide "V." Completely sober but no less brainless, we let out a slightly maniacal war cry, turned the wheels toward the gap, and went semi-airborne, half-sliding and half-steering down the embankment before miraculously landing right-side up and completely intact. Having never been at the bottom of a highway median before, we took in the scenery and downed a couple of half-crushed doughnuts. Then, with the Isley Brothers' "Pop That Thang" appropriately playing on the VW's tinny AM radio, we hit the gas again and crept up the opposite side through the grass and mud at an agonizingly slow pace, moving up a few feet and then sliding back a few. Finally, with the car about a yard from the road, we both jumped out, grabbed the door frames and pushed, stepping up on the running boards as the engine sputtered and the wheels wobbled on the asphalt. As it turned out, we were less than a minute away from becoming road kill.

We turned out to be excellent parking predators, finding a spot fairly near the State Department within about thirty minutes. That put us about a mile away from our bleacher seats for the parade and two and a half miles from the Capitol grounds where President Nixon would take the oath of office. It was good that we were young and had plenty of natural warmth because with the wind chill, the temperature couldn't have been more than 20°F. After just a few blocks we found ourselves scooped up into a crowd that seemed to double in size every few feet of the way along Pennsylvania Avenue to Capitol Hill. Overhearing conversations around us as we walked on the freezing pavement, it was clear that the herd we were in was politically diverse.

Some were vocal Nixonians wearing big commemorative buttons. Others were there just to see a presidential inauguration regardless of the president. Still others were there to protest the war in Vietnam. I remember a guy with hair down to the middle of his back shouting gleefully about an anti-war concert conducted by Leonard Bernstein at the National Cathedral and an older guy with a menacing voice calling him a "Commie." I remember the longhaired guy angrily calling the older guy a redneck. Mostly, I remember just wanting to get out of there before a riot started.

As we walked along, the presidential limousine, accompanied by the thunderous roar of motorcycles and the bright flashing lights of a vast security escort, seemingly came out of nowhere and rolled past us, close enough that I could see President Nixon sitting in the right rear of the car. Standing ahead of us on the curb yelling and shaking an angry fist at Nixon was a guy in an Army jacket with long greasy hair who literally reeked of something that smelled like rotting chicken. My first whiff of him made me sick to my stomach, and he seemed just seconds away from exploding like a keg of gunpowder, a possibility that made me more than a little jumpy. My concern, however, may have been needless. Sometime later I read that security was so tight that day that the protester could have been an undercover federal agent. If that was true and his job was to keep real demonstrators some distance from the motorcade, the man clearly deserved a raise. If acting like a maniac didn't make people back away, his stench surely would have.

Nixon's second inauguration was one of the most heavily guarded in history with more than 10,000 police and military personnel guarding the streets. News reports said that by the time the inaugural ceremony started at 11:30 a.m., some 35,000 people were assembled on the east side of the Capitol, the traditional spot for presidential inaugurations. The East Front of the Capitol, the side facing the Supreme Court and the Library of Congress, had been the site of all but four inaugurations since Andrew Jackson took the oath of office in 1829. That distinction would end in 1981 with the inauguration of Ronald Reagan. According to one story, inaugurations were initially held on the east side so that

American Presidents could face England and, albeit symbolically, flip the British monarch the bird. On this day, however, it was the American President who was being flipped off by anti-war protestors, estimated to be between 50,000 and 100,000 strong depending on who you listened to, who were spread out among the Capitol, the parade route, the Washington Monument, and the Lincoln Memorial. In fact, the number of protestors at the 1973 Nixon Inaugural set a standard by which all other inauguration protests since have been measured.

It is difficult, if not impossible, to convey the anger that drew so many demonstrators to Washington that Saturday without saying something about the tumultuous events that led up to it.

The nine years between President Kennedy's murder on November 22, 1963 and President Nixon's second inauguration on January 20, 1973 brought unprecedented change to America as the country faced some of the most socially divisive and politically explosive issues in its history.

There was much to discuss.

We were fighting a war in Southeast Asia that, at its peak in 1968, was claiming the lives of more than 40 American soldiers a day. Matters that had been simmering on the national stove for years like civil rights, gender equality, and sexual liberation were now boiling over. Meanwhile, conventional American culture was angrily colliding with new philosophies and the rising Baby Boomers, my generation, made up of 76 million Americans born between 1946 and 1964 whose size alone gave it unparalleled power to alter virtually anything.

It was the era of hippies, yippies, and peace signs, sit-ins, love-ins, civil rights and anti-war protests, *Easy Rider*, Archie Bunker, and LSD, the Cold War, long hair, Woodstock, bell-bottoms, and

Rizla. For those of us who were old enough to understand the major events of the time, it was like riding a giant roller coaster: exhilarating one moment and terrifying the next.

Although Americans had to do nothing more than look up at the moon to see the great things we were capable of, neither did we have to look very far to see horrifying things we couldn't stop. The assassinations of Robert Kennedy, Medgar Evers, and Martin Luther King, Jr. were direct assaults on everything good America stood for. Violent, bloody riots in Detroit, Los Angeles, Washington, D.C., and Chicago left people and property badly damaged, often beyond repair. Even more, the tragic shootings of four Kent State University students by the Ohio National Guard in 1970 left many wondering what kind of America would do such a thing and who might be next.

On our streets, on our television screens, and at our family dinner tables, America was at war with itself, and much of the worst of it was reserved for the issue of Vietnam.

Far more than just unpopular, the war in Vietnam angrily divided the American people and fractured the nation's trust in government. It was the nation's longest war, conducted in varying degrees over 25 years under six U.S. Presidents: Truman, Eisenhower, Kennedy, Johnson, Nixon, and Ford. Moreover, it was a seminal event in American history with perplexing sets of circumstances. As the U.S. position in Vietnam rapidly deteriorated during 1964, President Lyndon Johnson saw the United States trapped between the devil and the deep blue sea: withdraw from Vietnam and appear weak to our friends and enemies alike or escalate the war to a point that would allow the U.S. to win, but risk creating a far larger conflict that could potentially involve Communist Red China.

Clearly, these were not easily discernible options, particularly since America's involvement in Southeast Asia was driven by a concept called the Domino Theory. First articulated by President Eisenhower, the theory advanced the idea that if one country fell under Communist control, neighboring nations would follow, falling one after another in a chain reaction like a row of dominoes. Applying that premise to Vietnam, the map of vulnerable countries had the potential to include everything from Southeast Asia to India, the Philippines, and Japan. President Johnson made his position on the Domino Theory perfectly clear: "If we allow Vietnam to fall," Johnson said, "tomorrow we'll be fighting in Hawaii and next week in San Francisco." Although LBJ was frequently, and often brutally, demonized for expanding America's role in Vietnam, it's important to note that he held serious reservations about sending U.S. soldiers into harm's way and America's ability to ever remove its forces without virtually condemning the South Vietnamese to slaughter. Johnson also knew that losing the war he had inherited would have been completely unacceptable to the American people.

For the United States, the war in Vietnam wasn't about Vietnam. It was about stopping the advance of communism. Vietnam was simply the stage. To put the threat of communism into perspective for those who didn't live through the era, it's important to note that the Communist regimes in the U.S.S.R. and China were then the great evils in the world and, along with the threat of nuclear war, were every bit as frightening as terrorism is today. Ask any Baby Boomer who did "duck and cover" drills under their school desks in the early '60s, particularly around the time of the Cuban Missile Crisis. I lived in Miami, Florida in 1962, a concerning place to be because of its proximity to Communist

Cuba. At Miami Shores Elementary School, we also practiced pulling huge black curtains over our classroom windows so that attacking enemy aircraft wouldn't be able to see us inside.

At home, television was bringing war right into our living rooms for the first time in history. Never before had Americans seen the bloody, brutal realities of combat with their own eyes. Instead of U.S. Government-approved newsreels shown in movie theaters during World War II and Korea, the television networks brought vivid, uncensored images of real battles and real casualties to the evening news. Anti-war sentiments grew wide and deep as the realities of the war struck home and the horrific number of casualties on both sides mounted. Thousands of young men burned their draft cards and tens of thousands fled to Canada to dodge military service altogether, some helped by fathers who fought under Patton and MacArthur.

The anti-war movement also found a voice in entertainment on TV shows like *The Smothers Brothers Comedy Hour* and *All in the Family*. On the radio, songs like "Eve of Destruction", "Fortunate Son", "War", and "Ohio", about the Kent State killings, were at least in the Top 15 if not number one hits. Hundreds of thousands of protesters chanted, "Hell no, we won't go!" and "Hey, hey, LBJ, how many kids did you kill today?" In the wake of atrocities like the 1968 Mai Lai Massacre where 400 unarmed men, women, and children were slaughtered en masse by U.S. soldiers, some Americans began to see the military as cold-blooded murderers.

Instead of cheers and ticker tape parades, soldiers returning from Vietnam were sometimes met with cold stares and, reportedly, warm spit.

Had they wanted to, the anti-war protesters on Inauguration Day 1973 could have traced more than a few of the reasons they were standing in the bitter cold back almost twenty years to 1954. That year the French, who were then trying to reinstate their authority over Vietnam as a colonial possession after World War II, fell to violent resistance from Communists in the north fighting for Vietnamese independence despite more than $1 billion in U.S. support. In the interests of peace, Vietnam was temporarily separated north and south until elections could be held to unify the country. The elections plan failed, the division remained, and the struggle between Communist-backed North Vietnam (with its capital in Hanoi) and U.S.-supported South Vietnam (with its capital in Saigon) began. By the end of 1963, the U.S. had 16,000 military advisors assisting the South Vietnamese.

Waiting in the wings in August 1964 were three events that would eventually lead to the replacement of advisors with a half-million U.S. combat troops.

The first occurred on August 2nd off the coast of North Vietnam. The *USS Maddox,* a Navy destroyer cruising in neutral waters near the Gulf of Tonkin, reported that it had been fired on by North Vietnamese torpedo boats.

The second event, also in the Tonkin Gulf, happened on August 4th. In this incident, the *Maddox* and the *USS Turner Joy,* sailing in extremely rough weather, reported that the North Vietnamese navy had attacked again. President Johnson immediately ordered retaliatory air strikes on North Vietnamese targets.

The third event took place on August 7th when the U.S. Senate and House of Representatives passed the Tonkin Gulf Resolution, legislation that essentially gave the President a blank check to wage war in Vietnam without a declaration of war by Congress.

It would take until 1971 when top-secret documents were published in the *New York Times*, the *Washington Post*, and other major newspapers for Americans to learn that the Tonkin Gulf incidents largely consisted of half-truths and some very big, outright lies.

The story about the first attack was true, but only technically so. Although the North Vietnamese had fired on the *Maddox* on August 2nd, senior members of the Johnson Administration never mentioned that the *Maddox* had fired first with warning shots, leaving a question of whether the North Vietnamese actions were offensive or defensive.

The August 4th attack never even happened. Although the commander of the *Maddox* originally reported that they had been attacked, he amended his report to state that bad weather might have created false sonar and radar images that were mistaken for enemy vessels. Moreover, since there were no visual sightings of other ships, the commander thought that it was unlikely that either ship had been attacked. Despite this, the Navy insisted that the *Maddox* sank two North Vietnamese ships, although no corroborating evidence could be found. Moreover, President Johnson was not advised of the change in the *Maddox*'s report until well after the retaliatory strikes were completed.

The result of the events in the Tonkin Gulf and the Tonkin Gulf Resolution was a steep escalation of American involvement in Vietnam. After the Tonkin Gulf incidents, Johnson ordered the military draft doubled and began a covert bombing of the neighboring country of Laos. In 1965 the troop level increased to 185,000 and the U.S. began a continuous bombing campaign against North Vietnam that would last almost four years. By 1966, the number of U.S. military personnel rose to 390,000 and to 485,000 by 1967. By 1968, U.S. strength swelled to a peak of

540,000, or about as many people who live inside the city limits of Milwaukee, Wisconsin.

On January 31, 1968, North Vietnam mobilized some 90,000 troops during a two-day ceasefire celebrating the Lunar New Year and launched large-scale surprise attacks across South Vietnam. Known as the Tet Offensive, the objective was to strike down the U.S. and South Vietnamese leadership in Saigon, end the war, and unify the country under a Communist government. Although the Communist forces were defeated, the attacks stunned the U.S. and South Vietnamese military. Even more shocked were the American people who had been told repeatedly by the White House that the North Vietnamese army was wearing down and that victory in Vietnam was in sight. Considering that the Communists had enough men, munitions, and supplies to carry out these assaults, the optimistic claims of the Johnson Administration looked misguided at best. As a result, it became much more difficult to convince the nation that its leaders were taking the right course of action.

In March, President Johnson's advisors informed him that they did not believe America could prevail in Vietnam and that the U.S. should attempt to negotiate a peace agreement. On March 31, 1968, Johnson addressed the nation on television, saying, for all intents and purposes, that the U.S. would suspend its bombing of North Vietnam to induce the government in Hanoi to seek an armistice. Dejected over the course the war had taken and with his popularity plunging, Johnson also declined to run for another term as President, a real shocker if there ever was one.

The peace talks between the United States and North Vietnam began in Paris in May 1968. They would continue for nearly five years and produce nothing more than signed peace agreements that were never honored.

Richard Nixon was elected President in November 1968. Among his campaign promises had been a secret plan to end the war. With Nixon's first inauguration in January 1969 came a new approach called "Vietnamization", a plan to equip and train the South Vietnamese army to take greater responsibility for ground warfare as the U.S. reduced its combat presence. Between January 1969 and year-end 1971, some 400,000 of the 540,000 American troops in Vietnam returned home. "Vietnamization" did not, however, include reductions in U.S. air combat strength. From March 1969 until May 1970, the U.S. conducted a covert bombing operation of supply routes and safe havens in Cambodia and Laos that were being used by the North Vietnamese to stage attacks in South Vietnam. On April 30, 1970, President Nixon announced that U.S. and South Vietnamese ground forces would enter Cambodia to remove enemy troops entrenched on the Cambodian-Vietnamese border and the military safe havens.

Although successful militarily, the Cambodian incursion was viewed by many as an expansion of the war. Protests on college campuses across the country exploded virtually overnight, including some that were exceptionally violent.

On May 4, 1970, two students involved in an anti-war protest at Kent State University and two students walking to classes were shot and killed by the Ohio National Guard. Eleven more were wounded.

On May 8, 1970, 200 pro-Nixon construction workers attacked nearly 1,000 students protesting the invasion of Cambodia in the streets of Manhattan's financial district. On the same day, 100,000 demonstrators came together in Washington, D.C.

to march against the war. Some four million student protesters closed more than 400 universities and high schools across the country.

On May 14, 1970, two students were killed and five wounded by the Mississippi state police during an anti-war demonstration on the campus of Jackson State University. Altogether, there were aggressive confrontations between students and police or National Guardsmen at more than 30 colleges.

On the opposite side of the coin, some 100,000 people conducted a peaceful march through the streets of New York City on May 20, 1970 in a show of support for President Nixon's policies.

It speaks volumes about the tenor of the times that these events all occurred within a single month in 1970. Sadly, however, they were far from over.

On August 24 of that year, a bomb was detonated in the middle of the night in a building on the campus of the University of Wisconsin-Madison that housed a U.S. Army-funded mathematics center, killing a 30-year-old father of three.

The following year, in April 1971, Vietnam veterans tossed away hundreds of their medals on the U.S. Capitol steps while half a million anti-war protesters marched on Washington. In another demonstration in May 1971, 12,000 protesters were arrested. Although anti-war protests continued across the country in 1972 and 1973, they became fewer and farther between by 1974.

By the time the last U.S. Marine climbed into a helicopter on the roof of the U.S. Embassy in Saigon as South Vietnam fell to the Communists in April 1975, the United States had been caught up in Vietnam for a quarter of a century. Despite dropping millions of tons of explosive weapons on the enemy, sending three million troops, and spending the present-day equivalent of $900 billion, we lost. The bloodshed on both sides was horrific: 58,000 Americans died and 300,000 were wounded. Some 1.1 million North Vietnamese and 250,000 South Vietnamese military personnel were killed along with more than a million civilians.

With the pall of Vietnam, civil unrest, and winter clouds in the background, Capitol Hill had the quality of an old black-and-white photo about it on Inauguration Day.

The ceremony began with prayers and music from The President's Own United States Marine Band. Ignoring shouts of "Stop the War! Stop the War!" from protestors, Vice President Spiro Agnew stepped forward to greet Chief Justice Warren Burger and take the oath administered to all government officials other than the President, whose oath is specified in the Constitution. After Agnew was sworn in, the Marine Band played Ruffles and Flourishes and "Hail, Columbia", the Vice-Presidential march, not to be confused with "Columbia, the Gem of the Ocean".

Curiously, Vice Presidents were not sworn into office at the same time and place as Presidents until 1937. Before that time, Vice Presidents usually took the oath in the U.S. Senate Chamber, reflecting the Vice President's constitutional role as both Vice President of the United States and President of the United States Senate. It's interesting to note that one Vice President took the oath of office at his home in New York because he was bogged down with lawsuits and, incredibly, another in Cuba where he was ill with tuberculosis.

By the time another prayer was offered and another musical performance started, I'd been standing still on the hard, wintry ground so long that my feet were unconscious. The good news was that I could keep standing. The bad news was that I had apparently opened a hole in my right shoe. The worse news was that

I also had a hole in my right sock that was nearly aligned with the hole in my shoe. The cold was coming in so fast that my toes felt like frozen fish sticks. I found a few pages of *The Evening Star*, Washington's afternoon newspaper, on the ground and fashioned a makeshift patch for my shoe. Realizing that this wasn't going to be a permanent solution, I decided that I'd either need to buy a whole paper or prepare to hop down Pennsylvania Avenue.

We were in a roped-off area that was just close enough to make out two tiny figures on the inaugural platform who turned out to be President and Mrs. Nixon. While a small group of anti-war protestors yelled "Killer!" again and again, President Nixon swore to "protect and defend the Constitution of the United States" and followed two traditions that began with George Washington in his first inauguration in 1789: Nixon placed his hand on a Bible and added, "So help me God" after the constitutional oath.

A huge cheer rose from the crowd, and the Marine Band played four Ruffles and Flourishes followed by "Hail to the Chief". Then the military fired a customary 21-gun salute from cannons on the Capitol grounds.

It made me swell with pride for my country.

Moments later, President Nixon began his inaugural address. Able to hear the President over an audio system but barely able to see him, my friends were more than ready to move on to the Inaugural Parade even though it probably wouldn't start for almost two hours. First, the President would complete his speech. Then, he would attend a luncheon sponsored by the Joint Congressional Inaugural Committee where he would dine on shrimp cocktail, roast beef, and strawberries with cream. Finally, he would lead the parade from the Capitol to the White House.

Even though leaving early made perfect sense considering the crowds, I didn't want to go. My frosty newspaper-patched right foot was one reason. Just as compelling but less painful was my realization that I was watching a President being inaugurated in person. I remember seeing a minute or two of President Kennedy's inauguration in 1961 on a grainy black-and-white TV in a store window when I was five. I saw President Johnson take the oath of office in 1965 and caught part of President Nixon's first inaugural parade on an equally blurred black-and-white screen in my eighth-grade history class at W.F. Dykes High School in Atlanta in 1969. This day, however, there was no television. Everything was live, sharp, in living color, and unfolding right in front of where I was standing on the grounds of the capitol of the free world. As far as I was concerned, it was all so far out that there wasn't a word big enough to describe it.

Foolishly, I thought the hole in my shoe fulfilled the universe's need to show me who was boss. I was wrong about that.

As we walked down Pennsylvania Avenue, we ran into an utterly bizarre scene of dead and dying pigeons that grew larger and more gruesome the farther we walked. In fact, it was such a mess that you not only had to navigate around the cadavers on the ground but also stay alert for others falling from the trees. Although I was confident that the pigeons weren't trying to make a political statement, no one we spoke to seemed to know what was behind the calamity. The explanation that eventually came out was as strange as the carnage itself. For better or worse, Pennsylvania Avenue was, and still is, a popular spot with the pigeon crowd and, in 1973, the inaugural organizers apparently didn't want the parade tarnished by some of the less appealing things pigeons do, particularly if they decided to do it on the President of the United

States. So, the Inaugural Committee spent thousands of dollars to have the trees on the parade route treated with a repellant meant to irritate the pigeons' feet and subtlety tell them to get lost. But rather than getting the message, the pigeons stayed in the trees, ate the repellant, and fell mortally ill.

Believe it or not, this was not the first-time dead birds had been an issue at a presidential inauguration. Caged canaries were used to ornament the hall used for President Ulysses S. Grant's second Inaugural Ball a hundred years earlier on March 4, 1873. The temperature at noon that day was already an icy 16°F. When the sun went down, it plunged to -4° F and whatever the people who organized the Ball were using to generate heat in the building failed, forcing the shivering guests to quickly put on their hats and overcoats. In the rush to look after the partiers, the canaries were overlooked. With nothing to warm them, the sad little critters turned into feathery popsicles. Nearly as bad, or worse depending on your point of view, the champagne froze, too.

Folks less familiar with Washington, D.C. might be curious to know that Pennsylvania Avenue does not run uninterrupted between Capitol Hill and the White House. It comes to a dead end at 15th Street and resumes two blocks north to the left in front of the Treasury Department. Part of the traditional Inaugural Parade route, the path was often referred to by long-time Washingtonians as the "zigzag", a throwback to the days before Pennsylvania Avenue was closed to traffic after the 1995 Oklahoma City bombing. Before 1995, you could drive the stretch of Pennsylvania Avenue in front of the Treasury, the White House, Blair House, and the Old Executive Office Building. Since our parade seats were slightly west of the White House on the same side of Pennsylvania Avenue, our plan was to avoid the thick crowds along the "zigzag." We'd cross 15ᵗʰ Street, cut across the Treasury Department grounds, and stroll up East Executive Avenue, which was then open, too, until we reached the area behind the parade stands in front of the White House. Then we'd hang a left to our seats.

The plan looked great on paper; however, it failed to take a few things into account, including the District of Columbia police who quickly sent us back to the "zigzag." There, other officers told us to cross Pennsylvania Avenue towards the American Security & Trust Building, then turn left and walk behind the bleachers along Lafayette Park, a dilemma since our seats were on the opposite side of the street. However, since we knew where we were going and the harried officers didn't, it seemed perfectly reasonable to me to merely walk around the police and military, mosey down Pennsylvania Avenue a bit in front of several thousand fellow Americans, and cross the street in front of the presidential reviewing stand.

Of the many things I learned that day, one was that roaming higgledy-piggledy around a high-security area isn't something that will endear you to law enforcement. That goes at least twice if the area in question happens to be the White House. Nonetheless, in the brief shining moment before a very angry, red-faced policeman collared me and read us all the riot act, we were able to get an unusually good look at the stunning temporary structure the President would occupy during the parade.

Crowned by a colossal presidential seal hung right below the roofline, the brilliant white wooden building sat immediately outside the White House grounds. Large pillars on the far right and left of the stand supported a roof that covered a hundred or more seats. A smaller area centered in the front was glassed-in and covered by a separate roof that looked like an upside-down egg carton. Far from the cold, hard bleachers in our future, the President's box was carpeted, heated, and had exceedingly comfy-looking seats.

Come what may, it was clear that nothing frosty was going to touch a single presidential body part that afternoon.

At this point, it was almost taking us longer to get into the right seats than it did to walk from the Capitol. In the confusion, an understandably irritated officer sent us back in the direction we came from and loudly ordered us to climb up into the Lafayette Park bleachers. Rather than using our heads and showing him our tickets, we did what most kids our age would do: follow orders to avoid getting yelled at again.

So we climbed, throwing out one semi-sincere "sorry, pardon me, excuse me" after another to the people we stepped over and on. At one point I slipped, indelicately sending my left leg into the empty space between the bleachers and was jeered by a nasty old geezer with ear hair almost long enough to pass for sideburns. Minutes later my right shoe accidentally slaughtered someone's brownbag lunch. We looked back over our collective shoulders at the officer who was making a "keep on going," pushing-type motion with his right hand.

We went up a few more rows and, to our amazement, came upon four seats right under the parade announcer's booth and directly across from the reviewing stand. I swear that they were glowing with a radiant, almost divine, light. Next to the President's, these were pretty much the best seats in town, and we were amazed that the policeman had steered us to them. We sat down and waved to the officer. He waved back, although this time with a "move out of the way"-type of horizontal motion and consternation on his face as four fur-clad women who looked like they applied pancake makeup with a trowel kicked us out.

Even though the same policeman eventually helped us cross Pennsylvania Avenue to our seats just west of the presidential box, I swear that his "keep on going" motion meant for us to literally keep on going, not to a place to sit, but over the top of the bleachers, out into thin air and out of his sight forever.

As we settled into our seats, an icy wind pierced the thin, unlined brown trench coat I was wearing, the product of an ill-considered trade for my one and only Flying Burrito Brothers album. Because I'd obviously never given any thought to the fact that it was January and that January means miserably cold weather, I didn't have a hat, gloves, or a scarf. I ended up with ice-encrusted boxer shorts, brittle feet, and a leaky nose. If that wasn't enough, we were at the tail end of the parade route. Just before my eyeballs flash-froze, the sun mercifully came out and the parade started. When all was said and done, it surprisingly proved well worth the wait.

Aptly themed "The Spirit of '76" for the approaching two-hundredth anniversary of the American Revolution, the pageantry and precision were magnificent. In the lead were three men outfitted in colonial garb, two with drums and one with a fife, to resemble the subjects of Archibald Willard's famous painting, *The Spirit of '76*. Three motor coaches marked "First Family" carrying Nixon relatives followed a contingent of cavalrymen. Soon after, a procession of police cars and motorcycles escorted the motorcade carrying President and Mrs. Nixon who were standing up through the sunroof of the presidential Lincoln and waving to the crowd.

It was exciting. It was also an education in sharp contrasts.

At the corner of 14th Street and Pennsylvania Avenue, a cluster of anti-war protesters launched a fusillade of oranges that barely missed Nixon's limousine. Shortly afterward, the President and the First Lady entered the reviewing stand to the strains of "Hail to the Chief".

As the parade of 35 patriotic floats and more than 50 marching bands made its way toward the White House, another group burned 48 American flags on the grounds of the Washington Monument.

As thousands of American flags blew in the wind, clothing every inch of Pennsylvania Avenue in red, white, and blue, demonstrators in black shrouds with their faces painted stark white marched from the Lincoln Memorial to the Washington Monument carrying coffins that represented the men, women, and children on both sides who had died in the war.

After watching the parade nearly long enough to have lost the feeling in my legs, we danced around like accordion players in a polka band to get our blood flowing again, weathering some nasty catcalls from the people whose view we were blocking. With one of the four of us responding loudly to the crowd with a suggestion that was somewhere between anatomically impossible and probably illegal, we started snaking our way through the thick crowds and heavy traffic to get back to campus and change clothes for the evening.

As it turned out, we didn't leave a minute too soon. Those were the days before the Metro subway system in Washington, so much before, in fact, that the only visible signs of the subway's construction were mammoth planks covering holes on a hodge-podge of downtown streets. That meant that our merry band and thousands of other paradegoers who also wanted to get ahead of traffic ended up in a tangled, angst-ridden, gnash-your-teeth, bladder-busting mess of cars and buses.

It turned a regular thirty-minute drive to the American University campus into a two-hour journey that left our guests seething with rage unseen since the "little hotdog" incident.

I learned two more important lessons that night: one, never tell a lady that a fast-food joint is her dinner destination before a formal event, and two, remember that you usually get what you pay for. On the first matter, little more needs to be said since the stupidity of bringing onion rings in range of chiffon speaks for itself.

The second matter, however, was an entirely different issue. It took a lot of work to find tuxedos we could afford to rent, and once we did we virtually sprinted to the shop. The owner had us try on exceptionally cool outfits with wide velvet lapels and ruffled shirts, took our measurements and our money, and told us when they'd be ready. The clothes were so cool and we were so confident about looking good that we never even glanced at the suits until it was time to dress. To our great surprise, the rental fee we paid was apparently more than a tad short for 1973's top-of-the-line tux. In fact, it was probably short for a good tux during the Hoover Administration. Instead of velvet, mine came with mildew on the coat collar and a cheese-like aroma that I wasn't about to investigate for fear of finding out what it was. I splashed some Hai Karate on it, took a few sniffs to see if it had reasonably covered the smell, and sprinted out the door.

The evening's festivities were held at the Sheraton Park Hotel, one of the most prominent and historic hotels in the Nation's Capital. The Sheraton Park was torn down in 1980, and the Marriott Wardman Park Hotel now stands on the site.

Located in the same neighborhood as the Shoreham, the Wardman Tower Apartments connected to the Sheraton Park had been home to famous figures from Dwight Eisenhower, Lyndon Johnson, and Spiro Agnew to movie star Marlene Dietrich and Washington's "hostess-with-the-mostest," Perle Mesta, a former U.S. Ambassador to Luxembourg whose Washington dinner parties were the place to see and be seen during the Truman and Eisenhower years. In the early 1950s, the Wardman Tower was also home to *Meet the Press* which, curiously, used the basement as its original broadcast studio.

With its name, the Youth Inaugural Ball would have been easy to dismiss as something a notch above a high school prom. But to me at least, everything about it from the twinkling chandeliers and rich gold carpet decorating the ballroom to the smartly attired crowd roared preppy sophistication. The event was designated for the 18-30 set, and while I assumed that most of the partygoers would be closer to holding a mortgage than a dorm key, it surprisingly wasn't so: most people we met were only two or three years out of college, a fact that nevertheless made them seem ancient to us since that meant they were six or seven years older than we were. It was also well attended. The red-white-and-blue-colored tickets said the Youth Ball started at 9:00 p.m., but by 8:00 p.m. the line of expensive-looking people in tuxedos and glittering evening gowns waiting to get into the ballroom was so long that it wound around and back on itself almost all the way to the lobby. The Sheraton was appropriately proud of the fact that it had the largest hotel ballroom in the world. I don't know whether all or only a portion of the room was used that night; however, I clearly remember that there were so many people that there was barely room to squeeze onto the dance floor.

The good news was that the music more than made up for the congestion. In fact, for a Presidential Inaugural Ball immediately before disco took over America, it was almost edgy: among others, Micky Dolenz of The Monkees, the made-for-TV band that sold an unbelievable 50 million records, belted out "Proud Mary (Rolling on the River)", and the "King of Rock and Soul," Solomon Burke, a future member of the Rock and Roll Hall of Fame, blew the roof off with "Everybody Needs Somebody to Love", a classic that's been covered over the years by a collection of bands from the Rolling Stones and Led Zeppelin to the Blues Brothers.

But more than just the music, the atmosphere, and the history, I was learning a great deal about the diverse cultures and customs within our own society—social anthropology, really—or at least that's how I tried to sell it to my parents. It was true enough, though. At one end of the spectrum was the Inaugural Ball and a woman I saw there in a red, blue, and silver dress who was so exquisitely assembled in every way that the Earth must have trembled in awe under her feet. At the opposite end was a Grateful Dead concert I'd attended on the college baseball field in the fall and a girl there who was so drunk that she climbed on stage and showed the crowd how talented she was at taking off her shirt.

Something else rocked my world that night, enough that I literally thought I was going to die.

Minutes before the stroke of midnight, the noise in the ballroom was hitting the high end of the decibel scale: music was booming, people were dancing, laughing, and downing enough Cold Duck to keep the festivities going for four more years.

Then, just as the whole thing was about to explode, the music stopped so abruptly that some people kept dancing for a few moments after the sound ended. There was silence for several seconds before the music started again, but when it did it was far from a guitar riff. It was the sound of a drum and trumpets playing Ruffles and Flourishes and "Hail to the Chief" as the President, the First Lady, and their daughters, Tricia and Julie, walked onto the stage. At that moment, while every corner of the ballroom erupted in wild cheers and applause, my date and I stood twenty or thirty feet away from the First Family.

When the President reached down into the crowd to shake hands, the mob around us surged forward so quickly and violently that I had the wind knocked out of me and lost hold of my date's hand in the bedlam. The President then came down into the crowd, and another fierce surge on the heels of the first pressed me even tighter against the person in front of me, lifted me off the floor, and left me trapped, unable to move my arms or legs. I felt a muscular wave of terror come over me that turned to panic when I gasped for air and came up close to empty.

There was madness in the air, and it was alive in frenzied people with arms raised and hands reaching out, desperately trying to touch the President who was obviously hopelessly too far away and surrounded by Secret Service agents. Even with the security buffer, the President couldn't get back on the stage without being lifted into a sitting position so he could crawl backwards in a stance like a reverse pushup, knees bent and feet and hands flat on the floor. The crowd kept surging forward and then, in the blink of an eye, it suddenly stopped. In the two or three seconds it took President Nixon to step away from the edge of the stage, the tidal wave receded almost as swiftly as it came in.

Ensnared and struggling for air one moment, I was standing on my feet filling my lungs with air the next. Best of all, I found my friends safe and sound on the other side of the room, having somehow been moved out and away from the pandemonium by the shifting and turning of the crowd. As the clocked ticked and the First Couple danced to music better suited for their generation, the room relaxed like an unclenching fist. By a quarter past midnight the First Family had come and gone and the insanity had passed. The dance floor filled up again and, as far as I recall, the party raged on until at least two or three in the morning in the ballroom, moved to the lobby, and then, finally, to the parking lot despite the cold. Although we left when the crowd went outdoors, I heard that the hardcore revelers stayed on until five or six in the morning.

More hungry than tired, Mark and I literally counted our change, discovering that we could probably afford to buy everyone a cheap breakfast to match the even cheaper dinner we treated the ladies to at a burger joint the night before. We stopped by an all-night diner on Wisconsin Avenue where a future poster boy for "Just say no to drugs" sat at the counter muttering about somebody driving a Chevy over his hemorrhoids. With that and thick, forest-fire-level cigarette smoke as atmosphere, we calculated exactly how many pancakes we could afford before we ordered. We must have been a huge disappointment to the waitress who saw us come in decked out in formalwear. Nevertheless, we left a good tip and I learned an important lesson for future application.

Pancakes with lots of syrup and big, big glasses of water will make you feel really full.

Actually, more like really fluffy.

Either way, you won't need to eat again for a while.

Chapter Two

I WORK WHERE?

I can still see myself standing outside an office door in the General Services Administration Building near the White House. My hands were crossed in front of me, and my thin, cotton overcoat was neatly folded over my right arm.

I was sweating. So damn much, in fact, that I had to keep mopping my brow. As if that wasn't awkward and worrisome enough, I was convinced that somebody was going to think that I had typhoid fever, call an ambulance, and haul me away. Although I was nervous, most of my perspiration problem had to do with my wool suit which fit the bitterly cold February weather outside but not the temperature inside. At least in the area I was standing, the thermostat must have been set halfway between Florida in July and Death Valley.

An irritable middle-aged man with a mustache and a lime-green polyester shirt was responsible for putting me there. Barely looking at me during an exceptionally unmemorable visit in his office, he lazily thumbed through my paperwork, made a sweeping motion with his arm in the direction of a door that he said was down the hall, and told me to stand outside of it and wait until someone came to get me. He stressed that under no circumstances was I to knock on the door.

Doing my best to be respectful, I did exactly what I was told.

After what seemed like an eternity, the door finally opened and an equally grumpy woman walked out and immediately asked me why I hadn't knocked on the door. Before I could answer, she directed me to an office that held an elegant old wooden desk, red carpeting, and a tall, gold-fringed American flag on a stand. The lady seated behind the desk asked me my name and, in a more aggravated voice than the first woman, also asked me why I hadn't knocked on the door. Muttering something under her breath, she came around her desk and stood directly in front of the flag. She asked me to raise my right hand. Reading from a small black book, she administered the federal oath which I repeated word-for-word, swearing among other things to protect my country from "all enemies, foreign and domestic."

For a teenager, this was more than just an exciting moment. It was heady. With such ceremony, I had no doubt that a photographer would appear any second to take my picture in front of the American flag and I'd be handed some sort of handsome document suitable for framing to mark the start of my government career. Surprisingly, the photographer and the handsome document suitable for framing never arrived. Instead, when I completed the oath with "So help me God," the lady shook my hand, welcomed me into the government service, yawned, and reminded me to take my overcoat.

Although I was grateful for my new part-time job, the executive branch of government wasn't where I wanted to be. Between the November elections and Thanksgiving, I'd started looking for a part-time job or internship on Capitol Hill with a Member of the Senate or the House of Representatives by literally going door to door. Even though my success was limited to getting a few free cups of coffee, I kept at it in the belief that not everyone would throw me out.

As far as I was concerned, the legislative branch was where the action was and where I'd learn the most about government. Capitol Hill was also where several of the older political science majors I knew had internships. I was in more than slight awe of the fact that they would often come to class in business clothes rather than frayed bell bottoms so they could go directly to what they coolly called The Hill.

Desperately wanting to wear a wide tie and be on The Hill, but not exactly sure what The Hill was, I went to the library. I learned that the Capitol had been erected on top of a place called Jenkin's Hill and that the term Capitol Hill was often used as a metaphor for Congress. Additionally, it was used to identify an area that included the Capitol, the Senate and House Office Buildings, the Supreme Court, the Library of Congress, and a residential area near the Capitol. Because they were working for Members of Congress, my friends' reference to The Hill meant the Capitol and the offices where the Senate and House staffers worked which, in those days, were the Russell and Dirksen Senate Office Buildings adjacent to the Capitol on Constitution Avenue and the Cannon, Longworth, and Rayburn House Office Buildings on Independence Avenue.

Armed with a bit more knowledge but no perceptible plan, I wrote letters and made as many long-distance calls as I could afford to congressional offices over the Christmas holidays. My work produced a grand total of nothing, not surprising in retrospect considering that Congress wasn't in session and most of the United States was on vacation.

Occasionally, at least, I learned from my mistakes. When I came back to Washington in January, the first thing I did was make sure the government was open before I resumed my shoe leather campaign. My mom and dad were supportive of what I was trying to do and equally dead set against it, a dichotomy that only parents can truly understand. On one hand, they were proud of my enterprise. On the other, they felt my studies needed full attention, particularly since I'd skipped my senior year of high school and had only been in college three months. Fortunately, my first semester grades were good enough to reduce their concerns. If they hadn't been, this would be a really short story.

I have to say that almost everyone I met on Capitol Hill was very nice, if not downright charming, even as they were showing me the door. There were exceptions, of course. One was a large woman with an orangey bouffant and a hoarse, whiskey-soaked voice at a reception desk who stared at me over an ashtray full of lipstick-stained butts and bellowed "Not today, boy!" I had no idea what she was talking about; however, after seeing her light a match next to an open can of aerosol hairspray, it was clear that she was no more than one bad decision away from re-enacting the Hindenburg explosion. Another receptionist who I clearly remember smelling like rubbing alcohol simply stared at me and never uttered a word, even when I introduced myself. A real charmer who may have been pre-verbal, she grunted, then snorted when I said goodbye. I took that to mean that I impressed the hell out of her.

Making up for that in abundance were the people working for Sam Nunn, Democrat from Georgia, who was elected to his first Senate term in November 1972 and took office in January. Despite my being what I'd call a "mini-constituent," a kid from Atlanta who wasn't old enough to vote, their kindness and consideration was more than I could've ever hoped for. I even had an opportunity to meet the Senator, a very nice man who would go on to have a distinguished career in the Senate, including chairmanship of the Armed Services Committee. Although they didn't have a job available, they volunteered to forward my resume to some other offices.

They were good people, and they actually did it. In fact, the fine people in Senator Nunn's office inadvertently started a chain of events that taught me a lot about the mechanics of the universe.

Several months before any of this happened, probably as far back as September, in fact, I struck up a friendship with a particularly bright guy named Dave who lived on the same floor in Leonard Hall. One evening in late fall I ran into him on the elevator and noticed that he was wearing a coat and tie. My immediate assumption, of course, was that he worked on The Hill. Much to my surprise, however, he told me that he had a paid part-time job in the Old Executive Office Building. I had no clue what an Old Executive Office Building was. Looking back on it a few months later, I was happy to discover that I wasn't as dumb as I thought. Although I'd walked past it numerous times, there was no sign in front of the Old Executive Office Building to identify it. Someone had told me that it had once housed the Departments of State, War, and Navy, and that's all I knew.

Dave told me that he worked 20 hours a week as a clerk and messenger, making copies, delivering inter-office mail, and other, similar kinds of things as they came up. He found out about the job through friends of friends, interviewed, and was hired the same day. A few weeks after the inauguration, he told me he had an opportunity to do something more aligned with his major, that he wasn't going to continue in the job, and asked me if I'd be interested in it.

For at least a little while, I almost wished that Dave hadn't asked. It produced one of those moments in life when what you desperately want and what you desperately need come into severe conflict, like being willing to kill for a chocolate-covered dough-nut when you're three inches away from buttoning your pants.

I wanted to be on The Hill. I also didn't want to watch my wallet become worth more than what was in it.

I said yes.

Dave asked me if I'd like to join him the following Monday to see what the job was like.

I said yes to that, too.

We took the bus within a relatively short walk of the corner of 17th Street and Pennsylvania Avenue. Not surprisingly, some of the stands from the inaugural parade were still up, looking cold, forlorn, and uninviting without red, white, and blue everywhere. On the southwest side of 17th Street was the Globe Book Store. On the southeast side was the gargantuan Old Executive Office Building.

When we went inside the EOB, I had to sign my name on an official-looking list presented to me by a very serious-looking security officer. On the other hand, Dave only had to show a pass that he had on a chain around his neck bearing his photo and "EOB" in big block letters. The pass was cool beyond words, not just because I was a teenager but because anything more security-related than locking a door was unusual in my world. In fact, those types of things were unusual in most people's lives in that era. U.S. airlines weren't required to search passengers for weapons until 1973. A car alarm was the bark your dog made when somebody peeked in your car window. I even knew people who left their doors and first-floor windows open at night.

I can't imagine that the EOB's huge alternating black and white floor tiles wouldn't have been the first thing that struck me that Monday. They were exquisitely polished, stretching down every corridor like a colossal chessboard.

We climbed to the second floor on a wide, semi-circular staircase so dramatically designed that it could have easily come from the set of *Gone with the Wind*. We turned right at the top of the stairs and walked into a large room with neatly arranged desks, rows of olive green file cabinets, and a high ceiling that made the room seem considerably larger than it was. In the left rear corner was the door to a private office. A large, framed color photograph of President Nixon was hung in the center of the back wall beneath a bland government-issue black-and-white clock. Beneath the clock was a safe. On the front right section of the wall, flanked on both sides by high, metal file cabinets, was an open door to a supply room. Inside, Dave had a small desk that sat next to a huge copy machine.

It was immensely cool.

Dave introduced me to an assortment of people including his boss, Glen Stafford, with whom I had a lengthy and pleasant conversation. Then I shadowed Dave for an hour or two, delivering mail to other offices, making copies, and getting a feel for most of the other duties that made up his job. I must admit that I was a little overwhelmed by it all. Although I'd certainly been in offices before, I'd never worked in one. In fact, my last job had been selling newspaper subscriptions door to door in Alpharetta, Georgia, a then largely undeveloped Atlanta suburb. Although the boiling summer heat and long walks between farmhouses were no prize, it proved to be one of the most valuable jobs I ever had. I learned how to sell and, maybe more importantly, how to talk with people from all walks of life. I also learned a lot about the importance of listening to understand rather than to answer.

The hubbub of the office environment was energizing and the people were very nice. As I would find out, some were also quite intriguing.

After lunch with Glen and his assistant in the EOB cafeteria, I started back to campus, screwing up the simple instructions they gave me to get back to the bus stop at 17th and H Streets, N.W. I also completely forgot to write down the name of the group they might hire me to work for.

When I finally made it back to campus, something in the universe urged me to go straight to the dorm and take off my coat and tie. Just as I put my key in the lock, I could hear the black rotary telephone my two roommates and I shared ringing.

I hurried.

Telephone answering machines didn't come into widespread use until the 1980s, and caller I.D. didn't come on the scene until the 1990s. In 1973, if no one was around to answer the phone, you not only missed calls but wouldn't know if anyone had even tried to reach you.

I picked up the receiver on what was probably the last ring and was shocked to hear the voice on the other end ask for Mr. Stinson. It took me a second to realize that for the first time in my life the Mr. Stinson in question was me, not my dad. The man on the phone introduced himself as an aide to a Congressman from Georgia who had received my resume from Senator Nunn's office. He explained that they had a part-time opening available and asked if I'd be interested in discussing it. I immediately said yes, and he said he'd call me back to arrange a time to meet.

Reveling in my good fortune I stretched out on my bed, a top bunk with a mattress that curved up just enough to make you feel like you were sleeping in a rocking chair. No sooner than I put my hands behind my head, got the damn thing semi-stabilized, and took a deep breath, the phone rang again. I leapt to the floor, inconveniently bringing the mattress down with me, some of it right on top of my head. I answered the phone assuming it was the Congressman's aide calling me back; surprisingly, it wasn't. Instead, it was Glen from the "what's-its-name" group at the EOB asking if I was available to come back later that week. I immediately said yes to that, too, and he said he'd call me back to arrange a time to meet.

Now with not one but two job possibilities suddenly on the horizon I had skyrocketed from pleased to euphoric. Nature called, and I opened the door to walk down the hall to the restroom. Then I realized I had a problem.

I couldn't leave. I might miss their calls.

I barely slept that night, although it wasn't because I didn't answer nature's call. After a few hours of extremely uncomfortable thought the previous afternoon, I concluded that it was safe to wander down to the restroom when the business day ended around 6:00 p.m. Part of my restlessness was due to obvious excitement about my employment prospects. I'd also decided to turn my mattress over so that it had a hump rather than a curve, the idea being that my weight, all 140 pounds of me, would somehow straighten out the lump and I'd finally be able to lie flat. This, of course, didn't work, and all I got for my trouble was a stiff back.

Since I'd tossed and turned all night and didn't have any classes that day, I slept in a little bit. Around 8:30 in the morning the phone rang, and one of my roommates picked up the entire telephone and laid it and the receiver right next to my mouth. Still partially asleep, I mumbled into the speaker end of the phone and then sat up quickly, a bad idea since my rear end was on the mattress hump and the extra elevation made me hit my head on the ceiling. I grabbed the phone figuring that it was either the congressional office on The Hill or my new friend from the EOB.

It was neither.

Instead, it was a lady with a charming voice from a Senator's office who had also received my resume from Sam Nunn's staff. The person on the line mentioned that they had an opening for an unpaid internship and asked if I'd be interested. I immediately said yes to that, too. Mercifully for my nerves and bladder, she didn't tell me she'd call me back with an appointment time; instead we decided right then and there on Thursday at 3:00 p.m.

Somewhere between getting out of bed and boiling water with an electric coil to make instant coffee, I felt a chill run down my spine. I now had three opportunities, only two of which paid anything, and I had no clue how to handle any of it.

Under the circumstances, it would have been wise to get the advice of someone with experience in matters like these; for some reason that must have made sense to me at the time, however, I didn't. Instead, I let my imagination run wild about every conceivable terrible thing that could go wrong. With no idea how to avoid the utter catastrophe I had now convinced myself was coming, I felt like I was about to tumble off of a cliff.

Many years ago, a friend who describes himself as being a week older than dirt shared his observation that "sometimes you make decisions in life and sometimes life makes decisions for you." He could just have easily added that either way, your phone will never ring when you want it to.

Since I had no classes that day, I decided to stay in the dorm, work on a paper, and play The Rolling Stones' *Let It Bleed* album on my roommate's 8-track to my heart's content. Positioned on my desk just to the right of my trusty Royal typewriter was the phone. In the first hour, I probably picked up the receiver at least four or five times just to make sure there was a dial tone. In between dial tone checks I would look over at the little box the phone cord was connected to, apparently to confirm that an evil elf hadn't snuck past me and cut the line. I kept at it throughout the day and, although I can't recall how much progress I made on the paper, I know that I succeeded in making myself crazy.

Hours passed. Nothing happened.

Not even a wrong number.

By five o'clock that Tuesday afternoon I'd thrown in the towel and, wearing my immaturity on my sleeve, was thoroughly pissed that I wasn't at the center of everyone's universe and at the very top of their priority list. I was also thoroughly convinced that no one was ever going to call me.

Therefore, about 45 minutes after I became suitably verklempt, the phone rang.

◆

Glen Stafford was waiting for me at the same EOB entrance I'd come through on Monday. When he called on Tuesday afternoon, he asked if I could come down to see him at eleven o'clock on Thursday. I was more than happy to oblige, figuring that I'd have more than enough time afterward to make it to the Senate on schedule and even cruise through one of the Smithsonian buildings on the way. That would have made the logistics of my day pretty simple.

Life, however, tends to have a mind of its own and a quirky sense of humor to boot. As I was trying to tie what would vaguely resemble a Windsor knot that morning, the phone rang and a voice with a Southern accent asked if I could stop by at one o'clock. It was the Georgia Congressman's office. Despite having a bad feeling that I was on the verge of triple parking myself, I told him I'd be there.

As we walked up the stairway, Glen, whose kind, easy demeanor reminded me of Andy Griffith, told me that the purpose of my visit that day was to meet with a Navy captain whose private office I'd glanced at earlier in the week. The captain was the executive secretary of something Glen kept referring to as "sea-ep" which made me think it had something to do with the ocean. Just to be sure, though, I stopped at the top of the stairs to politely ask him what it was. I couldn't have been farther off the mark if I had thought it was a fish. "Sea-ep" was CIEP, which was an acronym for the Council on International Economic Policy, a group responsible for keeping an eye on things like foreign trade and making sure that America's economic policies and strategies for dealing with foreign countries were consistent.

Although I was a little short of knowledge about things like the General Agreement on Tariffs and Trade and balance of payments, CIEP sounded good to me if it came with a check at the end of the week.

My meeting with the captain was very nice considering that the most we had in common was being male. He was a naval officer. I'd never been in the Navy. He had a doctorate in economics. I was a college freshman. He had a big desk with stately flags behind it. I had a small desk attached to a wall and a tiny American flag taped to it. Perhaps most impressive of all was that he was a gentleman who didn't make me feel like I was a nobody. In fact, it was quite the opposite.

Our chat ended when he had to take a phone call. No sooner than I left and closed the door behind me, Glen opened the door, went in, and closed the door behind him. I sat in a chair by his desk. I looked at my watch. It was 11:45 a.m. When I looked at my watch again, it was noon. Knowing that I had to be on The Hill by one, I was as nervous as a cat in a room full of rockers.

Within a few minutes, Glen emerged from the office, put his hand on my shoulder, and asked me what I was doing. I had no idea what he was talking about. I muttered something like "Waiting for you, sir," scared to death I'd done something wrong. Then, with a completely serious look on his face he said "Well, get to work."

I must have looked completely flabbergasted because he leaned over and half-whispered, "That means you're hired."

When I looked like I understood, Glen shook my hand and laughed amiably. Everyone in the office must have been in on the joke because they all laughed, applauded, and made me feel exceptionally welcome.

Somewhere in the midst of all of this, I realized that I was going to have to make a very quick decision.

The EOB was fascinating, but I wanted to be on Capitol Hill. Considering my finances, however, the unpaid internship in the Senate made no sense. Working for CIEP would at least put $2.95 an hour, or about $16.06 in 2017 dollars, in my wallet. Although

I didn't know anything about the job in the Congressman's office, my grandmother always told me that "a bird in the hand was worth two in the bush."

With that, I decided to take the job with CIEP; however, I still had to do something about my other appointments. I explained my situation to Glen and told him that I'd like to go to The Hill, let the people there know that I'd taken another job, and personally thank them for their help. Glen liked my plan and sent me on my way. Unlike many of my decisions, that one turned out well. I spent a lot of time on Capitol Hill that spring and summer during the Watergate hearings and ran into those men and women more frequently than I could have ever imagined. They remembered my name and, judging by their smiles, seemed to think kindly of me. In fact, as Watergate turned darker and darker, one of the senior Senate staffers I'd met even stopped me one day to ask how I was doing and told me to let him know if I found myself in need of a job.

I also learned a lesson about anxiety from this experience that I've passed on to friends and family and have occasionally followed myself. You can worry all you want to about the uncertainties inherent in jobs, exams, relationships, or any of the hundreds of other torment-inducing things life serves up; in the end, however, it's all an utter waste of energy. When the time is right, the universe will not only influence what will happen and when but will probably wait until you least expect it to let you in on the plan. I chased 15 or more job possibilities for months with nothing to show for it and then landed three solid prospects in the space of just a few days. When events don't follow the path you'd like them to, keep plugging away. Things often work out better than you could have ever imagined.

I wanted to work on Capitol Hill but ended up at 1600 Pennsylvania Avenue, not exactly a poor consolation prize. Even more, through various other unexpected twists and turns and a problem called Watergate, I ended up experiencing some of the most fascinating aspects of both.

As embarrassing as it is to admit it, one of those fascinating things was finding out where I was. Because for at least the first few days, I didn't realize that I was working in the White House.

Looking back, I have no idea why or how I didn't grasp the significance of it all, except for the fact that I only entered and exited the EOB on the 17th Street side, which doesn't have a view of the White House. Whatever the reasons, I unquestionably recall the day that it all became shockingly clear.

The White House career I didn't know I had started in Room 204 of the Old Executive Office Building. I followed Dave around again for a couple of days. I studied copiers, learning how to load paper, refill toner, and clear paper jams, critical expertise that I was told could lead to becoming a Key Operator, the copier world's equivalent of a superhero. When a copier wouldn't copy and all hell was breaking loose, a little red light would come on and illuminate the words, Call Key Operator. If there was inky, torn paper hopelessly snarled in the machine's rollers, the Key Operator would get it back in service and make the world safe again for the mass reproduction of memos.

Along with learning the mechanics of copiers, I also practiced the ins and outs of sorting mail, applied myself to remembering names, and tried to figure out my way around a very old, stunningly beautiful building that looked virtually the same everywhere you went. Before the week was out, Dave had moved on and I was asked to clean out an office for a new occupant.

From the moment that I opened the door, it was abundantly clear that the former tenant wasn't big on organization. The office was a mess and if it hadn't been for the night cleaning crews probably would have been draped with cobwebs. Papers were haphazardly piled everywhere, and there were an unusually large number of fatally chewed yellow pencils scattered around. In fact, it looked as if the previous occupant had simply walked out of the building one day and never come back. The only things that were orderly were the disgusting pieces of chewing gum he'd stuck under the lip of the desk top. They were lined up evenly in rows of three.

One of the desk drawers was so stuffed with various kinds of junk that I had to pry it open. Like many in those days, the top drawer had slats that were made to hold stationery. I pulled out the contents and looked at the letterhead.

In raised blue ink across the top it said "The White House" on one line and "Washington" on the next.

I was absolutely stunned.

My immediate reaction was to assume that someone must have stolen it and that they were going to be in a lot of trouble with the government. Not completely sure what to do, I decided that I needed to find someone I could trust with my amazing discovery.

I walked across the hall to a lovely lady from Kentucky who was a secretary to one of the big bosses. I cautiously showed her the White House letterhead.

"Can you believe what I found?" I asked excitedly, positive that her eyes would pop out of their sockets as much as mine had.

Instead, she was very calm.

"We have all kinds of interesting things here in the White House," she said with a warm smile.

Although I don't precisely remember my reaction, I wouldn't be surprised if I did a very comical double-take.

Sitting behind her typewriter, she patiently explained that the Old Executive Office Building and the White House were part of the same complex and that most White House staff offices were in the EOB. I must have had an odd expression on my face because at the end of the work day, my kind friend literally took me around the corner to show me Vice President Agnew's office in Room 274 and to the next floor down to see the door to President Nixon's office in Room 180 of the EOB, a hideaway of sorts where he could go to escape the madding crowd and where many of the Watergate tapes were recorded.

By the time my tour concluded, I was in at least a modest state of disbelief if not downright shock. Although it may sound funny, it reminded me a little of how I felt in the aftermath of the infamous "Heidi game" between the Oakland Raiders and the New York Jets in 1968. With a minute left in the 4th quarter, the Jets ahead by three points and the ball in Oakland's possession, NBC abruptly switched from the game to *Heidi*, a children's movie, and left millions of viewers thunderstruck. My dad and I were so stunned that we could barely speak. We had to wait for the eleven o'clock news to learn that while Heidi was traipsing around the Swiss Alps, Oakland had scored two touchdowns in 9 seconds and won 42-32.

I also felt something else that was much more important than amazement that day. My friend could have easily laughed at my ignorance and made me feel foolish. Instead, she was kind and sweet and treated me in a way that kept my dignity intact. I was grateful for that. I remember that she had attended Georgetown College, a liberal arts school north of Lexington, Kentucky. Every time I've heard that college's name mentioned over the years, I've thought of her and smiled.

As an American history enthusiast, learning that the EOB was part of the White House and that the EOB had its own breathtaking story to tell was like winning the mega-bucks lottery.

If you stand on the Pennsylvania Avenue side of what is now called the Dwight D. Eisenhower Executive Office Building, one of the largest, most ornate, historically significant, and least known government buildings in the Nation's Capital, the sheer massiveness of it can be a little deceiving. While it's clearly big, few people realize that it covers more than 217,000 square feet, making it 2.5 times larger in square footage than the Empire State Building. Originally called the State, War, and Navy Building when it opened in 1888 because of the executive offices it housed, the construction took 17 years and cost the current-day equivalent of $500 million. For their money, the American people took delivery of nearly 10,000 breathtaking feet of black-and-white-tiled corridors, more than 500 rooms, 100-odd fireplaces, 18-foot ceilings, eight curved granite staircases, four skylight domes, and two stained glass rotundas.

They also bought an exterior that was disparaged nearly from the beginning.

Built of gray granite and cast iron in the French Second Empire architectural style that was popular in Paris in the 1860s, the design was already out of vogue by the time construction was completed. Mark Twain called it ugly. In fact, the public criticism was said to have contributed to the architect's suicide in 1890. A proposal to raze the EOB and build a new facility was presented to the Eisenhower Administration in 1957; however, the high costs of the project combined with First Lady Jacqueline Kennedy's interest in preserving the building ultimately saved it from bulldozers.

The EOB was also a place to feel the energy of remarkable people and momentous events that lived on in the building's atmosphere.

William Howard Taft, the only person to have ever served as both President and Chief Justice of the United States, had an office in Room 232 of the EOB during his term as Secretary of War. A young Franklin Delano Roosevelt worked in the building as Assistant Secretary of the Navy during World War I under President Wilson as did his cousin, Theodore Roosevelt, before him in Room 278 under President McKinley. From time to time, FDR may have shared a hallway with a State Department clerk named James Thurber, who would become one of America's most famous writers, and Douglas MacArthur, who would later command all U.S. Army Forces in the Pacific and accept the Japanese surrender that would end World War II.

On December 7, 1941, Secretary of State Cordell Hull met with Japanese emissaries in Room 208 after the attack on Pearl Harbor had begun and promptly threw them out. My friend from Georgetown College worked in that very spot.

There were stories about British Prime Minister Winston Churchill ambling down the building's corridors during his wartime visits to Washington. There was a tale of John "Black Jack" Pershing, General of the Armies, riding his horse up and down one of the EOB stairways one afternoon. In the 1930s, it wouldn't have been unusual for a young Dwight Eisenhower, who would become America's 34th President in 1952, to be summoned to

Pershing's office in Room 274. President Herbert Hoover used the same room as his temporary office after a fire in the West Wing of the White House in 1929. Room 274 would later be occupied by Vice Presidents including, up to that time, Lyndon Johnson and Spiro Agnew. Following President Kennedy's assassination, Johnson spent his first days as President in Room 274.

And all of that happened just on the floor where I worked. For a history nerd like me, it was heaven.

The story of the EOB in many ways mirrors the history of the United States itself, the growth of its geography and population, the increase in the size and scope of government, and America's emergence as a world power.

Odd as it may seem, there was once a time when American presidents didn't have hundreds of aides to help them carry out their responsibilities. Congress simply wouldn't provide the funds. Concerned that a government without checks and balances could rule with absolute power, the founding fathers drafted a Constitution that forced the executive, legislative, and judicial branches of government to compete for power. Accordingly, they gave the President only limited authority, which also meant limited resources. Thomas Jefferson had to pay for his two aides out of his own pocket. President Lincoln had three assistants, only one of whom was paid with funds appropriated by Congress: the other two were on Cabinet department payrolls. Only ten more people were added in the thirty-five years between the end of the Lincoln Administration and President McKinley's re-election in 1900, and only 15 more were added over the next two decades.

The size and stature of the American Presidency remained largely unchanged until the Great Depression of the 1930s when the demand for strong presidential leadership during the nation's worst domestic crisis led to massive expansion of the Federal Government. With the Navy and War Departments having moved to new headquarters by 1938, the White House started moving selected offices to the State, War, and Navy Building the following year. The location was perfect: the West Wing of the White House and the State, War, and Navy Building were separated by nothing more than a fairly narrow street. In 1949 the building was turned over to a newly created entity called the Executive Office of the President, which, among other things in 1973, included the Executive Office of the President, the Council on International Economic Policy, the Office of the Vice President of the United States, the National Security Council, the Council of Economic Advisors, and the White House Communications Agency.

The good news for me in all of this was that the expansion of the presidency and the advent of copiers collided at just the right time to provide me with work. However, when I learned that making copies would be part of my responsibilities, I didn't realize it meant changing my name to Gutenberg.

One of my first literally weighty jobs for CIEP involved the biggest copier machine I had ever seen and a huge three-ring notebook containing several hundred loose leaf pages of something somebody thought was vital for America's future. It was a special mission. I had to make eight copies of each page, collate them, three-hole punch them, make dividers, and place the sheets in order in separate binders. Today, that's not a particularly impressive feat considering that there are machines that will do all that and wash, dry, and fold your laundry while you're waiting. Back then, however, it required a lot of labor.

Glen sent me to a giant machine in a big, busy room on the ground floor of the EOB. Because there were no automatic feeders, I had to take each page out of the master notebook individually, place the sheet on the glass, pull a floppy rubber cover over it, turn a dial for the number of copies, make the copies, collate them by hand, and three-hole punch them myself. That wasn't a big deal if you were doing, say, twenty copies of twenty pages. But eight copies of 300 pages was a whole different bag of cats.

My work schedule was organized around my class schedule and, at that time, I worked 20 hours a week over Monday, Tuesday, Thursday, and Friday. I started the project on Monday with a broad smile, energy, and youthful enthusiasm. By Tuesday afternoon, my smile was fading and I started counting how many pages were left, a bad idea with a project that large unless you're also ready to start tying a hangman's noose. By the time Glen stopped by on Thursday to give me another 20 pages, I was down and funky with the shake, rattle, and roll of the machine. By the time I finished the last book on Friday, I had every move from placing the original on the glass to neatly putting the copied pages in binders choreographed in my head to the Hollies' "Long Cool Woman (In a Black Dress)". On the very last note, I'd hit the three-hole punch with my fist.

Rock 'n Roll.

Within the first week or two of my employment I had to fill out forms for the Federal Bureau of Investigation. Strange as it may seem considering the last 40-odd years of White House history, law enforcement agencies actually tried to establish that you weren't a criminal if you were going to work around classified documents and some of the most powerful people in the world. The investigation included asking your friends, neighbors, and family questions about you. If I passed muster, I got a permanent

EOB credential to wear around my neck and kept my job. If I failed, I was history.

Although I had nothing to be concerned about, the kid part of me worried about one of our Atlanta neighbors grumbling to the Feds about the '64 Chevy Bel Air I drove over the summer. The guy I got it from, believe it or not, had painted the exterior white with a brush, the kind of you'd use on a house, and covered the dash with red paint that got so tacky under the hot Georgia sun that the smears of red left on your hand if you touched it made it look like you'd been on a five-state killing spree. The front license plate said "Love Machine" in psychedelic Day-Glo script and mercifully came off with a screwdriver and a quart of turpentine. The fact that the car's mere presence in our driveway drove down local property values wasn't the biggest problem: it was the noise when I cranked it up. With a V8 that punched out 340 hp with a single Carter 4-barrel, everybody in the neighborhood knew I was leaving. For that matter, so did half of North America. Smirk if you will, but when I drove off in my hand-painted Chevy blasting "Brandy (You're a Fine Girl)" on the radio in my turquoise sports coat, dark blue shirt, and white pants, I was something to behold.

As week after week went by without hearing a thing about my EOB pass, I was starting to sweat. After the first week, I asked my boss about it so often that I had surely become an insufferable annoyance. I was starting to think I'd made a huge mistake going to work there instead of The Hill, although I figured that at the rate I was going I'd be back up there looking for work soon anyway. Just about at the end of my rope, I even started to ask folks I worked with about how long it took them to get their security clearances. Their responses weren't comforting: most everyone said that it took about three weeks. I was still wearing a visitor's badge almost at the end of five.

As I was honing my skills in the copier room one early Friday afternoon, a friend stuck her head in to let me know Glen wanted to see me. Without the need for a substantiating reason, I immediately assumed I had done something wrong. When I arrived at his desk he was giving me a very serious look.

"Don," he said, "I need to tell you something important."

"Yes sir?" I replied as I choked back the urge to revisit my lunch on his desk.

"You need to see the Secret Service before you go home tonight," he said, handing me a piece of paper with a name and room number on it. "They've been waiting to see you."

The combination of the words "Secret Service" and "waiting to see you" in the same sentence drained the blood from my face. Now, along with lunch, I was also trying to hold back a high-pitched, panic-filled scream. In my mind's eye I saw a federal agent the size of a tree leaning over me saying, "We know all about the Chevy, kid" and then escorting me out of the building in handcuffs. I decided I was better off to get the nerve-wracking suspense about the Secret Service over with and went to their administrative office in the building prepared for the worst. When I walked back upstairs with my new EOB pass hanging around my neck, Glen and more than a few co-workers were waiting for me. They gave me a round of applause which I was sure I deserved but just didn't feel right about under the circumstances. After all, how did they know what I'd been doing?

"Congratulations, Don," Glen said, trying so hard to suppress a laugh that he was almost crying.

I looked around, puzzled.

"Did they tell you they've had it for three weeks?" he asked, now laughing out loud so hard he was about to expel his spleen.

With my eyes slightly squinted and a sideways smile on my face, I simply shook my head the way most of us do when we realize we've been had. Glen had been holding out, making me sit on pins and needles as a rite of passage of sorts. Suppressing a strong urge to commit homicide, my face opened into a broad smile.

◆

Although I was never the kind of person to purposely get into trouble, there were some things I simply couldn't resist. Although my pass only gave me access to the EOB, not the White House itself, I could cheat a little by walking out onto West Executive Avenue and casually inching my way towards the West Wing. That proved productive for excitement. On one of those walks, a Secret Service agent suddenly approached telling me to step aside a few feet and not move. Seconds later, President Nixon came out of the West Wing basement, passing me as he walked up the stairs of the EOB to his hideaway office. A week later I ran into H.R. Haldeman, the White House Chief of Staff, as he left the EOB bound for the West Wing.

The week after that, I was walking south on West Executive down the middle of the street rather than on the sidewalk. As I approached the interior entrance to the EOB known as the "ramp," a car horn that was loud enough to wake the dead blared right behind me. I jumped and turned around to see a long black Cadillac Fleetwood limousine. Behind the limousine was a station wagon with several men in it. One of them stuck his head out of the window and yelled "Move!" in a tone that clearly meant business and motivated me to get on the sidewalk as quickly as possible. As the Cadillac rolled by I saw Vice President Agnew sitting in the back seat, making it a good bet that the guys growling at me were Secret Service agents. Agnew's car turned right and pulled up in front of the swinging brown doors on the ground floor of the EOB. As it slowed to a stop, an agent jumped out of the still-moving wagon and got in front of the right rear door of the limousine where the Vice President was seated. Once the other agents were out and in position, he opened the door, Agnew got out and, together with the retinue of Secret Service agents, walked into the EOB.

Comings and goings of that sort were always interesting, and after the second or third encounter I developed a curiosity about the vehicles in the Secret Service fleet.

One story I came across was almost beyond belief.

On December 8, 1941, the day after the attack on Pearl Harbor, President Franklin Roosevelt traveled from the White House to the Capitol to ask Congress to declare war on Japan. Roosevelt's trip to the Capitol and the speech he delivered there are, of course, well-known historical facts. There's also a widely circulated story about the car that took the President to the Capitol.

Because Congress refused to authorize the necessary funds, the Secret Service didn't have an armored limousine for presidential transport in 1941. On the afternoon of December 7, aware that America was on the verge of war, agents in Washington realized they had only a matter of hours to produce a vehicle that would ensure Roosevelt's safety. With astounding good luck and some help from the Internal Revenue Service, they located a 1928 Cadillac sedan fitted with bullet-resistant glass and more than a ton of armor, which the IRS had confiscated and impounded in

Washington a decade earlier. The car the President of the United States of America traveled in that December day had previously belonged to a Chicago resident who had been convicted of felony tax evasion. His name was "Scarface" Al Capone, one of America's biggest gangsters, whose crime syndicate generated as much as $100 million annually in the 1930s, or roughly $1.9 billion today, from illegal liquor sales, prostitution, racketeering and gambling.

The story, as interesting as it is, is disputed, however. There are claims that Capone's car had been shipped to England before World War II and remained there until it was sold to a buyer in Toronto in the 1950s. If it wasn't Capone's car that took FDR to the Capitol, it's clear that somebody didn't let the truth get in the way of a good story.

On another occasion, as I walked down West Executive Avenue after one of my many brown bag lunches in Lafayette Park, I saw a large black Lincoln Continental sitting in the middle of the street with its engine running and Secret Service agents surrounding it. For some reason, I was allowed to walk past it on the sidewalk. As I reached the corner by the EOB ramp, I ran into a guy I knew from the National Security Council who was staring at the car.

"Waiting to see the President?" I asked.

"Not really," he responded. "I'm looking at the car."

"Cool, isn't it?" I said.

"Cool? How can you call that cool?" he replied, looking at me with the kind of stare reserved for someone who had just kicked his elderly mother in the shin.

"Don't you know what that is?" he asked.

I shook my head side to side.

"That's the car President Kennedy was assassinated in."

For some reason, I doubted the accuracy of his observation, probably because the car didn't resemble the dark blue Lincoln Continental convertible I'd seen time and again in newspapers and magazines over the previous decade. As I learned some years later, what he meant was that the car had the chassis of the convertible President Kennedy rode in on November 22, 1963.

Although, like many people at the time, I'd read everything about the assassination I could get my hands on, the fate of the limousine had never crossed my mind. The Secret Service and Ford Motor Company, which leased the car to the U.S. Government, had it stripped down to the chassis, redesigned, and painted black. The government also had armor and bullet-proof glass installed, a surprising fact, at least to me since I assumed that President Kennedy's car would have already been equipped that way. Not so. The Secret Service considered it a parade car that was to enhance the President's visibility, not, oddly, to provide protection. The car was used through the end of the Carter Administration and today is on exhibit at the Henry Ford Museum in Dearborn, Michigan.

If the Secret Service, the limousines, and the commotion that went with them could be called exhilarating, my first step into the West Wing would be best described as electrifying. In fact, my first visit to the West Wing was also my first time inside the real, honest-to-goodness-see-it-on-postcards-and-in-history-books White House.

I'd had a chance to take a public tour one Saturday morning in the fall of 1972 but missed it, at least in part because of the movie *The Exorcist*. About an hour before three or four of us were going to leave for the White House, some other friends stopped by to see if we were interested in going to Georgetown University instead.

Warner Bros. was going to film what turned out to be one of the movie's earlier scenes, a group of students protesting on the steps of Healy Hall, and they needed extras. Everyone preferred a chance at stardom to the White House, and I decided to blow off both. Looking back, I should have at least gone to Georgetown. One of the guys made nearly $100 because of the length of time he was on camera and became immortalized in a famous motion picture.

The buzz the studios created about how scary the movie would be was incredible for the time, and the gimmicks included parking ambulances on the street outside theaters, obviously implying that somebody was going to be nearly scared to death. I only saw about half of the movie. Early in the film when the door to the bedroom opens to show Regan, the little girl who was possessed by a demon, and her bed floating several feet off the floor, my girlfriend, Melissa, buried her face in my shoulder in one very quick, lunging sort of motion. Being a tough, macho kind of guy, I buried my face in her hair and the two of us huddled like a pair of hamsters until we decided to walk out, our eyes half closed.

Although the special effects were below the digital fare produced in Hollywood these days, they were terrifying enough to have earned the film the title as the "scariest horror movie ever made" in several polls. I knew more than a few people who admitted to sleeping with the lights on for months after seeing it, something I did, too, but refused to concede. Just about the time I felt it was safe to turn the lights off at bedtime, I found out that the book version of *The Exorcist*, which spent more than a year on the *New York Times* bestseller list, was based on a story about the 1949 exorcism performed on a 13-year-old boy from Cottage City, Maryland, a suburb of Washington, D.C.

I immediately turned on the lights again.

◆

The mission of my inaugural trip into the White House was to deliver something from the big boss in our corner of the world, Peter Flanigan, the Assistant to the President for International Economic Policy. Improbably, I knew who Peter Flanigan was before I worked for CIEP. In a wild coincidence, I had chosen a 1972 *Time Magazine* article about him as part of a high school English assignment. A graduate of Princeton, a World War II Navy carrier pilot, and managing director of New York investment firm Dillon, Read & Co., he was also a great-grandson of Adolphus Busch, the co-founder of Anheuser-Busch. Flanigan had known Richard Nixon since 1959. In 1960 he served as the national director of volunteers for Nixon-Lodge, and he served as Nixon's deputy campaign manager in 1968. Among other accomplishments, he had been a major force behind America's decision to build the Space Shuttle.

The sealed brown envelope was addressed to someone on the second floor of the West Wing. Glen, who had a White House pass, could have easily taken it himself and made less work out of it; instead, he was the kind of class act who shared the wealth. Inevitably knowing that he was about to make my day, Glen told me where to go and how to get there and picked up the phone to arrange clearance with the Executive Protective Service (EPS), the uniformed branch of the Secret Service sometimes referred to as the White House Police. Once that was done, and despite being told that the envelope wasn't a rush delivery, I flew down the EOB stairs at near breakneck speed and ran across West Executive Avenue. Just before I got to the West Wing basement's double doors, enough healthy nervousness luckily set in to at least reduce my speed from a gallop to a medium trot.

As I opened the door and crossed the threshold into the building, what I expected and what I saw were two somewhat different things.

In my mind, the White House was a very big place filled with people who were always doing something important.

The first thing that surprised me was that the physical area of the basement was both a lot smaller and appeared to have a lot more in it than I had imagined. I walked to the modest security desk that was in an open area to my right, introduced myself to the middle-aged EPS officer sitting there, and extended my hand for a hearty handshake. To my delight, rather than the often-gruff responses I usually received from the EPS, the officer shook my hand, smiled broadly, and welcomed me to the West Wing. As the officer reviewed my badge and wrote down my name, I had a chance to look around for a few seconds. I remember being struck by the beautiful dark wood doors everywhere, most of which were closed, and the sign on one that said Navy Mess, which I thought was a joke rather than a military term for a dining room. Then, I saw two more things that astonished me.

The first was that the people in the open area were just milling around, chatting and laughing with one another rather than doing something that looked significant.

The second was that there was a men's room sign in the corner over my right shoulder as I stood in front of the desk. Why that caught me off guard I have no idea, except for the weird possibility that I believed people in the White House either didn't go the bathroom or weren't allowed to. In any event, after I spent a few more moments marveling at the fact that I was standing almost directly below the Oval Office, the officer directed me to a narrow elevator and told me to check back with him before I left. Then I headed off, delivered the envelope, and, admittedly more than a little intimidated by it all, went straight back to the elevator and pressed "B" to return to the basement. I breathed a huge sigh of relief that nothing embarrassing had happened, one of the huge concerns that casts a shadow over your life when you're a teenager.

Not too many weeks later during a similar West Wing trip, however, I stepped onto the elevator on the second floor, pressed the "B" button and, as the elevator came to "1", the floor where the Oval Office is located, it came to a halt. The door opened and John Ehrlichman, second only to the Chief of Staff at the top of the White House food chain, walked in. By that time in March 1973, Ehrlichman was already drowning as a central figure in the Watergate scandal. I remember that his face was quite red, that he said hello to me, and that I was too shocked to respond with anything more than a slightly goofy look. Considering what must have been on the man's mind, his simple "Hello, how are you?" was very thoughtful. Six weeks later, President Nixon demanded his resignation. In 1975, he was convicted of perjury and conspiracy to obstruct justice and served 18 months in federal prison. In 1977, he would be quoted as saying, "If I had any advice for my kids, it would be to never, never, never defer your moral judgments to anybody: your parents, your wife, anybody."

On my way out, I stopped to see the EPS officer. After he marked my name off the clearance list, we chatted for a few minutes about where I was from, my college studies, and other things. He asked me if I had been to the Oval Office "yet," as if it was simply expected that I would stroll by when I had a minute.

I told him I hadn't. He was an extremely nice man, ancient from my perspective although probably about the same age I am now.

"Tell you what," he said, "if your boss will let you, stop by around one o'clock one day and I'll take you up there myself."

We shook hands again and I walked back to the EOB with a huge smile on my face.

As you might expect, all I could think about from that point forward was seeing the Oval Office. And, just like my job hunt, opportunity knocked on the door when I least expected it.

In fact, that day was rather unusual all around, and it started with a visit to the Selective Service System, otherwise known as the draft board.

In 1973, men were required to register for the draft within a period of thirty days before to twenty-nine days after their eighteenth birthday. Since my eighteenth birthday was coming up, I decided to take the bus downtown to the draft board and take care of business before I went to work. When I arrived, I was given papers to fill out and told to take them to a lady sitting behind a metal desk when she was free. At the moment, the lady was busy being nasty to another guy who looked like he was about to punch her out.

When it was my turn, I sat down in a gray metal chair to her left, introduced myself, made a polite little joke, and damn near choked to death on her perfume, heavy, eye-stinging stuff that smelled like the deodorant in portable toilets. In response to my wheezing over her aroma, she gave me a creepy look that suggested that what she lacked in a sense of humor she made up for in violence. All the same, I just couldn't let an opportunity for a few laughs pass me by. She looked at my paperwork and noted that I was a Georgia resident but lived in the dorms at American

University. Then she suggested, somewhat under her breath but not quite enough, that people from Georgia were stupid. I told her that I was prepared to "give up my Georgia citizenship" if she thought I should. Short of that, however, I told her that I'd appreciate it if she could arrange to have me drafted into the "Georgia Army" so that I could be with "my own kind." This led to a five-minute tutorial about the difference between U.S. and state citizenship, a curt denial that there was a "Georgia Army", and yet another nasty look when I asked, "Are you sure about that?"

Then she served up a question so perfect in every way that it couldn't have been better if I'd spent a hundred years writing it myself.

"Outside of a family member, who will know where you can be found for the next five years?" she asked.

"My boss, I guess," I answered.

"And what is his business address?" she inquired.

"1600," I said. "1600," she repeated. "Pennsylvania," I continued. "Avenue."

"1600 Pennsylvania Avenue?" she said, turning her red-tinged eyes towards me sharply. "Stop it, young man. Everybody knows what that is," she said.

"Well, that's where I work," I said, showing her my EOB pass.

She looked at it, stood up, told me to stay where I was, walked over to an empty desk, and completed whatever was necessary for my draft card. She walked back, handed the card to me, and, in a cold, dead voice told me to get out. I thanked her profusely in the deepest Southern accent I could muster.

At work after partying with the Selective Service, Glen sent me to perform one of my usual duties, shopping for exotic items like copier paper, pencils, and typewriter ribbons at the General

Services Administration store a few blocks away. The place was amazing. They had almost every office supply imaginable plus car tires and TVs. I'd walk over with my modified grocery cart, fill the orders I had, and pay for everything with a rudimentary form of a government credit card. I could only imagine someone with one of those credit cards at the counter saying, "I'll take two reams of copier paper, a stapler, and four tires for a '71 Pinto." I never heard of anyone buying tires or TVs, but they certainly made for interesting conversation.

That day I was particularly overloaded—so much, in fact, that the supplies were stacked above the top of the cart. I must have been something to watch. It's not every day you see someone doing a modified version of the cha-cha behind a cart, swinging back and forth to keep a pile of teeter-tottering office supplies on board. Even though the walk wasn't very far and the weather was chilly, I worked up enough of a sweat that my rayon and polyester shirt stuck to my chest and my polyester tie stuck to my shirt.

Frequently, the scenery on these excursions was more fascinating than the destinations. Whenever the opportunity came up, I particularly enjoyed walking by The Octagon House, the national headquarters of the American Institute of Architects and purportedly one of the most haunted spots in the Nation's Capital. Little more than a block from the Old Executive Office Building, the three-story brick building at the corner of 18th Street and New York Avenue was built at the turn of the 19th century by John Tayloe III, a moneyed plantation owner, at the behest of his friend George Washington who wanted to see the new capital city grow. What few people other than history enthusiasts are aware of is that The Octagon was used as a temporary residence by President

James Madison and his wife, Dolley, after the White House was burned by British troops during the War of 1812.

Two hundred years after its construction, The Octagon remains busy with an assortment of interesting occupants and visitors, many of whom, whether they know it or not, are dead.

Dolley Madison, whose spirit is said to be accompanied by the smell of lilacs, has reportedly been seen in the ballroom and the garden. Lively in her old age, Mrs. Madison has also been seen in the White House Rose Garden and smiling at pedestrians from the porch of 721 Madison Place in Lafayette Square where she passed away in 1849. She is said to be kept company in The Octagon by the apparitions of slaves, a gambler, a British soldier, and two of John Tayloe's daughters, among others. Curiously, both of Tayloe's daughters allegedly died following arguments about their romantic interests with their disapproving father, and both fell over stair railings, one from the second floor and the other from the third floor. A coincidence? Perhaps. Whatever the case, the ghost of one of the girls is said to manifest itself as a candlelight floating up the staircase. The other is said to be a dark shadow that haunts the space between the second and third floors.

By the time I put the supplies away it was lunchtime and one of the extra-large hot dogs in the EOB cafeteria was calling my name. I believed a treat was in order after the morning's events, and I loaded that puppy up with as many diced onions and clumps of sauerkraut as the laws of the physical world would allow. After the dog, a big soda, and a bag of chips, I felt more than a little overstuffed and decided to go out on West Executive Avenue to walk off the damage. Instead, I ended up proving that Murphy's Law of whatever can go wrong will go wrong was very much alive and well. Damp, onionated, and slowly bloating with fermented cabbage, I ran straight into my favorite Executive Protective Service officer who asked if I was ready to see the Oval Office.

Doing my best to hold back what was sure to be a revolting, if not also deafening, belch, I told him I was.

Back in the basement of the West Wing, my new best friend led me up two flights of stairs to the first floor and down a central corridor to a spot where another EPS officer was seated in a chair. Over the officer's right shoulder was an open doorway which had a burgundy velvet rope with mirrored gold hooks suspended across it. While my mind was grappling to accept the fact that I was standing outside of the President's office and not a replica in a museum, my friend nodded to the officer in the chair who stood up, released the rope, and let me take a step through the doorway.

It would be difficult, if not impossible, to walk into the Oval Office and not be moved by the rich history indelibly etched on its walls. Its celebrity makes it all the more interesting to know that the physical structure most people are familiar with today isn't the original one. It's the third Oval Office and the fourth presidential office in the West Wing since the beginning of the 20th century.

The first presidential office in the West Wing was constructed in 1902 for Theodore Roosevelt. It was rectangular. President William Howard Taft built the first Oval Office in the center of the West Wing in 1909, and President Hoover had the Oval Office rebuilt in the same location in the aftermath of a West Wing fire in 1929. Several years later, President Roosevelt had the Oval Office moved to the southeast corner of the West Wing where there was better lighting and better access to the White House residence for his wheelchair. Apart from a few nips and tucks, the Oval Office occupied by Richard Nixon in 1973 was virtually the same one Franklin Delano Roosevelt designed 40 years earlier.

I stopped to take a deep breath.

Curiously, the first thing I noticed wasn't the room but the air, which somehow seemed lighter or cleaner as if they had pumped a higher mix of oxygen through the ventilation system. Although it's more likely that my senses were elevated from excitement or tickled as the harsh taste of sauerkraut in my mouth vanished under the weight of a Peppermint Lifesaver, the moment sparkled, making everything seem brighter and sharper.

I took my time looking around.

The brilliant blues and yellows of President Nixon's Oval Office gave the room an extraordinary energy. There was an enormous royal blue oval rug with a golden yellow presidential seal in the center and a border of golden yellow stars. Dark yellow drapes, better described as saffron, as I later learned, and a matching valence outlined the windows behind the President's desk, and similarly colored fabric covered the armchairs and two sofas. There were at least a dozen representations of American eagles in the room, including a medallion of the presidential seal in the ceiling. My friend had me look up to see that the rug was positioned so that the eyes of the eagle in the presidential seal looked directly into the eyes of the eagle in the ceiling. On the left side of a credenza that held Nixon family photos and a bust of Abraham Lincoln stood an American flag. A dark blue presidential flag stood on the right. Farther to the right were five military parade flags with gold tassels representing the Army, Marine Corps, Navy, Air Force, and Coast Guard. A black leather chair with a back that would have come as high as the Chief Executive's shoulders sat behind the President's double-pedestal mahogany desk, known as the Wilson Desk, a stunning piece of furniture with a quirky history and at least a pinch or two of bad luck.

Woodrow Wilson, the 28th President of the United States, was America's wartime Commander in Chief during World War I and a Nobel Peace Prize winner for his leadership in founding the League of Nations, the forerunner of the United Nations. A keen admirer of Wilson's, Richard Nixon used what he understood to be President Wilson's desk during his eight years as Vice President from 1953-1961. When he became President in 1969, Nixon, a Republican, not only had the Wilson Desk moved into the Oval Office where he noted its distinguished history in a nationally televised speech but also had a portrait of Wilson, a Democrat, hung in the Cabinet Room.

At some juncture, a White House curator was assigned to delve deeper into the desk's history and, rather than finding something that added to its nobility, was forced to deliver some unfortunate news: although the Wilson Desk had indeed been used by a Wilson, it wasn't President Wilson. Instead, the Wilson in question was Vice President Henry Wilson, who served under President Ulysses S. Grant. Vice President Wilson fell asleep in a bathtub in the Capitol Building one day in 1875, caught a chill, suffered a stroke, and literally died in his office. He's said to haunt the Capitol at night.

Apparently not believing in quitting while they were ahead, further research by the curators discredited their own findings, claiming that the desk had never been associated with either Wilson and had been purchased by William McKinley's first Vice President, Garret Hobart, in 1897. Hobart, who also fell a tad short of the cache of a Woodrow Wilson, was best known for two things: first, his untimely death in 1899 that opened the way for Theodore Roosevelt to succeed to the Presidency after McKinley's death in 1901 and, second, a penchant for extravagant spending on his office in the U.S. Capitol which, among other things, included the desk and a silk robe made to match the cushions on a new couch.

While the fate of Hobart's robe may be unknown, his desk sat in the Oval Office until 1977 when President Carter replaced it with the Resolute desk used by President Kennedy and made famous in photographs of little John F. Kennedy, Jr. playing behind the desk's hinged privacy panel while his father worked. The desk was built from the timbers of the British Arctic Exploration ship *H.M.S. Resolute* and given as a gift to the United States by Queen Victoria. The Wilson Desk was consequently moved back to the Vice President's Room in the U.S. Capitol, where it reportedly resides today.

Frankly, I'm not so sure about the Wilson Desk. Think about it. Vice President Hobart used it and died in office. Vice President Nixon used it and lost the 1960 presidential election. President Nixon used it again and resigned. President Ford used it and lost the 1976 election. Last but not least, President Carter used it for a little while after his inauguration and lost re-election in 1980. Not that there were any other factors, of course, but if I were President, I believe I'd leave that desk right where it is.

As I walked away that afternoon, I marveled at my good fortune. I'd had an extraordinary excursion, learned some fascinating things, and managed to keep my potentially volatile lunch under control. After that day, it was clear to me that the Oval Office and I were made for each other. I decided that I'd take advantage of everything I could sneak into or hang around near the President's office until somebody with a gun heaved me out onto Pennsylvania Avenue.

All I had to do was to figure out how to do it.

Fortunately, I'd learned something the previous summer that helped.

A group of us decided to meet in the ticket line for a rock concert one night. Everybody arrived on time except for one of our friends who worked as a coach at a kid's day camp. When he finally showed up, he said that he was broke but that he could get in for free. While we waited in line, he slid off the rubber band holding his long ponytail in place as he walked to the side entrance of the building. With nothing more than his clipboard and white T-shirt that said "Staff" on the front, he walked past a security guard and through the backstage door without a soul stopping him. We couldn't believe it. After we took our seats, our minds were completely blown as we watched him walk across the stage, tap on a microphone, say "Check, 1, 2, 3", and walk back behind the curtains.

After the show, which he watched from behind a table loaded with refreshments, he explained why he thought his maneuver worked. He said that most people assume that you belong wherever you are, especially if you wear something official-looking, carry something important-looking, and look like you know what you're doing.

If you tried his stunt in most places today, you'd be lucky to avoid getting arrested. In the era before layered security became necessary in so many venues, however, blending in worked pretty well if you took it seriously.

I did.

I picked out a place to stand in front of the Roosevelt Room, a conference room built in the original location of Theodore Roosevelt's office, only steps away from the Oval Office. I kept an inter-office envelope tucked under my arm and tried to look like

I was waiting for somebody. Although there were two mammoth Secret Service agents who would tell me to get lost the moment they saw me, my loitering paid off over time. I came across a collection of people from key Members of Congress and the Cabinet to two future Presidents, Gerald Ford, then the House Minority Leader, and George H.W. Bush, chairman of the Republican National Committee.

I even helped the very uncomfortable-looking head of a foreign government into a restroom.

Well, sort of.

Chapter Three

SWEAT, SENATORS, AND SOVIETS

From the day I went to work for the Federal Government in February 1973, I started living in two radically different worlds.

In the world in which I had the most fun but spent the least amount of time, I wore a blazer, a tie, and shined shoes and worked for grown-ups who had important jobs. In the world I enjoyed the least but spent the most time in, I went to college and lived in a dormitory. At work, I was in the company of people with doctorates in economics. In the dorm, I lived near a guy who called himself Muz and wore an old-fashioned top hat.

Not surprisingly for the early '70s, Muz wasn't the only thought-provoking figure on campus, although he was the only one who claimed to be a political refugee from another planet. In fact, to suggest that we only had a handful of eccentrics walking around would be like saying that Custer wasn't well-received at Little Big Horn. It would be the height of understatement. There was a student who wore a parka in frigid temperatures, but no shoes or socks. Another guy answered every question with a question. If you asked him his name, he'd ask yours instead. If you asked him for the time, he'd ask you why you wanted to know.

Impatient people often belted him. We even had a fellow scholar who liked to put on pince-nez glasses and a Rough Rider uniform and pretend he was Teddy Roosevelt. He said "Bully" a lot and talked about riding up San Juan Hill. The only one who worried me a little was a guy who carried on a conversation with himself in the mirror every morning while he shaved. Today, you'd assume that he was chatting on a mobile phone. In 1972, you assumed that he was a few feathers short of a chicken.

As imposing as this group was, however, they were nothing compared to what walked out of a dormitory shower one morning.

As I stepped out of a shower stall, I saw someone with waist-length blonde hair standing about ten feet away from me. Considering that there were more than a few guys with hair that long in 1972, I didn't think much of it. Then she turned around to display every naked millimeter of her spectacular body. While I was high-fiving myself for my decision to go to college, she smiled at me, said hello, threw her only towel over her shoulder, and walked out into the hall completely au natural.

Although I desperately wanted to say hello back, I couldn't get out more than a ragged gurgle that must have sounded creepy.

It turned out that she lived with her boyfriend in one of the dorm rooms. Even though living arrangements like that were unusual and a little shocking in those days, I did my best to remain as absolutely open-minded about the situation as possible. As luck would have it, I would run into this divine creature many more times in the future, although never again without her clothes on no matter how much time I spent in the shower, which, not coincidentally, was a lot.

As you might expect, the characters who were openly connected to drugs gave off a whole different vibe than the dancer, the shoeless guy, or even Teddy Roosevelt did. Ambitious, sociable, and never without a life-sized human skull tucked under his arm, Muz became well known for regularly hosting bong soirees that drew 10 or 15 of his followers to his tiny dorm room. With a supply of cold pizza and wet towels jammed under the door to keep the smoke in, the party-goers would stay for days at a time. One afternoon they opened a window and the door at the same time. So much thick smoke bellowed out of the window that a passerby called the fire department and almost everybody near the door got high. I can vouch for that.

At the opposite end of the hall was a guy who became known as "The Moron" because of an incident that involved a powerful sedative called Quaalude. Some users would combine Quaalude with alcohol to achieve a drunken, sleepy high that could cause death or a combination of respiratory arrest, delirium, and coma that would eventually kill you. One evening ""The Moron" took a shower and, for reasons I doubt were even clear to him, decided to dry his wet pubic hair with a hot comb. Everything apparently went well until the Quaaludes wore off. High temperature hot combs were made to straighten curly hair on the top of your head, not down around your tender vittles, and he ended up in considerable pain. After failing to convince his roommate to rub butter on his scorched groin, he decided to pour a cold beer on it. That idea proved to be a poor choice, too.

Just as people began to believe that we had already seen a living legend in action and that no one could possibly outdo first-degree crotch burns from a hairstyling appliance, a challenger arrived on the scene. His name was "Ed, man," and he lived in the middle of the hall.

Standing about 5'5", with dark hair down to the middle of his back, a beard, and mustache, "Ed, man" was a dead ringer for Cousin It on *The Addams Family*. No one, including his room-mate, even knew his last name. When meeting someone for the first time, and sometimes for the sixth time, he shook hands and simply said "Ed, man." In fact, I never heard him say a third word.

"Ed, man's" more than fifteen minutes of fame arrived one Friday night when he passed out cold at his own party. Very stoned themselves, his guests decided that rather than try to bring him to, it would be a lot more entertaining to put him on display like a circus sideshow attraction. One guy thought it would be funny to strip him naked, so they took all of his clothes off. Another suggested putting him in a wire grocery cart someone had swiped from the neighborhood supermarket, and they hoisted him into it. Then, the craziest one of the bunch rolled him, naked as a jaybird in the wire cart, into one of the elevators and punched the down button. I heard that "Ed, man" was in the cart a good part of Saturday riding the elevator up and down and sleeping off whatever put him there in the first place. Not surprisingly, he drew a big crowd and more than one person had their picture taken with him, although he was in no condition to say "cheese," at least from the front end.

Eyewitnesses said that "Ed, man" eventually got out of the cart by simply throwing a leg over the side and jumping out. Some people thought it looked like he'd done it before. I never saw "Ed, man" in the cart, but I did see him walking down the hall shortly afterward. His entire backside looked like it had been pressed in a waffle iron.

Meanwhile, back in my other world, there were places to go, people to see, and mistakes to be made.

One of my best worst moments started one afternoon when I innocently stepped into the hallway to go to the men's room. Mr. Flanigan's secretary, Marge, had a sixth sense for knowing where to find me, and she stepped out in the hallway at almost the same moment and waved to get my attention. She had a very serious, almost anxious, look on her face and, before she said a word, pressed several coins into my hand.

"I need you to go and buy two bottles of Pepsi out of the machine and bring them back here right away," she said. "And I mean right away."

This did not appear to be the right time to ask questions, so I took the money, flew down the hallway and down the stairs towards the first vending machine I knew of. I put the money in and pushed the Pepsi button.

Nothing came out.

I tried again.

And again.

After coming up Pepsi-less for the third time, I went to another machine and bought two Cokes. As far as I was concerned, there wasn't much difference between the two.

In old horror movies, there's typically a moment when the camera comes in for a close-up of the first ill-fated person to see the monster before it chows down on the town. The poor soul's flesh looks blood-drained, their eyes bulge, and their screams slice the air like a knife. When Marge saw me approaching with two bottles of Coca-Cola, her reaction was strangely similar. She was holding a silver tray with two glasses, a small bucket of ice, and silver tongs.

"I told you to get Pepsi. Why did you get Coke?" she said in a hard whisper.

"The machine didn't work," I replied. "They're the same thing."

If looks could have killed at that instant, I would have been six feet under.

"Well, it's too late," she said with anxiety dripping from her voice. "Stay right here. Don't move."

She poured the liquids into the glasses, put the bottles on the floor behind her desk and, with a deep breath, opened Mr. Flanigan's office door, entered, and closed the door behind her. I knew I was in trouble, but couldn't figure out exactly why.

Less than a minute later, she came back out and told me to take a seat. A few seconds after that, I heard loud laughter coming from inside Mr. Flanigan's office.

Marge went in.

I heard my name mentioned.

Marge came out.

Marge asked me to go into Mr. Flanigan's office.

Sitting there were Mr. Flanigan and a gentleman I hadn't met, both of whom had apparently been laughing so hard that they were turning red.

Mr. Flanigan introduced me to his visitor whose first name also happened to be Don. Don asked me in a very pleasant voice why I bought Cokes, and I explained that the Pepsi machine wasn't working. He asked which cola I preferred.

"Coke," I answered.

"Don, this is Don Kendall. He's the chairman of PepsiCo, the company that makes Pepsi," Flanigan said

I don't remember what, if anything, I said in response, but I probably realized that things weren't cool even though the other Don gave me a warm smile. After about a minute, which felt like an eternity, Mr. Flanigan thanked me for coming in and sent me on my way.

Looking back on it so many decades later, I think about how both men could have made a huge, nasty deal of my mistake and put me out on the street right then and there. In later years, I certainly came to know enough executives without a moral compass who would have done so simply because they could. Instead, both men were very gracious and, by being so, taught me an important lesson about how to treat people who make honest mistakes. A few weeks later, Mr. Kendall sent me a very nice letter, a stack of vouchers for free bottles of Pepsi, and a suggestion that I give Pepsi a try. Because of that, I've been a Pepsi drinker ever since.

After making enough trips to the West Wing to have learned names and faces and find my way around without a map, I sort of became the "go-to guy" when something needed to be taken there. Although I eventually suspected that the reason I was the "go-to guy" was because people wanted to see what kind of mess I'd get into next, I nonetheless relished every opportunity to go. On one occasion Glen even cleared me to deliver something to the White House Social Secretary, the executive in charge of arranging White House social events, a trip that took me beyond the Oval Office through the ground floor of the main White House building to the East Wing. I wanted to stop about every five feet just to look around but decided it wouldn't be cool to become the White House staff equivalent of a tourist in Bermuda shorts, black socks, and wingtips.

My security badge gave me to access to the EOB but not the White House proper, and going all the way to the East Wing without a White House pass required that I stop at multiple security checkpoints along the way. The route I was sent on was circuitous to say the least. My first stop was to see my friend in the Executive Protective Service in the West Wing basement, then across the basement area and up a flight of stairs that took me to the White House Press Office, bypassing the Oval Office and the walkway through the Rose Garden that connected the West Wing to what insiders called the Residence. Then, I cut through the Press Office, walked outside, and presented myself to another EPS officer sitting in an area I later learned was the White House Carpenter Shop. Next, I was sent through an area near the White House florist's shop that was bursting with the delicious smell of fresh flowers and around to an entranceway that opened into a long colonnade with windows and a view of Jacqueline Kennedy's Garden and the South Lawn on my right. At the end of the hall, I presented myself to yet another EPS officer sitting near a very large bust of Abraham Lincoln. Finally, I reached the Social Secretary's office and left the envelope I'd been charged to deliver.

It had been a modestly interesting trip, but not very exciting. Having fulfilled my critical mission, I realized that it was about lunchtime and gave myself full permission to make things a little more thought-provoking.

Had I known more about security matters, I might have avoided my first mistake of the afternoon.

It didn't occur to me that the same EPS guards that I had checked in with on my way over to the East Wing would be expecting me to check out on my way back. Although I stopped to see the officer stationed next to Lincoln so that he could sign me out, I thought I'd see what happened if instead of returning to the EOB by walking around the Residence as instructed, I simply walked through it. So, I strolled back down the colonnade. Instead of going to the door in the foyer that would take me outside, however, I made a left onto the wide, red-carpeted center hall that, to me, looked like a movie set.

The Library was the first room on my right as I walked down the hall, and, since it was very inviting and no one was there, I walked right in. Since I'd never toured the White House before, I wasn't completely sure what the room was used for. There were shelves filled with elegantly bound books, expensive-looking knick-knacks, sofas, tables, chairs, and a fireplace. The room reminded me of every store I'd ever been in with signs that read, "You break it, you buy it." Despite that, I explored the room's nooks and crannies and, like a much more respectful version of Goldilocks and the Three Bears, I tried out the couch and at least one of the chairs to find out which one felt "just right."

While the question of the most comfortable seat in the Library was debatable, the question of how long it took to get thrown out of the Library wasn't: it didn't take more than a few minutes. There was another EPS officer posted about 30 feet away at the foot of some marble stairs leading up to the first floor where the East Room, the State Dining Room, and the Red, Green, and Blue Rooms are located, and we couldn't have missed seeing each other by more than a second or two. Apparently, though, he had the same spooky flair for having eyes in the back of his head that my mom did, and he scared the living daylights out of me when he asked "Who are you?" in a deep, authoritative voice that thundered over my shoulder from behind.

I jumped again when I saw him, a man clearly over six feet with the size and angry bearing of an NFL linebacker. At this point, of course, the question wasn't whether I was in trouble: the tenor of his voice told me it was simply a matter of how much.

My gut instinct was that I wasn't going to squirm out of this pec-
cadillo easily.

Then I thought it probably wouldn't be bad at all.

Then I learned to trust my gut in the first place.

About the only thing the officer didn't do was put me in
handcuffs which, considering how mean and agitated he looked,
was something I'm sure he'd thought about.

After ordering me out of the Library and interrogating me
about who I was and what I was doing there, he picked up the
telephone next to the dark red upholstered chair at his station and
called someone who presumably was also in the Secret Service. I
was so nervous that I broke into a sweat all the way down to my
ankles and my right leg started to shake involuntary, develop-
ments that made me worry that I might also involuntarily wet
the rug. Despite my saying that I was sorry several times and
swearing that I would never wander around the White House
again, he paid no attention. In fact, the less he said, the more of a
wreck I became. After a minute or two, another officer arrived to
take his place and the fellow who busted me told me in a sharp,
no-nonsense tone to come with him. I sort of limped along like a
pile of wet laundry with one good leg, the other one still moving
around the way you shake it the "Hokey Pokey". With me closely
in tow, the officer gave me a razor-sharp tongue-lashing about
doing what I was told, advice that wasn't exactly a great revelation
to me under the circumstances.

Eventually, he led me back on the same route I had traveled
and back to my friend, the EPS officer in the West Wing basement. After giving my friend an earful about my transgressions
and giving me a couple more verbal whackings, he walked away
and left me there. Frankly, this was the worst punishment I could

have imagined short of the Secret Service calling my dad. I felt like I'd let down both my friend and my boss. I desperately needed a change of clothes. I could barely speak and was on the verge of launching a vomit rocket right on the wall of the White House. It was not the kind of mark I had planned to make there.

My friend cleared his throat, looked down at a piece of paper, and wrote something. He put the paper in my hand and, in a brusque voice, said, "You need to go back to your office now."

I walked outside onto West Executive Avenue and opened the note.

It said, "He's a jerk. Don't come back for a while, but don't worry."

Until I had my first unspeakably abusive boss with no conscience and breath like an iguana, I never realized how fortunate I was to work for people who were thoughtful and didn't make me nauseous.

One way they demonstrated their kindness was by letting me occasionally attend special White House events without having to invite myself. In early March I was given time off to join a colorful sea of cheering, flag-waving fellow employees on the South Lawn in welcoming a former Milwaukee, Wisconsin schoolteacher by the name of Golda Meir who had become the Prime Minister of Israel. Giulio Andreotti, the Prime Minister of Italy, came to town in the middle of April, and I had permission to attend a welcoming ceremony for him, too. Unfortunately, a copier emergency raised its ugly head at the last minute and I had to bid my plans arrivederci.

Although I was disappointed, it may have been one of the best bad things that ever happened to me. An hour or so after the ceremony was over and the crowd had returned to work, Glen came by to tell me to hurry up and follow a parade to the East Room.

Having no idea why I was headed into the Residence, and a tad jumpy about it considering my recent history, I blindly fell in behind a large group of women and a handful of men snaking their way out of the EOB toward a set of outside stairs in front of the West Wing. Eventually, we reached the ground floor center hall of the Residence with its remarkable vaulted ceiling and were then directed up the stairs by a White House usher. When we reached the first floor, we walked down the red-carpeted Cross Hall and into the glittering East Room where several men were gathered around a grand piano across from George Washington's portrait.

Flanking the piano were musicians who looked ready to play, a single microphone on a stand, and 40 or 50 folding chairs. I grabbed a seat at the end of the front row which, like a game of musical chairs, was the only one available when we were asked to sit down. With no real idea what we were there to see, I didn't quite get why there was so much excited chatter, not to mention occasional squeals from the women in the audience.

Having failed to learn that discretion is the better part of valor, I turned to the lady next to me and asked what all the excitement was about. Rather than utter a word, she simply looked at me like I was the village idiot. The good news was that it didn't take long to learn why.

When I looked up, a broadly smiling Frank Sinatra was standing at the microphone.

Sinatra said something lighthearted about "bobbysoxers", and the women in the audience went wild, something I didn't think anyone north of 30 could do without blowing a vital organ.

The applause was loud, skirting the edge of shockingly rowdy, and was mixed with barely muffled shrieks and a wolf whistle that was wholly inappropriate for all sorts of reasons. Most of the audience was so keyed up that you could literally feel their energy, so intense and commanding that I wouldn't have been surprised to learn that every lady in the room had spent the morning mainlining sugar.

Although I was apparently surrounded by "bobbysoxers" in the East Room that day, I'm not sure I'd even heard the term until Sinatra lobbed it out to the frenzied throng. When I looked into it later, the explanation surprised me. I thought Elvis and the Beatles were the first to make teenage girls delirious. Not so. America's first teen singing idol was Sinatra who rose to national fame in the 1940s. Although my mother went to see him perform in Brooklyn, New York and didn't find the experience quite as exciting, he nevertheless attracted a multitude of other young female fans who wore black-and-white saddle shoes and white cotton socks folded over at the ankles. In the 1950s they added wide, brightly colored "poodle" skirts to the ensemble, so named because they had a poodle design sewn on the front and not because they were made of poodles as one major-league pothead I knew once assumed.

While it's not clear how the socks got their name, it's very clear that Sinatra and the "bobbysoxers" made a major impact on the record industry and literally transformed American culture. Before Sinatra came along, record producers largely targeted the over-30 crowd because only adults could afford the relatively high cost of vinyl records. Curiously, neither the term "teenager" nor the consumer group of young men and women between the ages of 13 and 19 even existed at that time. People in that age group were simply considered to be older children and had none of the buying power they have today. With Sinatra and his screaming, fainting, hysterical fans, the focus began to shift towards younger people and, with the introduction of relatively inexpensive 45 rpm records in 1950, the youth music market exploded. As funny as it may seem, every current-day entertainer from The Rolling Stones and Radiohead to Beyoncé and Jay-Z owes their ability to make a living as musical artists to Frank Sinatra.

Sinatra was in the East Room to rehearse for his performance at the state dinner honoring Prime Minister Andreotti that night. One thing that became patently obvious as he took the microphone was that it was a lot different listening to Frank Sinatra sing from twenty feet away than in Row 70-something of the Kennedy Center. I was so close that I could feel the vibration of his silky baritone. At such close range, it took more than a little time to wrap my mind around the fact that I was not only within spitting distance of Frank Sinatra but that I was within spitting distance of Frank Sinatra inside the White House. He sang several songs including "Ol' Man River" from the Broadway musical *Show Boat*, and I'm not ashamed to say that tears welled up in my eyes. I was in awe and could feel goosebumps running up and down my arms. I'd never heard anything so moving; moreover, I've never heard anything so emotionally penetrating in all the decades since.

When he reached the last note, the East Room came unhinged. The audience stood up nearly in unison to give Sinatra a standing ovation. Then he introduced the members of his band and thanked us for coming as everyone fell in line for the walk back to work.

By now, it shouldn't be surprising to learn that I didn't catapult myself to the front of the group heading back to the EOB despite my run-in with the Secret Service.

Sitting as close as I was to the front, I heard Sinatra ask a member of his entourage for a drink of water. Being younger and faster, I turned around, reached the water pitcher first, poured a glass, and offered it to Sinatra. Then I poured a glass for myself. Having absolutely no clue what to say, I asked him what he thought of some rock group I liked that he'd never heard of and then blurted out something about liking his daughter Nancy, a beautiful blonde whose song "These Boots Are Made for Walkin'" had been a huge hit several years earlier. He ruffled my hair, told me I had balls, and suggested that I "look him up" if I ever got to "Vegas." My happy shock quickly dissipated, however, when, to my complete horror, I absentmindedly turned my glass of water over on his left sock. It was my lucky day that there was only enough water left to moisten it, not drench it. He took it reasonably well, although it sort of put a damper on our conversation.

Still, I was confident that I would take Mr. Sinatra up on his invitation. With a head filled with dreams of hitting the Vegas Strip in a limo with "the Chairman of the Board," I couldn't wait to call the airlines to price a ticket. Then, after hearing the discouraging news that the cost was four times what I'd probably ever have in my checking account, I embraced the sad reality that it would be a long time before I'd get to hang out with the Rat Pack, a "hip" group of "Vegas swingers" that included Sinatra, Sammy Davis, Jr., Dean Martin, Peter Lawford, and Joey Bishop.

Despite taking time to rub elbows with "Old Blue Eyes", I was able to catch the tail end of the conga line going back to the Executive Office Building, excellent timing since the EPS officer who was about as far from being on my Christmas card list as Attila the Hun was now standing at the base of the marble stairs. He looked at me and scowled and, as much as I wanted to stick out my tongue at him, I smiled and saluted, which probably only aggravated him more.

Back at work an hour or so later, I was given another sealed manila envelope to deliver to the West Wing, this time to the White House Press Secretary's office. I was in the middle of flirting with a very tall, very cute, very smart girl in her twenties who also worked for CIEP and whose mother was the secretary to one of the very biggest White House bosses. I liked her a lot and we had any number of excellent, easy conversations on a wide range of subjects, a matter she bemoaned while giving me a ride back to campus one evening. She said that most of the guys she dated were pretty much stuck on single topics like fly-fishing or bowling, subjects she found okay for occasional discussion but not as a steady diet. She was 23 and I was barely 18, an age disparity that wouldn't have made much difference in later years but was a huge gap then. She said she wished that I was older. I did, too.

Being much more interested in things other than work that day, I took my time delivering the envelope. When my head finally came out of the clouds, I put on my suit jacket, stopped by the cafeteria for my usual afternoon "double," two Pepsis that I drank one after the other, and then wandered across West Executive Avenue.

The shortest route was to walk the length of the West Wing basement and take a modest flight of stairs to the press office area where future ABC *World News Tonight* anchor Diane Sawyer worked. The basement was teeming with Secret Service agents, and it took more than a few aggressive "excuse me's to navigate the herd and make it up to the press office. Going back the same way was another matter. Just as I approached the stairs, a wall of meat the size of the Chicago Bears offensive line came up and curtly pushed me out of the way. I was semi-shoved into an area crowded with American and Italian officials between the press office and the Roosevelt Room and found myself in the same nasty fix faced by countless people stuck in bumper-to-bumper traffic jams: I'd had entirely too much to drink and had nowhere socially acceptable to put it. Worse, I started to panic when I realized that I had no practical way to get to the closest men's room which was back at the entrance to the basement.

Then I remembered that there was a restroom near the West Wing lobby that the EPS officers had explicitly told me to stay away from. Naturally, I went straight to it.

It proved to be quite something.

While I'd had the pleasure of visiting more than a few fine restrooms at that point in my short life, this one clearly took the game up a few dozen notches. The room was a small but magnificent "one-holer" with the same blue-and-saffron color scheme that decorated the Oval Office. Among other amenities, the toilet seat had a blue cover with a saffron eagle in the center and saffron stars around it. It made you proud to be an American.

Alone and grinning ear-to-ear as I got down to business, I had absentmindedly forgotten to lock the door. That unfortunately allowed a Secret Service agent to walk up behind me and yell "Get Out!" in my ear at point-blank range while I was urinating. Not only was I caught by surprise, but I jumped in the clumsiest, most awkward way possible, barely missing his legs with a good soaking as I instinctively turned towards the sound of his voice. Although my heart was thumping in my throat and my head felt like it was going to detonate, these were far from my worst problems.

For one thing, I couldn't simply pull the plug on nature without a potentially disastrous outcome.

For another, there was an old guy in a dark suit next to the agent with the same terror-filled look I'd had on my face minutes before.

The old guy and I locked eyes in the sort of High Noon moment you see in old Westerns where two gunfighters square off against one another. In this case, however, it was clear what the old guy wanted and that the U.S. Secret Service was going to get it for him. Seeing no options except bad ones, I pulled myself together as best I could and brusquely pushed past the agent and the old guy, semi-walking and semi-hopping around the lobby to the stairwell to get to the basement men's room. Largely thanks to the fact that my plumbing was still pretty new, I made it just in the nick of time.

The next day I saw a picture of the old guy in the *Washington Post*. It turned out that he was the Prime Minister of Italy.

It just goes to show that when you've got to go, you've got to go, regardless of who you are.

Since my White House toilet violation inexplicably never raised its ugly head to my bosses, I was still on the job a week or two later and was asked to help bring a college intern on board for the summer. Our intern was the son of a distinguished Member of Congress, and Glen thought it might be more pleasant for him if he already knew someone his own age in CIEP before he arrived. So, I was given his name, telephone number, a list of topics to review, and unclear instructions about having the call placed by a White House operator. Without a clue what it meant to have a call "placed" or where to find a White House operator, I scrambled to find my loose-leaf White House employee's guide to figure it out. As I should've expected, all it said under White House Operator was "Contact the White House operator."

I quickly learned that the White House telephone operators were amazing. Using the kind of upright switchboards you see in old movies with a million wires going every which way, the operators were highly respected, not only for their efficiency and professionalism but for their astonishing ability to find anyone the President wanted to reach, anywhere on earth. There are scores of funny stories about how people were located over the years, not to mention what the operators occasionally had to do in the days before caller I.D. to convince someone that they were being contacted by the White House and that the call wasn't a practical joke. When I stopped by the operators' center in the EOB, they couldn't have been nicer in unraveling the mystery of having a call placed: I was to simply give them my name, the name of the party I was calling, and their number. If the operator connected with them, they'd ask the person to hold and then put me on the line. If the person wasn't available, the operator would either leave a message or keep dialing until they reached them.

This, of course, sounded unbelievably cool, and I gave it a try as soon as I got back to my desk in the storage room. Sure enough, the operator called the Congressman's son and I stayed on the line to listen. When his roommate reported that he was in class, the operator simply said, "Please ask him to call the White House operator" and provided the area code and number. What surprises me in retrospect is that there was no "call White House Operator Number 2" or something like that to recognize and route the return call. With what had to be an incredibly high number of calls going in and out, the operators were somehow able to keep everything straight among them. I'm still blown away by that. I was even more blown away by what happened when the call was returned and the operator dialed my extension. When I picked up the phone, she said "Mr. Stinson, this is the White House operator. I have Mr. John Doe on the line." Even I recognized that this was not good for my head, and it was the next to the last time that I ever had a call placed. The last one had a bad ending.

The Congressman's son turned out to be a great guy and, despite his father's position and relationship with the President, didn't act any differently than any of my other teenage friends. He was a cool kid who more than once even volunteered to help me collate some of my more challenging copying projects, an act truly worthy of sainthood. Unfortunately, I couldn't say the same for at least a few of the other interns who regularly came by our office to visit him that summer.

One of them was particularly reprehensible.

Smart, with classic good looks, an expensive wardrobe, a sports car, a rich father, and high-level connections, he trashed every one of those gifts with a vicious attitude and a venomous tongue that spat out nasty comments about people who were clearly in earshot.

One morning, I ran into a young woman I knew and liked, a widow with two small children, who had the displeasure of working with this bloodsucker. Tears were running down her cheeks because he had apparently browbeaten her into taking his laundry to a cleaner a few blocks away and ordered her to pick it up for him late Friday afternoon and leave it on his desk for him to collect on Monday. The jerk didn't even give her the money to pay for it, and, to add further insult to injury, she was going to have to miss a function at her daughter's school to get his precious shirts and underwear on time. Since I was slightly less broke than she was and had some free time on Friday afternoon, I offered to pick up the laundry, advance the money for it, and deliver it exactly where he wanted it. I even stopped by while I was at work on Saturday just to make sure that the laundry hadn't sprouted legs and run away.

With that amount of diligence, you can imagine my utter surprise on Monday when she called to tell me in a laughter-laced whisper that the laundry had been in a terrible accident. Over the weekend a dark, thick, dirty, smelly something had mysteriously formed on the ceiling very high above his desk and dripped all over the brown paper the laundry was wrapped in. Even worse, it had also managed to leak through the paper and through each of the folded garments inside, leaving everything in desperate need of either sterilization or burial. The bully, of course, was beside himself with rage but couldn't say a word without admitting that he'd forced a government employee to do his personal chores. Even he knew that that would get him into trouble.

To this very day, I believe that incident to be one of the most unusual I've ever come across. One of the building engineers looked at the ceiling but couldn't figure out how the gross substance could have possibly originated there. It looked more like someone had projectile-vomited their lunch up into the air. He said it smelled like rotten milk, coffee grounds, and clam chowder, which, by sheer coincidence, had been on the cafeteria menu on Friday.

Damn good guess.

I worked on Saturday mornings whenever possible. As well as having many good uses for the extra money, including gas for the cream-colored Ford Pinto I'd bought with every penny of my life savings, I found it helpful and fun to be in the office when it was quiet. Saturdays opened opportunities to do things that were verboten during the week. Not only could I park my Pinto in spots that were reserved for important White House staffers Monday through Friday and venture into the West Wing a little bit without clearances, I could use the cool electric typewriters and correction tape in the CIEP offices to write my college papers.

I usually went in around 7:30 in the morning after having breakfast at a popular diner on Pennsylvania Avenue that was almost always packed with interesting characters from all walks of life. Among them was an otherwise normal-looking guy in a jacket and tie who would take off his black wing-tip shoes and put them on the counter for what he said was "safe keeping." Along with good, cheap food, the diner had incredibly robust, flavorful coffee. That made me curious, and I asked the guy behind the counter why the coffee was so good. He had a bald head festooned with the tattoo of a hula dancer whose hips swayed a little when he scrunched up his forehead. He shot me an aggravated look and simply said, "We never wash the pots."

One Saturday morning, I was working away at a typewriter when one of CIEP's high-ranking executives stuck his head in the door and asked me to come to his office right away. On the mistaken assumption that I was competent, he handed me a sheet of paper and told me to send it by something that sounded like "desk" to White House Press Secretary Ron Zeigler who was in San Clemente, California. Roughly halfway between Los Angeles and San Diego, San Clemente was the location of President Nixon's home, La Casa Pacifica, which was often referred to as the Western White House. As the high-ranking CIEP executive loaded papers into his briefcase and grabbed his suit jacket, he told me to call the White House operator "later" to reach Zeigler and let him know that the document was coming. With that, he headed out the door at warp speed and left me confused, anxious, and sick to my stomach with worry about what I was supposed to do.

Trying to sort it all out, my first concern was with the word "later." Did he mean that I should call the White House operator in ten minutes or at 6:00 p.m.? Was I supposed to talk to Zeigler and just say that something was on the way or say "Good morning" too? I had no clue. My concern quickly turned into panic as I realized that I didn't know what he meant by a "desk" either. To soothe my nerves, I immediately went to the cafeteria to get a glazed doughnut and a cup of coffee and, after loading up with more than enough sugar and caffeine to launch myself into lunar orbit, started walking up and down the halls frantically in search of someone who might know something.

One lesson I learned that day was the importance of properly phrasing a question, particularly when you need help. Instead of saying, "Excuse me. I've been asked to send a document to the Western White House. Can you help me?" in a calm, measured voice, I walked up to people and spewed out a string of vaguely connected words that were met with cold stares and unenthusiastic good luck wishes. Eventually, I came across an EPS officer who at least minimally understood what I was saying and directed me to the White House Communications Agency, the group that handled presidential communications. Rather than joining in my panic, the guy I spoke with at WHCA looked excruciatingly bored, asked me if I meant LDX, short for Long Distance Xerography. That sounded like a winner to me. I nodded my head "yes" and he pointed me to a machine. After realizing that I had no idea how to work the LDX, a frequently used term for a fax machine, the WHCA guy told me that he'd send the document.

Feeling confident for all the wrong reasons, I dialed the White House operator at about 8:30 a.m., explained that I had orders to call San Clemente, and asked to be connected to Mr. Zeigler. Completely oblivious to the fact that it was only 5:30 a.m. in California, I obviously wasn't expecting a very groggy man to answer the phone. "Yes?" he asked in the kind of husky voice that usually means that the victim of your call was in a very deep sleep. The White House operator said something I couldn't make out because my heart was thumping in my ears. Paralyzed over not knowing what to say, I blurted out "It's me."

"Who's me?" growled Ziegler.

"That's right," I said and quickly hung up.

◆

By the time my college classes ended in May 1973, the Select Committee on Presidential Campaign Activities, otherwise known as the Senate Watergate Committee, was brought to order on Capitol Hill.

Scores of books and articles have been written about the Watergate scandal over the past four decades, and I'll leave the lengthy and often intricate details that led to President Nixon's resignation to those authors and historians. For purposes here, the short version of the Watergate story began in 1972 with two burglaries, one in May and one in June, at the Democratic National Committee headquarters in the Watergate office complex in Washington, D.C. located on the east bank of the Potomac

River adjacent to the Kennedy Center. As odd as it may seem considering the influence the scandal has had on American politics, the objective of the break-ins has never been clearly established. Speculation has run the gamut from gathering intelligence about prospective Democratic presidential nominees to determining what Democrats knew about purportedly illegal Nixon campaign contributions to destroying records about an alleged prostitution ring. Regardless of the motives, in May a group of five burglars rifled through files, photographed confidential documents, and violated federal wiretapping laws by placing telephone listening devices in the Democrats' offices to eavesdrop on private conversations. When the burglars returned in June to search for more documents and install additional wiretaps, they attracted the attention of a security guard and were arrested by District of Columbia police. Within a short time, all of the burglars were found to have connections to the Nixon re-election campaign.

On October 10, 1972, less than a month before Nixon's landslide re-election, *Washington Post* reporters Carl Bernstein and Bob Woodward, who had been working on the story since the break-in in June, reported that an FBI investigation had concluded that the Nixon campaign had conducted widespread political espionage and sabotage of which the burglaries were merely the tip of the iceberg. In response, White House and re-election committee officials denied any wrongdoing.

In February 1973, only weeks after Nixon took the oath of office for a second term, the U. S. Senate formed the Select Committee on Presidential Campaign Activities consisting of four Democrats and three Republicans to investigate the wiretapping and break-in, the alleged cover-up of those felonies, widespread violations of campaign finance laws, and allegations of spying on the Democratic presidential campaign. In March 1973, the Committee, headed by its chairman, U.S. Senator Sam Ervin (D-North Carolina), held its first meeting and, in May, began to hear the testimony of subpoenaed witnesses including many of the President's top aides. Also in May, a separate Watergate investigation was begun by an independent prosecutor in the U.S. Department of Justice, Archibald Cox, a former U.S. Solicitor General and Harvard legal scholar who, as coincidence would have it, was a descendant of both the attorney who defended President Andrew Johnson in his 1866 impeachment trial and one of the signers of the Declaration of Independence. Cox reported to the Attorney General of the United States.

Ervin's committee and Cox's office joined U.S. District Court Judge John "Maximum John" Sirica, so named for his penchant for handing down stiff prison sentences, who was presiding over the trials of the Watergate burglars, in a three-pronged legal spear that would eventually be pointed directly at the Oval Office.

In July, former White House aide Alexander Butterfield testified before the Ervin Committee that President Nixon had a tape-recording system in the Oval Office, the Cabinet Room, his office in the Executive Office Building, and at Camp David, the presidential retreat in the Catoctin Mountains in Maryland. Although Nixon followed Presidents Roosevelt, Eisenhower, Kennedy, and Johnson in recording conversations, he was the first to use a voice-activated, rather than a manual, system, meaning that every conversation, not just those that the President purposely selected, was recorded.

On the assumption that the recordings might contain conversations pertaining to the Watergate burglaries, both the Ervin Committee and Prosecutor Cox immediately asked Nixon to turn over the tapes. Nixon refused, suggesting that some of the conversations concerned highly sensitive national security matters. The President also argued that he had a responsibility to protect the confidentiality of communications he received from people whose unfettered advice was essential to helping him carry out his duties.

In October 1973, Nixon offered a middle-ground solution in which 72-year-old John Stennis, a six-term Democratic Member of the Senate from Mississippi who was hard of hearing, would listen to the tapes and provide Cox with a summary.

When Cox refused the compromise, Nixon ordered U.S. Attorney General Elliott Richardson to fire Cox.

Richardson refused and resigned in protest.

Nixon then ordered Deputy Attorney General William Ruckelshaus, the second-highest official in the Justice Department, to fire Cox.

Ruckelshaus also resigned.

Finally, the third-highest Justice Department official, the Solicitor General of the United States, carried out the President's order.

This all happened on one night, Saturday, October 20, 1973. It became known as the "Saturday Night Massacre." I watched the reports on TV with my jaw on the floor.

On November 5, 1973, Houston lawyer Leon Jaworski, once a prosecutor in the Nuremburg trials, the post-World War II prosecution of Nazi war criminals, was named to replace Cox. This time, however, the Watergate Special Prosecutor could only be fired with the consent of the Senate Judiciary Committee.

In April 1974, Nixon turned over edited transcripts of some of the conversations instead of the actual tapes that had been subpoenaed by the Judiciary Committee of the U.S. House of

Representatives, which was considering impeachment proceedings against him. The transcripts were rejected by the House committee, and prosecutors turned to the Supreme Court to force Nixon to release the tapes.

In July 1974, the Court ruled in *United States v. Nixon* that the President had to release the tapes. Among the recordings was a conversation from June 23, 1972, only a few days after the second Watergate break-in, in which Nixon agreed with aides that officials of the Central Intelligence Agency should tell the FBI to drop their investigation into the burglaries due to national security concerns. Coining it the "smoking gun" tape, prosecutors took the position that Nixon's approval of the action made him a party to a conspiracy to obstruct the criminal justice system, a felony. The conversation was released to a shell-shocked American public on Monday, August 5, 1974. With impeachment pending in the House of Representatives and almost certain conviction by the Senate, Nixon resigned effective at noon that Friday, August 9, and turned over the presidency to Vice President Gerald Ford.

Watergate was both a political nightmare for the country and the first circus I had the chance to watch from a ringside seat.

To put the national interest in Watergate during the spring and summer of 1973 into perspective, an estimated 85% of Americans with television sets tuned in to at least one portion of the hearings. Earlier that same year, only 43% of Americans with television sets watched the Super Bowl between the Miami Dolphins and the Washington Redskins. While that's not an apples-to-apples comparison, it offers some insight into how intensely curious the public was. Watergate was like a train wreck. You knew it was going to be horrible, but you just had to watch it. Even John Lennon and Yoko Ono sat in the gallery during the hearings one day.

Television back then was a much different critter than it is today. Watergate happened long before the birth of cable and satellite television, the 24-hour news cycle, and home video recorders, which meant that you could only watch a program when it was being aired, not hours or days later. In fact, most households still had black-and-white sets with a huge picture tube sticking out in the back and twin antennas known as "rabbit ears." I had a friend who'd put the rabbit ears on his little sister's head and make her walk around until he got a good picture. Then he made her stay exactly where she was until his program was over.

Along with the fact that a remote control was my dad telling me to get out of my chair and turn the dial, TV stations usually went off the air at midnight right after playing the national anthem and switching to a test pattern, often a strange-looking thing with an Indian head at the top and circles around it, and the irritating sound of static. Despite the medieval nature of the times, all three networks, NBC, ABC, and CBS, covered the hearings from start to finish for the first full week, eventually taking turns until the initial round ended in August of that year. The sole exception was when former White House counsel John Dean gave more than 20 hours of astonishing testimony linking President Nixon and others in the obstruction of justice. For that show, all three networks broadcast Dean simultaneously.

If there was ever a case of someone unintentionally stealing a scene from a lead actor, it was Maureen Dean, John Dean's drop-dead gorgeous 28-year-old wife. While her husband implicated President Nixon and others, including himself, in the attempted cover-up of the burglaries before the Ervin Committee, Mrs.

Dean sat attentively in the gallery several feet behind him to his right. With flaxen hair fashioned in a bun on the back of her head, perfectly elegant posture, and dressed in exquisitely tailored suits, she was so beautiful and sophisticated-looking that she made more than one man gasp for air, me included. Not surprisingly, it seemed that the guys running the TV crews aimed their cameras in just the right direction to keep her in frame throughout the day. Forget Watergate. I knew guys who would turn on the hearings just to look at Maureen Dean. If there was a beautiful princess among all the trolls in the Watergate saga, she was it.

While Sam Ervin was becoming a household name as chairman of the Senate investigation, I was shuttling sealed, plain manila envelopes given to me by a White House secretary to the offices of Republican Senators on Capitol Hill and bringing similarly nondescript sealed envelopes back to the same White House secretary. At least once a day, I had to fight the terrible urge to open one of those nondescript manila envelopes. In fact, I became so preoccupied with my preoccupation with the envelopes that my teenage mind went to work on the problem and convinced itself that opening one would not only be some sort of act of treason but something that my dad would be mad at me for doing. Had I been a lot older at the time, my overriding concern would've been doing anything that might put me in jail. At 18, however, the thought of my old man knocking the daylights out of me was what was really terrifying.

Even though Capitol Hill could be a great playground, I hated leaving the comfort of the air-conditioned EOB. Having a talent for sweating at the drop of a dime, the humid weather that usually started to raise its ugly head in late May and continued into October often made me miserable. I read somewhere that Washington, D.C. had originally been swampland that neither Maryland nor Virginia wanted and gladly gave to the Federal Government for a capital city. The idea that I was living in swamp weather made sense. In the short time it took to walk out to Pennsylvania Avenue and hail a cab, I'd grow large, uncomfortable splotches of sticky perspiration on my chest, back, and under my armpits. Few, if any, of the D.C. cabs I caught in those days from the White House to the Capitol for $1.15 including tip had air conditioning, and I'd sometimes resort to sticking my head out of a window like a dog to try to cool down. It got to the point that I kept at least two fresh shirts and a big bottle of underarm deodorant in the office just so I could stand to be around myself. I thought about putting underarm deodorant all over my face and neck, too, but ultimately dropped the idea. I was afraid that it might clog my pores and make my head explode.

Somewhere along the way I gained the nickname "The Little Senator" from my White House bosses, partly because they were wise guys and partly because I was able to get my hands on things that other people seemingly couldn't or, more likely, wouldn't put much effort into getting. In one case I got a file that was allegedly being withheld from the people I worked for by an undersecretary of State for something-or-other.

I walked down to the State Department and returned to the EOB an hour or so later with the file.

A much older staffer who had tried to get the file and failed made a very big deal over what I'd done in a nasty tone, even suggesting that I might have stolen it. If he didn't like me beforehand, he certainly didn't care for me after I told him and everyone within earshot the simple truth: all I had done was to ask for it. He said that that was impossible, called me something nasty, and stomped off in a huff. I didn't say a word, although I surely wanted to. The then-popular expression "sit on it and rotate" would have fit him and the moment perfectly for a variety of reasons. Unfortunately for everyone concerned, he was one of those unendurable souls that even Mother Theresa might have punched out. I was reminded of him in another time and place years later when a going-away party was thrown for a similarly obnoxious individual who left the company we both worked for. The next day there were leftover potato chips and vegetables lined up on a table for anyone who was hungry. A guy walked up to the snacks and asked a co-worker, "Where's the dip?"

"He left yesterday," she replied.

My bosses were also pleased that I had become friendly with a variety of secretaries, guards, elevator operators, and other folks on Capitol Hill who saw me so often that they thought I worked there. I also developed nodding acquaintances with Senate Minority Leader Hugh Scott of Pennsylvania and Senator Barry Goldwater of Arizona.

Not unexpectedly, I met Senator Goldwater, the 1964 Republican presidential nominee, and the mustachioed, pipe-smoking Scott on a "Senators Only" elevator I had absolutely no business being on.

I had arranged a ride just for the hell of it with one of the operators in exchange for a book of matches with a raised engraving of the White House on the front and the presidential seal on the back. Just as the door was closing, the Senators hopped on board and gave the operator and me the knowing, friendly look of grown-ups who had just busted you but could remember breaking more than a few rules themselves when they were young.

When we reached their floor, all that was said was "Have a good afternoon, gentlemen."

Although it wasn't often, whenever I ran into Senator Scott afterward he'd chuckle, puff on his pipe, and wryly ask, "I know you from somewhere, don't I?" I'd say "Yes, sir", and we'd both laugh and move on. On the other hand, where Senator Scott was a talker, Senator Goldwater was a "saluter", and whenever I came across him in the Russell Senate Office Building, he'd give me a little salute of recognition and I'd salute right back. I must admit, though, that I often wondered if he was acknowledging someone else, sort of like when an attractive woman smiles at you and you glance over your shoulder to see who she's really looking at. Oddly enough, we sort of got to know one another although without ever speaking a single word.

We did, however, get close once.

Walking by his office one afternoon, I saw Senator Goldwater standing in the reception area cleaning his trademark black-framed glasses with a handkerchief then holding them up against the light to see if the lenses were clear, a procedure that apparently wasn't working. Fearlessly taking command of the situation, I walked in, fished around in my pocket for a cleaning cloth I had for my own glasses, and handed it to him. Happily, it did the job but, just as he began to form the words "thank you," one of his assistants said something and he quickly turned away, nevertheless placing the cloth back in my hand as he did. Damned if he didn't look back and salute me as he hurriedly walked back towards his office. While a little short of being a crowning moment in either of our lives, Senator Goldwater got a clean pair of glasses and I was happy that he'd be able to read the legislation he'd be voting on, which is more than can be said for most of Congress these days.

Ironically, one of my more eye-opening moments on Capitol Hill had to do with the man Richard Nixon defeated for the Presidency the previous fall. Beneath the U.S. Capitol grounds is a subway which, in those days, connected the Rayburn House Office Building and the Russell and Dirksen Senate Office Buildings to the Capitol Building. The cars were roofless and a blast to ride because they gave you the feeling of being on one of those little, child-size trains that sometimes run along the perimeters of zoos and parks. While the purpose of the subway was to speed Members of Congress to the House and Senate floors when votes were called, a variety of congressional assistants, visitors, and people like me looking for a cheap thrill also rode them right along with the lawmakers. One day, while taking a needlessly long, winding route back to work, I hopped on the train at the Russell Building.

To my great surprise, I found myself sitting next to George McGovern.

One of the funny things about being so young was my tendency to see adults as something other than real people. Just as it was almost impossible to imagine your parents as children, your teachers as students, or your boss as a low-level employee, it was equally difficult to see someone famous as much more than the cardboard character they had been made into by the media. In this case, because Senator McGovern had been labeled a loser by the press as well as his own party, that's how I saw him, too. To say that the presidential election had been a disaster for the Democratic Party and McGovern would be the understatement of the century. Winning less than 38% of the national vote and only 17 of the 537 votes cast in the Electoral College, McGovern carried only Massachusetts and the District of Columbia and lost the Presidency by one of the largest margins in history. While Americans tend to love underdogs, they don't generally like losers. On election night, in fact, it appeared that the network TV reporters in the room were making the story more about the magnitude of McGovern's loss than the size of Nixon's victory, something I thought was unfair to both sides.

Ironically, the lopsidedness of the election was at least partially due to McGovern being cast as a pacifist and soft on the use of military force against America's enemies, a label that stuck even though he had flown more than 30 missions over Nazi-occupied Europe as a World War II bomber pilot and had been awarded the Distinguished Flying Cross for heroism.

Although he had lost so spectacularly, sitting next to anyone who had received 29 million votes for President was still impossibly cool as far as I was concerned, and I immediately shook the Senator's hand and introduced myself, albeit leaving out the part about my working for the White House. Even in this very brief crossing of paths, I found that it would have been very hard not to like George McGovern who radiated warmth and seemed every inch a kind and gracious man. I was quite struck by him, in fact, and my interest in learning more about who and what he was taught me a great lesson about the fleeting nature of fame.

In the fall of 1973, Senator McGovern was invited by the Kennedy Political Union, American University's non-partisan lecture bureau, to address students and faculty in a huge outdoor setting in the Woods-Brown Amphitheater. I was there and can vouch for the fact that the crowd was so large that evening that "Standing Room Only" couldn't begin to describe it. People were even hanging out of dorm windows to hear him speak. A year or so later he was invited back to campus, and I heard that the audience on that go-round apparently topped out at around 50 people.

That had to hurt.

Even if it had been 500 people it had to hurt.

I watched the rest of his career in the Senate and as the U.S. Ambassador to the United Nations Agencies for Food and Agriculture, a position he was appointed to by President Clinton in 1998 and continued to hold into the first year of the Bush Administration. George McGovern's devotion to the fight against hunger in the world, including his work with former Republican Senator Bob Dole in developing the McGovern-Dole International Food for Education and Child Nutrition Program, which fed millions of children and improved school attendance, was extraordinary to say the least.

Over time, I had begun to sense that my life was destined to move quickly from the sublime to the ridiculous with no stops in between. Consequently, I was not unduly surprised that my meeting with Senator McGovern was soon followed by two guys in trench coats who looked like refugees from an adult movie theater.

Most of the time, my first duty in the morning after inhaling breakfast at the People's Drug Store counter near the corner of 15th Street and New York Avenue was to stop by one of the Executive Protective Service command posts and sign for copies of the daily CIA briefing. The briefing book, which was the size of an average edition of *Time* or *Newsweek* in those days and bound like a magazine, was a detailed, riveting, and sometimes even provocative report of what was happening around the world. Or so I gathered. Since access was restricted to specific individuals near the top of the government food chain and I wasn't among them, I simply delivered the books as assigned and left it at that. One day, though, an official I occasionally chatted with about world politics stopped me as I passed his office and showed me parts of a story that was at once titillating, grisly, and exceptionally disturbing, somewhere between a bodice-ripping romance novel and an autopsy report. I can remember my eyes bulging, my mouth opening wide in shock as I read it, and his laughter-laced comment that "that's not something you're going to learn about in college, is it?"

No, I wouldn't learn about that in college, I thought. He was certainly right about that.

An interesting character, this same executive simplified the history of world economics for me. "Somebody has something you want," he explained. "You offer him something you think is valuable in exchange. If he doesn't agree, you kill him."

Funny, but not all together inaccurate.

Even though Washington is a town that thrives on long working hours, I wasn't used to seeing many people around the EOB at seven o'clock in the morning. You can imagine my surprise, then, when I stepped off the elevator at that hour one day and came face-to-face with two short, portly guys in trench coats whom I'd never seen before. Utterly charming, they didn't introduce themselves and gruffly demanded that I give them the CIA reports I had in hand. Probably around 40 years old, they looked like bookends in their long coats, a particularly odd wardrobe selection on a May morning that was already a humidity-laced 70 degrees. When I told them that I wouldn't give them the books without my boss's approval, they got more than a little nasty.

Reacting like a normal teenager, I took off running down the grand staircase towards the Executive Protective Service's offices with the idea in mind that with longer legs, thirty pounds, and twenty-odd years working in my favor, I could make them eat my dust. Eventually, we got everything worked out with the help of people with badges, guns, and big offices and I learned that they were going to be working in what was a converted closet filled with wires, machines, and blinking lights on something that had a vague connection to the briefing books.

I never found out who they were or what they did, but I became convinced that they wore trench coats and sometimes sunglasses to give the impression that they were with the CIA. Stranger yet, when I had something to drop off for them I'd have to knock on the door and wait. In a minute or so the door would open just enough for a hand to pop out to take whatever item I had, much like Thing on *The Addams Family*. Sometimes I couldn't resist faking out the hand by brushing it with a piece of paper and then jerking the paper away so all it could grab was air, which it reacted to by snapping its fingers twice in sort of an agitated manner. I quit after realizing that the hand didn't have its own personality.

As the calendar inched closer to June, the White House was up to its neck in preparations for the visit of Leonid Brezhnev, General Secretary of the Central Committee of the Communist Party of the Soviet Union.

As a microscopic part of that, I was sent to the Soviet Embassy every few days to deliver metal canisters of 35mm film about American industry and agriculture. The Embassy would, in turn, ship the movies to officials in the Kremlin. Just like a vacationer today might access information from the internet about a country they are going to visit, Brezhnev and his people wanted to know more about America. Since the internet didn't exist in

1973, movies were among the better alternatives, even though I'm sure that they were crushingly boring.

Until the day I walked through the gate and into the Soviet Embassy's courtyard four blocks from the White House, I had never met a Russian and my view of the Russian people, frankly, was embarrassingly one-dimensional. Growing up during the Cold War, I had child-size memories of the 1962 Cuban Missile Crisis during which the United States and the Soviet Union came terrifyingly close to unleashing their nuclear arsenals against one another. I also remembered then-Soviet Premier Nikita Khrushchev's speech in which he threatened to bury the United States, a statement which was taken with considerable alarm in America but which Khrushchev later claimed was used figuratively to mean that communism would bury American capitalism.

For better or worse, many of my little friends and I gained some of our impressions of Russians from cartoon characters. Boris Badenov and Natasha Fatale, who were often featured on *The Rocky & Bullwinkle Show*, were among them. Incompetent spies who spoke in Russian-sounding accents, Boris and Natasha were from a country called "Pottsylvania." Week after week, their fiendish plots to steal secrets or do other bad things were foiled by Rocket J. Squirrel and Bullwinkle T. Moose, proving, at least to us, that "Pottsylvanians" were bad and Americans were good.

Of course, the world outside of *Rocky & Bullwinkle* was never quite that simple. As I would see for myself two decades later in Moscow, the Urals, and Siberia a few years after the Soviet Union's collapse in 1991, the average person who had lived under Soviet oppression wanted the same happy, healthy, and productive lives for themselves and their children as the average American did. They were also as kind and thoughtful or as mean and thoughtless as anyone I had met anywhere else in the world. That included my own neighborhood in which there were more than a few folks no country would have wanted to claim. The evil in the U.S.S.R. lived inside its leaders, not its citizens.

With large, stately mirrors and ornate, gold-trimmed furnishings, the Embassy's lobby was so richly decorated and imposing that it looked, ironically, like it belonged to global oil barons, not Communists. About 15 feet or so straight ahead through the entryway was what appeared to be the official welcoming committee, a stern, albeit bored-looking Red Army soldier standing in front of a small desk. As I approached, the soldier stepped aside to reveal a man about 30 years old with blonde hair and wearing a business suit. He looked up from the desk and said "hello" in an accent that sounded exactly like he was from somewhere in the Midwest.

I introduced myself and learned that his name was Sasha. More than a little curious, I asked him how he got a job in the Soviet Embassy which, to me, sounded cool and interesting.

"I am in the foreign service," he said.

I had no idea that Americans were assigned to foreign embassies," I replied quizzically.

"No," he said. "I am in the Russian foreign service."

"Then how did you learn to speak English like an American?" I asked.

"From watching *Mr. Ed*," he replied, referencing a popular '60s TV show about a talking horse.

Although Sasha and I never became buddies, we usually chatted for a few minutes whenever I delivered something and, in the course of things, I discovered that he had a good sense of humor. It also came to light that despite Sasha's familiarity with American television, a few things escaped him. One day he asked me why Americans got excited over things that were "at a distance." I didn't understand what he meant and asked him to give me an example. "Well, when Americans really like something they say it is 'far out,'" he said. I guess that expression came along after *Mr. Ed* went off the air.

During another chat inside the Embassy, I made a very politically incorrect comment about free speech in America and the absence of it in the Soviet Union. Sasha told me that there was just as much free speech in the U.S.S.R as there was in the United States.

"In the United States," he said, "you can go outside and yell 'Nixon is a fool' and nothing bad will happen, right?"

I nodded my head in agreement.

"Well, in the Soviet Union, I can go outside and yell 'Nixon is a fool' and nothing bad will happen to me either."

I was sad when Sasha simply vanished one day. When I asked the Red Army soldier who'd been right there with us on every one of my visits where he was, the soldier said that he didn't know who I was talking about.

Chapter Four

SPIRO WHO?

The arrival of Soviet leader Leonid Brezhnev on June 18 was a huge event in Washington. So big, in fact, that nearly everyone I knew wanted to get into the White House arrival ceremony, including some of my new friends on Capitol Hill.

Despite what was called détente, an easing of Cold War political tensions between the United States and the U.S.S.R., and President Nixon's historic visit to Moscow in 1972, the Soviet Union was still very much our enemy. In fact, Brezhnev, who had succeeded Nikita Khrushchev in a bloodless coup in 1964, had recently increased the size and scope of the Soviet military to expand Russia's influence around the globe. Not surprisingly, we were curious to see the ugly, overweight man with bushy eyebrows who had nuclear warheads that were aimed at the United States and led what President Reagan would one day aptly call the "Evil Empire."

We were also fascinated by Brezhnev's peculiar personality. Reportedly a textbook-definition narcissist, he was big on giving himself lots of highly prestigious war medals that he didn't deserve. An old joke had it that if a bear ate Brezhnev, it would cough up metal for a month.

The pomp and circumstance associated with the visit of a foreign head of state to the White House blows a million watts of electricity into the air. In 1973, the event started with the distant whir of helicopter blades as a dark green Sikorsky Sea King bearing the words *United States of America* on its fuselage carried the visiting head of government from Andrews Air Force Base in the Maryland suburbs past the Washington Monument and onto a landing pad on the Ellipse, an open, elliptical-shaped field across the street from the South Lawn. From there, a motorcade led by police motorcycles and cars with flashing lights and sirens roared up 17th Street and through the southwest gate of the White House past hundreds of flag-waving White House and State Department aides and guests to the entrance to the Diplomatic Reception Room. The Marine Band played Ruffles and Flourishes, and trumpets announced the guest's arrival as it might have been done in medieval times. By the time both countries' national anthems had been played, a 21-gun salute had been fired, and the President and his guest completed a ceremonial review of the troops, most people I knew had a serious case of goose bumps.

Just as Brezhnev wasn't just any head of state, the person I brought as my guest wasn't just any friend. She was not only very sweet but stunning, sort of a college freshman version of Maureen Dean, whom I obviously regarded as the gold standard of American womanhood. I remember the two of us standing at a window adjacent to Mr. Flanigan's office with a picture-perfect view of the South Lawn. Seeing that a crowd of thousands had already assembled for the ceremony, we started to walk down the wide, black-and-white-tiled hallway to the stairway.

Just as I took the first step down, a familiar female voice loudly, and all too clearly, called out my name.

I shuddered.

The voice belonged to the sweet but stern woman who sent me to and from Capitol Hill. Knowing in my heart that my walk to the South Lawn was about to go up in smoke, I nevertheless turned around and shot her my saddest puppy dog eyes just in case whatever I had to do could be put off for an hour. Unbelievably, she proved to be immune to my charm. She was so immune, in fact, that her next words were "right now."

This gave me two immediate problems at hand and one I didn't even know about yet. The first was to quickly explain to my friend that I had to go and was going to leave her behind in the company of people she didn't know. The second was finding someone to leave her behind with since she had to be in the company of someone with clearance. The explanation went well, and my friend, who proved to be mature well beyond her years, graciously understood. I looked around quickly for Glen or anybody else I knew who would be kind and take her under their wing. All I found were unfamiliar faces. Then, proving the truth of Murphy's Law once again, I saw the worst familiar face I could have imagined.

We called her the Wicked One.

With no other choice but to escort my poor, innocent friend out of the building, I had to leave her in the care of the nightmarish old biddy whose career and sullen wardrobe probably pre-dated electricity. She was certainly the nastiest person I had ever met up to that point in my life and in the Top 10 worst I've met since. With a face like a bulldog licking urine off a cactus, she went out of her way to say or do anything that could hurt someone's feelings, make their day more difficult, or embarrass them. I thought that perhaps she was just misunderstood and that showing her a smile and a little kindness might help. As it turned out, I could have better spent my time watching paint dry.

I started off towards Capitol Hill as fast as I could go, sweating from the summer humidity and fearing that the Wicked One would send my friend running for the nearest exit, never to be seen again. There was, however, a huge problem. Traffic was nearly in gridlock. Pennsylvania Avenue was like a parking lot, and I couldn't find an empty cab anywhere. So, I part-walked, part-ran to the Senate side of the Capitol. Having been so preoccupied with the Soviets that day, I never bothered to look at the address on the manila envelope I was carrying and simply assumed that it was going to the Russell Senate Office Building. The destination, however, read The Vice President's Room, The Capitol. I had no idea that the Vice President even had a room in the Capitol or why he needed one, much less where it was. With time working against me, I eventually found it right outside of the Senate Chamber. Then, because I couldn't find a cab again, I hoofed the mile-and-a-half stretch back to the office, praying that I'd either make it back for the ceremony or at least see my friend before she had to leave. I failed at both.

The next day, she told me that the Wicked One had gone on at length about how much I was disliked by everyone and how lucky everyone was that I had been sent away. My friend, who apparently didn't find character assassination amusing, told me that she asked the old buzzard if she was of Russian heritage.

"Why would you ask that, dear?" the old rat inquired.

"Because you and Brezhnev look so much alike," my brilliant friend explained.

Brezhnev, by the way, was not only ugly and mean but allegedly a first-class bastard to boot. While working in Russia in the mid-1990s a former government official told me that it was a well-known secret that Brezhnev had a young girl, usually between the ages of 16 and 18, delivered each weekend to entertain him. A family, he said with a smirk on his face, considered it an honor to have their daughter spend private time with the General Secretary of the Communist Party of the Soviet Union.

I asked if that was true.

He said no, but it was considerably better than being shot.

Some weeks later, I bumped into an FBI agent I had become friendly with. Although I can't remember how it got started, we had a little joke between us that had to do with my calling home on a regular basis. When I'd see him, he'd ask me if I'd let my parents know that I was still alive, I'd say "no" even if I had, and he'd say something about my "poor mother, sitting by the phone, waiting to hear from her only child." One day he asked me if I had written home recently. I told him that I hadn't. "Well, next time you do," he said, "let me know. We have some great photos of you going in and out of the Soviet Embassy. Your mother would love them."

He laughed. I didn't. Then I felt the kind of paranoia that came with watching entirely too many spy movies. "What exactly had been in those film canisters?" I asked myself. "Was I somehow connected to Sasha's disappearance?" Even though I thought that my friend might be jerking my chain, I never took it further. Besides, my mother would have broken out in hives if she'd known that I'd been hanging around with the Red

Menace, as Soviet Communists were sometimes called in those days. For that matter, my poor mom broke out in hives when I got on a bus.

◆

If anything good came of my sprint to the Capitol and back, it was that my very short visit to The Vice President's Room raised my curiosity about what Vice Presidents did.

In high school, I'd read William Manchester's book *The Death of a President* about President Kennedy's assassination and found myself fascinated by the scenes related to presidential succession. Vice President Lyndon B. Johnson was two cars behind Kennedy in the motorcade in Dallas, Texas on November 22, 1963. With shots ringing out, Secret Service agent Rufus Youngblood jumped over the front seat of the Vice President's open car, pushed Johnson to the floor of the vehicle, and covered him with his body. When the cars pulled up at the emergency entrance at Parkland Memorial Hospital, agents placed the Vice President and his wife in a small room that could be quickly secured. After President Kennedy was pronounced dead, the Johnsons were rushed to Air Force One in unmarked police cars where, an hour later, Lyndon Johnson was sworn into office onboard the plane by Federal Judge Sarah Hughes. Standing where that historic event took place many years later, I tried to imagine the weight that LBJ must have felt on his shoulders at that moment. There was no information to construe if the assassin acted alone or if Kennedy's murder was part of a far larger plan aimed at toppling the U.S. Government. For all Johnson knew, he had just become the Commander in Chief of a nation that was under attack.

Considering that President Kennedy was the eighth Chief Executive to die in office since 1841, the sixth to have had a serious attempt made on his life, and the fourth to have been assassinated since 1865, one would assume that the Vice Presidency had always carried great importance. Not so. Vice Presidents were neither considered particularly important to the Framers of the Constitution nor to the Chief Executives they served with for nearly the first 200 years of our history. At best, they were an afterthought.

Although the Constitution was clear on the matter that the Vice President was granted the powers and duties of the Presidency in the event of a vacancy, it didn't clearly say that the Vice President became President. In fact, it may never have been clarified had it not been for Vice President John Tyler's insistence on taking the Presidential oath when he succeeded William Henry Harrison in 1841. By refusing to be an acting President, Tyler created an informal precedent that stood for 126 years until it was clarified by the 25th Amendment in 1967.

There was also no legal provision for a President to fill a Vice-Presidential vacancy until 1967, either. When Truman became President after the death of Franklin Roosevelt in 1945, the country went without a Vice President until Truman was elected President in his own right and sworn in in 1949. LBJ didn't have a Vice President from November 1963 until January 1965. Had something happened to 55-year-old Johnson, who had already had two major heart attacks, the next in line to the Presidency was the 73-year-old Speaker of the House of Representatives, John McCormick.

DONALD M. STINSON

Not surprisingly, Vice Presidents didn't get much respect or give themselves much respect, either. Harry Truman knew nothing about America's development of the atomic bomb, the horrifying fury of which we would unleash on Japan to end the war in the Pacific, for the first two weeks he was the Commander in Chief. Vice Presidents weren't automatically provided with Secret Service protection until 1962, although Presidents had been protected since 1902. An old joke had it that "A mother had two sons: one went to sea, one became Vice President of the United States, and neither was ever heard from again." Senator Daniel Webster turned down the Vice Presidency because "he did not wish to be buried until he was dead."

The root of the matter lies in the Constitution, which gives the Vice President only two jobs. The first is to assume the powers of the Presidency in case of "the removal of the President from office, or of his death, resignation, or inability to discharge the powers and duties of the said office." The second is to serve as the president of the Senate, but he or she "shall have no vote, unless they be equally divided."

That's it. That's the whole thing. In fact, the Vice President doesn't even have to show up to work if he or she doesn't want to.

Part of the reason for the dream job description is that the Vice Presidency was originally something of a consolation prize given to the presidential candidate who received the second-highest number of votes in the Electoral College. Had that never been changed, for example, Hillary Clinton would have been Donald Trump's Vice President after the 2016 election. Because forcing political adversaries to serve together tuned out to be pretty much a train wreck, the process was changed in 1804 and provided for the President and Vice President to be elected together.

The joint election of the President and Vice President has worked both for and against American Vice Presidents. On one hand, the President can't fire the Vice President. Believe it or not, the Vice President could spend every day calling the President a moron and the President couldn't do much about it, at least legally. To be removed from office, Vice Presidents must be impeached and convicted of high crimes and misdemeanors the same way that Presidents are. On the downside, it limited many Vice Presidents to doing much more than representing the United States at funerals. The reason was simple: bosses rarely want to hire anyone they can't fire. Fortunately for the country, Vice Presidents have been much better utilized since 1977 when President Carter gave his Vice President, Walter Mondale, an office in the West Wing and regularly consulted the former U.S. Senator from Minnesota on important issues.

Frankly, what I knew about the Vice President of the United States who worked down the hall from where I held court as a Key Operator was underwhelming. My family had been in Miami visiting friends during the 1968 Republican National Convention and, for me, who was bored beyond belief, the most enjoyable part of the trip was collecting Donkey and Elephant pins being given away as premiums at Gulf Oil stations. In fact, there were only two campaign-related things that I remember. One was a huge banner hanging from the roof of a hotel for then-California Governor Ronald Reagan, who came in a distant third behind Richard Nixon and Nelson Rockefeller in the race to become the Republican nominee that year. The other thing, oddly enough, was a comedian on television making cracks about somebody named Spiro Agnew whom Nixon had just named as his running mate.

On the flip side, other events of 1968 were exceptionally clear: the images of Martin Luther King, Jr.'s murder in Memphis in April, Bobby Kennedy's assassination in June, and the Democratic National Convention in late August where anti-war protesters violently clashed with the police and National Guardsmen, turning the streets of Chicago into a bloody war zone. I remember looking at the long, snaking line of voters waiting to get into my high school's gymnasium on Election Day while I walked to classes. Moreover, I remember that it took until noon the next day to learn that Nixon had won a razor-thin victory over Vice President Hubert Humphrey and Alabama Governor George Wallace.

I can't recall paying any attention to Agnew until one of my teachers brought up a speech that the Vice President made in November 1969 denouncing NBC, ABC, and CBS for what he claimed was politically biased news coverage.

"I am not asking for government censorship or any other kind of censorship," Agnew said. "I am asking whether a kind of censorship already exists when the news that 40 million Americans receive each night is determined by a handful of men responsible only to their corporate employers and filtered through a handful of commentators who admit to their own set of biases."

It was an interesting and intensely controversial comment that the news media attacked quickly and vigorously. Right, wrong, or indifferent, Agnew's comments were a hit with the American people. At the end of the year, a national poll showed that the three most admired men in the nation were, in order, President Nixon, evangelist Billy Graham, and Spiro Agnew.

Agnew was virtually unknown to the American electorate when Richard Nixon tapped the first-term Governor of Maryland as his running mate. "I agree with you that the name of Spiro Agnew is not a household word," he said at his first press conference. He was not the choice of Republican convention delegates in all corners that year. Some, who wanted a name brand like George Romney, Nelson Rockefeller, or Ronald Reagan on the ticket, even chanted "Spiro Who?" on the convention floor.

Whether Americans knew Agnew or not at that moment was probably of little concern to Richard Nixon. What was important was that Agnew represented the working-class and middle-class Americans whose vote Nixon needed to win the general election. Romney, Rockefeller, and Reagan did not. Dartmouth-educated Rockefeller came from massive wealth, Romney had been the president of American Motors, and Reagan, of course, had been a Hollywood actor. Agnew was the son of a Greek immigrant who owned a restaurant. He grew up during the Depression, fought in the Battle of the Bulge, earned four battle stars and a Bronze Star during his service in World War II, served in the Korean War, went to Johns Hopkins University, and earned his law degree from the University of Baltimore at night on the G.I. Bill. During the day, he worked as an insurance adjuster. His wife, Judy, was quoted as saying that his political career began in the PTA.

In the end, Spiro Agnew became an entirely larger presence in American politics than anyone could have predicted: not only a highly recognized name but a public figure whose love of alliteration and proclivity for stirring controversy attracted both respect and ridicule. As Vice President, he was hailed as a voice against anti-war protesters and bias in the news media and a champion of law and order, famously referring to various groups as "nattering nabobs of negativism," "hysterical hypochondriacs of history," "impudent snobs," and "pusillanimous pussyfooters." A political moderate as Maryland's chief executive from 1967-1969, Governor Agnew supported tough laws against water and air pollution and enacted open-housing laws prohibiting discrimination in selling or renting housing.

He was also a pop icon whose face was on everything from T-shirts and trash cans to a popular wristwatch that used a cartoonish Agnew in red-white-and-blue-striped short pants as the centerpiece on the dial à la Mickey Mouse.

Had he remained in office, of course, Agnew, not Gerald Ford, would have become the 38th President of the United States when Richard Nixon resigned in 1974. He was also a very popular candidate for the Presidency among Republican voters looking ahead to 1976.

◆

Now that I knew where I worked, I frequently looked down the hall at the Vice President's office.

Richly made American and Vice-Presidential flags with gleaming hardware stood on either side of the entrance to the reception area along with two or more large Secret Service agents whenever Agnew was in his office. Among the special agents assigned to protect the Vice President was Jerry Parr. Many years in the future, Parr would push President Ronald Reagan into the armored presidential limousine when gunfire erupted outside of the Washington Hilton on March 30, 1981. His quick thinking and decision to take Reagan to the hospital was widely said to have saved the President's life.

As if the armed bodyguards and flags weren't impressive enough, the vice-presidential seal was affixed over the door. For those of us with an unhealthy interest in these kinds of obscurities, it was the old vice-presidential seal which was designed in 1948 and used during the terms of Vice Presidents Barkley, Nixon, Johnson, Humphrey, Agnew, and Ford. The seal was redesigned in 1975 at the urging of Vice President Nelson Rockefeller who made it more closely resemble the presidential seal.

Coming out of the men's room near our office one afternoon, I lined up not only too quietly but too closely behind a gentleman who was filling his coffee percolator at an adjacent water cooler. Long before the advent of double venti-vegan-light-foam-free-range-two-shots-of-espresso-shot-of-soy-milk-three-pump-vanilla-whipped-cream-mocha-half-decaf-with-room brews, the cutting edge of coffee technology was the percolator. Usually made of stainless steel with a small see-through chamber at the top so that you could see the coffee "perk," percolators made a "whoosh-puh, whoosh-puh" sound that let you know that your eye-opening cup of Joe was only moments away.

Provoked by God knows what, I proceeded to unleash a thunderous sneeze that made the gentleman jump like a frog out of boiling water and spill the entire contents of the percolator on the floor. The exceptionally nice man I found myself quickly apologizing to, who was so classy that he was simultaneously apologizing to me, turned out to be one of Vice President Agnew's senior aides.

After exchanging enough friendly greetings over the next few weeks to be pretty sure that he didn't hold my sneeze against me, I decided to go out on a limb and ask him what it was like to work for the Vice President and how he got his job. I was floored when, rather than turning me away with the disdainful "you're wasting my time, kid" look that frequently came across the faces of people over 30, he invited me to his office to chat. Despite probably not understanding half of what he said considering the ocean-sized difference in our worlds, I got so pumped up from the conversation that I decided to try to get a job on the Vice President's staff. With his help, I was able to get an interview with the Vice President's Deputy Chief of Staff, who asked me about my background and what my university studies were like.

Then, he asked me the question that interviewers often ask but for which I was completely unprepared: "So, why would you like to work for the Vice President?"

I was stumped.

Thinking that the answer "because it would be neat" was not my best move, I pondered the matter for what was probably only a few seconds but seemed like an eternity. After rejecting a few other responses that were bouncing around in my head, I settled on one that seemed to be the least lame, although not exactly profound.

"Because I think he'll be the next President of the United States," I said.

"That's an interesting response," he replied.

With that, he stood up, shook my hand, and told me that they'd be in touch.

Since I was used to simply being hired, or not, on the spot for the jobs I'd had in the past, the concept of someone taking time to think about employing me was completely alien and very nerve-wracking. I immediately jumped to the conclusion that the Vice President's Deputy Chief of Staff really meant "Don't call us, we'll call you."

Waiting for me at the end of what seemed like a very long walk back to my desk was a very smart, adorable co-worker with big eyeglasses and an ever-present smile on her face. She was the only person I'd told about my secret mission.

"What happened?" she asked in the excited tone of voice that only very good friends use.

"I blew it," I said.

"Did he say that they didn't have any openings?" she replied.

"No," I said. "I was stupid. I told him that I wanted to work there because I think Agnew's going to be the next President."

She looked at me like I'd lost my mind.

"What do you think would have been a better answer? That you wanted to make copies for him?"

Laughing, I started to feel better right away.

In the final analysis, if my answer to why I wanted to work for the Vice President wasn't the best, it must have not been the worst because I received a call a few days later to schedule an interview for a job in the Vice President's Correspondence Office.

The day after the interview, and after telling my friend that I still didn't think I'd get the job, I was offered $3.46 an hour, or $18.78 in 2017 dollars, to read, categorize, and respond to the Vice President's mail. With gas at 39 cents a gallon and eggs about 60 cents a dozen, or $2.12 and $3.26, respectively, today, those were righteous bucks.

"You're a putz," my friend said, giving me a hug.

Despite being excited about my new job, the first few weeks before I moved to the Vice President's staff were filled with fear that I had suddenly lost my mojo.

When President and Mrs. Nixon opened the South Lawn of the White House to staffers and their families to watch the 4th of July fireworks, I took some friends along. Before it got dark, I decided to show them the Oval Office from the outside, walked with them towards the West Wing, and was sent back by EPS officers with my tail between my legs in a New York minute.

I had bought a used Pinto, a model that would later be the focus of the largest safety recall in history up to that time because of gas tank explosions in rear-end accidents. It was not the coolest car on the road to begin with, and it didn't help that the passenger door sometimes swung open when I made sharp right turns. That even happened when it was locked.

Maybe worst of all, no one in the coed dorm I was living in that summer seemed to care that I worked in the White House. Fed up with being ignored, I sat down with a group that was watching a replay of that day's Watergate hearings on PBS. When the White House was mentioned, I snootily blabbed something like "I work there." Instead of a response like "Really?" or "Cool!" that my ego was looking for, a girl glared at me and said, "Bastard" in a sharp Boston accent. To add to my self-inflicted wound, I couldn't make out what she said and asked her to repeat it. She did, only louder.

I was starting to feel a crisis coming on. I was barely 18, and my arrogance was headed for assisted living.

Thankfully, far bigger things happened that month that took my mind off my self-importance.

On July 12, President Nixon was taken to Bethesda Naval Hospital with a 102-degree fever. Doctors diagnosed the problem as viral pneumonia, and the President remained in the hospital for a week. In the aftermath, there was more than one rumor that Nixon's illness was something worse, possibly a stroke, and that Alexander Haig, the White House Chief of Staff, was effectively the acting President.

On July 16, the Watergate hearings produced a revelation that President Nixon had listening devices in the Oval Office and other locations that started recording conversations whenever he walked into a room that was bugged. The equipment was tied to the presidential locater system that kept the Secret Service advised of the President's whereabouts in the White House around the clock. I think I saw the then-very-rudimentary system being used one day about a year later. While I was walking behind the President and the Secret Service in the bleak, mostly empty Palm Room, an agent stopped and opened the door to a box mounted on the wall. He then inserted a key, turned it, removed the key, and closed the door. Someone told me that a red light corresponding to the room the President was in would blink on a panel inside the Secret Service command post.

On July 17, Vice President Agnew cast his first deciding vote as President of the Senate to break a 49-49 tie that essentially opened the way for passage of the Alaskan Pipeline bill.

On July 18, Nixon ordered the recording system to be shut down.

Ironically, the minority counsel for the Senate Watergate Committee who asked former White House aide Alexander Butterfield about the existence of the recording system, a question that played a key role in bringing down the Nixon Presidency, was, in later years, better known to most Americans for his work in Hollywood than for his work in government. Fred Dalton Thompson, who would later become a United States Senator from Tennessee, was a well-known face in films and on television for his acting roles in *Days of Thunder, In the Line of Fire, The Hunt for Red October*, and *Law & Order*, among many others.

From then on, Watergate was a boiling cauldron of problems that seemed to get bigger every day.

On July 23, the Senate Watergate Committee demanded that President Nixon turn over a range of White House tapes and other documents. The next day, Nixon refused, based on executive privilege, an assertion that as an equal to the judicial and legislative divisions of government the executive branch could refuse their demands for documents and other information. Two days after that, the Committee issued subpoenas for the materials. President Nixon ignored the subpoenas and set up a landmark legal fight that eventually went before the United States Supreme Court a year later.

Sometime during all of this, a friend who claimed she knew of the recording system took me on a tour of where the $199 Sony 800-B tape recorder and other equipment had been housed in the basement of the West Wing. She also showed me the room in the EOB where the reel-to-reel tapes and John Dean's files were held and guarded by the Secret Service. I can't say for sure what was inside the room, of course, but I can say that the agents in front of the door were two of the largest guys I'd ever seen. In 1968, I met legendary Baltimore Colts defensive end Bubba Smith who was 6'7" and 260 pounds. Both agents could have given him a run for his money on the size scale.

There was one other thing that happened at the end of July that would have huge repercussions, although only a handful of people knew about it. A letter was being drafted by the U.S. Attorney in Baltimore regarding a criminal investigation of the Vice President for conspiracy, extortion, bribery, and tax evasion. The letter was addressed to the Vice President's personal attorney and hand-delivered to him on August 1.

Ironically, the July 30, 1973 edition of *Newsweek* magazine contained an article by journalist Stewart Alsop with the headline "President Agnew?" In it, Alsop described the Vice President as "a serious man partly because he epitomizes a mood, an attitude, that a great many Americans share. If he became President before 1976 he might be a most difficult President to defeat."

◆

One thing was obvious from the moment I stepped into the Correspondence Office on the 5th floor of the EOB: Vice President Agnew received a lot of mail, piles and piles and piles of it, more of it, I was told, than any other Vice President before him.

I joined a team of very smart, fun people on the 5th floor of the EOB. My job, which was full-time in the summer and part-time during the school year, was to open mail, categorize it by topic, select the proper pre-approved response, and print a letter and envelope on what was known as a Magnetic Card Selectric Typewriter. Now gathering dust in museums, they were the Daniel Boone of word processors, blazing a trail for all the generations that would come after them. The card, which was inserted into a reader connected to the electric typewriter, stored several thousand characters and could automatically type letter after letter error-free, a development that was wholly revolutionary. If you made a mistake typing a regular letter, the machine also had erasure tape built into the ribbon, eliminating the need for messy correction fluid that often somehow ended up as a wet white spot on my nose. Instead of the basket of long bars found in other typewriters, the Selectric had a golf-ball-looking thing that spun around faster than a Chihuahua in a clothes dryer, struck the inked ribbon, and printed the characters on paper as you typed.

After a letter and envelope were personalized with the correspondent's name, address, and a salutation, they went to a lady who oversaw quality control. She would return both for a do-over if, for example, the apartment number in the address wasn't listed before the street address. The apartment, suite, and house numbers, up to 100 as I recall, had to be spelled out, too. In other words, it was to read "Mr. John Smith, Apartment Two, One Hundred Elm Street, City, State, Zip Code." All these years later, I think of her every time I address an envelope.

When all of that was done, the letters were sent down the hall to a retired Air Force sergeant who had spent most of his career assigned to Air Force One. Along with a lot of other things, like the vice-presidential flags and seals, he controlled the autopen, an amazing contraption that signed the letter with either the Chief of Staff's or the Vice President's signature depending on the content.

The autopen was great fun to watch and experiment with when no one was looking. To use it, you selected the matrix, essentially an engraving, of the signature you wanted to reproduce, put whatever pen you liked in the machine's hand, placed a document under the pen and, at least with the model we had, stepped on a pedal that would start the machine's robotic arm in motion.

Then, in a slightly jerky manner, the arm would move up and down, more like drawing the signature than writing it.

I signed more stuff with that machine than I can count, including the cuff of one of my business shirts.

At least in the old days, autopen signatures were fairly easy to identify because they had odd, tiny squiggles in them that the human hand would be very unlikely to make. At a dinner party in the 1980s, I watched in horror as our host took on a $100 bet from a guest that a John F. Kennedy autograph on White House stationary he owned wasn't real. He took the letter out of its frame, wet his finger, rubbed it over the signature and, after virtually destroying it with saliva, declared that it was real because the ink smeared, ostensibly proving that the signature wasn't stamped or printed. Sadly for him, President Kennedy was said to have six or seven different autopen signatures, and the fact that the ink smeared meant nothing because the autopen could reproduce a signature with virtually any pen.

While some people think that having a machine sign a document for you is deceitful, the reality is that movie stars, politicians, athletes, and other celebrities who receive thousands of requests for autographs on everything from photos and letters to baseballs would otherwise spend most of every day signing things. Believe it or not, the first President to use a version of an autopen was Thomas Jefferson. The first President to admit using one was Gerald Ford. Just as astonishing is an opinion issued by the U.S. Department of Justice in 2005 that concluded that Presidents could sign bills into law by directing a subordinate to affix his or her signature with an autopen.

I still remember what a Spiro Agnew autopen signature looks like. Not that there's a lot of call for it these days, of course, but I can still tell the difference between an autopen and a real autograph.

All of this aside, my favorite part of the job was reading the mail. Along with correspondence about significant issues like high gasoline prices, the mounting Watergate scandal, and the war in Vietnam, there were cute letters from elementary school classes, young adults interested in government, and people seeking everything from autographs to recipes. There were also folks who opened my eyes to things that would have certainly never crossed my mind.

One guy wrote an 8- or 9-page letter every week about making the cranberry the official vegetable of the United States, which included a promotional plan for the government to use entitled, *Cranberries: America's Silent Hero*. Cranberries are fruits, not vegetables, but I wasn't going to tell him that. He didn't seem like a guy who would take it well.

Another sent a dozen color photos of a New York Yankees baseball cap-wearing golden retriever on a toilet holding a picture of Richard Nixon in his mouth.

One woman complained that wearing the Republican Party's elephant symbol on her dress made her look fat and suggested that the GOP use a thinner animal. Another felt that it was important for us to know that a local doctor had given her a shot of something that made her want to take her clothes off and stand naked in front of her picture window. She said that she was 76.

From political manifestos, senseless manifestos, old quilt patches, and used movie tickets, to a badly withered French fry, if it was strange it came addressed to the Vice President. In one single work day, I came up with a bumper sticker that said

"Honk if You Love Meat," a suggestion about how large-scale ear wax excavation could be helpful to our troops in Vietnam, and 26 pennies wrapped in a clearly used handkerchief, with a note from the sender that said he didn't know what else to do with them.

As impressive as these were, however, there were fellow Americans waiting in the wings with the capacity to take the game to a whole new level.

For reasons that are still not clear, the most interesting correspondence consistently came out of an about two-hundred-square-mile area of the Midwest. From this sweet spot in America's heartland came letters from a family that was under attack by Martians, a tome about a home besieged by heavily armed chipmunks who were holding the family's Siamese cat hostage, and a note from a woman who communed with an apparition of President Grover Cleveland that liked to steal socks, sometimes while people were wearing them. The late President, I learned, apparently favored argyle.

When I came back to work one afternoon after spending an uncomfortably humid half-hour with a brown bag lunch across the street in Lafayette Park, I found a small cardboard box on my desk addressed to "Speero Agnoo" with a note on it from my boss.

"I saved this one just for you," it said.

A little wary of the huge potential for a practical joke, I carefully lifted one of the box flaps and peeked inside. A perfectly innocent-looking wad of aluminum foil peered back at me. After I let out a breath of relief, I took it out of the box, turned it around a few times, and realized that it was a hat with wing-like arms sticking out of the front, back, and sides. It was made for a small head. Symbols of some sort were scrawled in black marker across the top of the middle section, and an arrow pointed to what I guessed was the front. In the box was an envelope addressed to the Vice President. On the back of the envelope "Nat'l Scurity" was written across the flap in red crayon.

The letter inside was handwritten in pencil by a self-described mother of three. She started out by explaining that she and her children had been "cranially wired" by visitors from Mars who had relocated to Ohio. Their goal, according to the writer, was to exert mind control over her family and take control of several local grocery stores. She said she could tell that the grocery clerks were Martians because they had big heads and did a poor job of bagging groceries, particularly bread, which was often crushed by their long, alien fingers.

The real giveaway, though, was that they couldn't help anyone find the butter or carrots. They also didn't want anyone to see their hands which, she surmised, were probably green. She complained that many of the aliens had bought homes in her neighborhood and were overcrowding public transportation and making everybody late for work.

The lady had made foil protective helmets for herself and her children. She was confident that they worked and sent one as a prototype for the government.

She was no doubt a national treasure.

Her only request was that the U.S. Government would consider building a ranch for the aliens anywhere but Ohio and preferably in New York because there were more buses there.

It all made sense to me.

She wrote a couple more letters and was then never heard from again. Nevertheless, every time I go into a grocery store I watch the checker put my bread in the bag. If they squish it, I try to catch a glimpse of their hands, just in case. And I always keep plenty of aluminum foil nearby.

As uniquely interesting as these things could be, there could also be a very dark version.

It had never crossed my mind that the United States Postal Service allowed brown paper grocery bags filled with stuff to be sent through the mail. Obviously, it did, because I found one sitting on my desk one morning. It was half-covered in stamps and addressed to "VP Stinky Agnew, Washington, D.C." Not surprisingly, it was missing a return address. The bag was stapled multiple times at the open end and, by the way the top was folded over, it looked like it contained something that filled about three quarters of it.

All of our mail was put through an X-ray machine before being forwarded to our office and, assuming that this had been, too, I popped the staples and took a look inside. From a weirdness standpoint, the contents were far from disappointing.

The first thing I saw was a pair of electric scissors that had one of its blades broken off. The scissors were sitting in a thick pile of paper clippings, each about a third of the size of an index card, that turned out to be a collection of pornographic photos that the sender had probably cut out of magazines, possibly with the electric scissors.

That was moderately creepy.

The really disquieting thing, which was about an eight out of ten on the creepy scale, was a rag that was scrunched up in the right corner. It was stained with a dried, brownish-looking substance. Although my mind was trying to convince itself that the brownish stuff was ketchup or paint, another part of me thought that it might be blood. Since the cryptic, bizarre contents were obviously not meant to brighten up the day, I followed procedure and took the bag to the Secret Service, specifically the Vice-Presidential Protective Division. Although I was sure that I was holding something of life-and-death importance, none of the agents thought that it was all that special. That suggested to me that there was a level of creepiness in America so unnerving that it made the garbage bag guy look like a two-bit amateur.

Nonetheless, the agent I spoke with, whom I knew from his frequent post outside of the Vice President's office, took it seriously and told me that he'd take care of it.

Then he turned and said, "Don, meet Mr. Hill."

I politely shook the gentleman's hand, thanked the agent for his help, and walked towards their coffee pot to steal a quick cup.

"Don't you know who that is?" the agent whispered to me. I answered with a question mark on my face, failing to make a connection.

"Idiot, that's Clint Hill," he said.

I was speechless.

Clint Hill was the first genuine American hero I ever met. While our country is blessed with many brave men and women who have performed acts of great heroism, I have never known of anyone who out-heroed Clint Hill.

On November 22, 1963, Special Agent Hill of the United States Secret Service was assigned to protect First Lady Jacqueline Kennedy. He was in a backup car directly behind the limousine carrying President and Mrs. Kennedy and Texas Governor and Mrs. John Connally. When the first shot was fired, Mr. Hill jumped off the running board of the moving Secret Service vehicle, ran to the President's car even as it accelerated, stepped up on the bumper, climbed over the trunk, and threw himself over Mrs. Kennedy and the President, who had already been fatally shot.

Mr. Hill did this in a matter of seconds.

For those of us who grew up in the shadows of that horrible day, Clint Hill's bravery is an indelible part of our collective memories. When I met him in the summer of 1973, he had been promoted to Assistant Director of the Secret Service.

I turned around and walked back to Mr. Hill, extended my hand a second time, and, with deep respect, said, "It's a great honor to meet you, sir."

Indeed, it was. I count that brief, chance meeting as one of the highlights of my life.

Although I didn't appreciate it for quite some time, history was becoming much more than just an academic endeavor in a classroom for me. I was meeting the people who made it. With Clint Hill, I had now met two men who had been inside the presidential car on that horrible Friday in 1963.

While still working for the Council on International Economic Policy, I had been on the third floor of the West Wing one day and, just as I pushed the down button on the elevator, a hand reached in to pop the door open. The hand belonged to former Treasury Secretary John Connally who introduced himself as if I had no idea who he was. I unquestionably knew who he was. Moreover, I knew that he had been seated in front of President Kennedy when the shots were fired and sustained wounds to his right back, right chest, right wrist, and left thigh. His injuries were part of the Warren Commission's still much-debated "magic bullet" theory that contends that one of the three shots fired by Lee Harvey Oswald entered President Kennedy's neck and continued through Connally's body.

Secretary Connally and I had a brief chat on the elevator that continued when we reached the ground floor of the West Wing. I particularly remember the conversation because I desperately wanted to ask him questions about the assassination but thought better of it. Instead, I asked him something about inflation that had come up in a controversial way in one of my college classes. To my astonishment, he answered my question at some length and well past what I understood. On top of that, he sounded so much like his mentor, Lyndon Johnson, that it was almost spooky. At the end, Secretary Connally shook my hand and wished me well in my studies. There's an old saying that if you want to learn about somebody, watch how they treat the people who can do nothing for them. In that regard, if no other, John Connally was good in my book.

In the wake of Vice President Agnew's resignation a few months later, Secretary Connally was said to have been Nixon's first choice as a replacement. The 25th Amendment allows the President to appoint a Vice President in the event of a vacancy with the approval of both Houses of Congress. For a variety of reasons, including the fact that the secretary had been a registered Democrat until early in 1973, Nixon decided that Connally's nomination might be too hard to pull off and chose House Minority Leader Gerald Ford instead. Connally ran for the GOP presidential nomination in 1980 but came in behind Ronald Reagan and George H.W. Bush.

It may not have been the first time that Nixon had the idea of replacing Agnew with Connally. There was a story that Nixon had considered arranging a job for the Vice President as the head of a conservative television network and tapping Connally as his 1972 running mate. Reportedly, the idea didn't move ahead because of Agnew's popularity with Republican voters and donors. In a poll of GOP voters in the spring of 1973, more than a third named Spiro Agnew as their top choice out of a crowded field of potential 1976 presidential candidates. Ronald Reagan was far back in second place.

◆

In August, I moved into a $75-a-month basement apartment in a home near the university. It was more than perfect for a college student. Nicely furnished, there was a private entrance, a working fireplace, a window air conditioner, and room to park my Pinto. If there was a downside, it was that the bathroom was in the unheated garage and, in the winter, I had to be very sure that I needed to use it before I walked out there. I mentioned that to my dad once. When he was done laughing, he reminded me that if that was my biggest problem, I didn't have a problem.

Although I'd planned to move off-campus in the fall anyway, I sped up my exit a little because of a neighbor in the dorm I had been living in that summer. He played Mountain's "Mississippi Queen" repeatedly at high volume every day until the wee hours of the morning. Complaining to the guy didn't work. He just turned up the volume. Complaining about him to the resident assistant didn't help, either. The RA didn't like confrontations. The only thing that sort of worked but made everybody suffer right along with him was stuffing about a half pound of limburger cheese under his door. After I moved out, I heard that somebody broke into his room, doused his bed with spoiled milk, and left a psychotic-looking note scrawled in crayon that said something about beating his 8-track player to death with a blunt object. That apparently worked like a charm. It was all the scarier that the suspected criminal was 5 feet tall, 90 pounds, wore big, square-shaped eyeglasses, and always had a little smile on her face. It made you worry about what was going on inside her head.

Like many Baby Boomers, the first thing I did after getting up in the morning was to turn on the TV news. Then, I'd make myself a cup of instant coffee with my trusty heating coil, take a shower, and catch the morning headlines between the time I dressed and left to catch the bus. My apartment came with a well-worn black-and-white console TV set with rabbit ears and a surprisingly good picture.

On Tuesday, August 7, I probably turned the TV dial to WTOP, the local CBS affiliate, because the network had just started a new morning news program with Hughes Rudd and Sally Quinn, the strikingly attractive wife of *Washington Post* editor Ben Bradlee. At some point, I heard the words "Agnew" and "investigation" and was understandably perplexed and concerned. As soon as I got to the bus stop, I bought a copy of that morning's paper. A front-page story explained that the Vice President had been notified by the U.S. Attorney's Office in Baltimore that it was "investigating allegations concerning possible violations...of federal criminal statutes" related to extortion, bribery, conspiracy, and tax fraud. The investigation concerned the awarding of state contracts while he was Governor of Maryland and federal contracts while Vice President.

The Vice President was quoted as saying that he was innocent of any wrongdoing, that he had complete confidence in the criminal justice system, and that he was equally confident that his "innocence would be affirmed." The article also noted that the investigation was not associated with Watergate.

By the time 8:30 or 9 o'clock rolled around that morning, our little band on the 5th floor was pretty much in shock. I wasn't even in the mood for my daily 10:00 a.m. glazed doughnut and coffee with so much cream and sugar that it was more like a molten birthday cake.

Sometime later in the morning, a memo came around that reiterated the Vice President's statement. It made everybody feel better.

I doubt that any of us believed that the charges were true. Every day we read what Americans from all walks of life thought about the Vice President and how highly they regarded him. As for us, no one ever had anything other than kind things to say about him and his family. In fact, the first time I met the Vice President, I was taken aback by how approachable and down-to-earth he was. At 6'2", urbane, trim, and dressed in an exquisitely tailored suit, he was warm, friendly, and, to me, bigger than life. I remember being surprised that the brief chat we had had nothing to do with him and everything to do with me. That was a lot more than I could say about my interactions with a lot of far lesser people. Some of them would have found it annoying to stop talking about themselves long enough to ask me my name.

Early in the afternoon of the next day, August 8, Jim stopped by my desk to ask me to help him with a few things. In no time, we were rushing an American flag, the vice-presidential flag, the vice-presidential seal, and all the related hardware, poles, and flag stands to Room 474 of the EOB, the auditorium where the press conference would be held. It was the same auditorium, in fact, where President Eisenhower conducted the first-ever televised presidential press conference in 1955.

Incensed that the confidential letter from the U.S. Attorney to his counsel had been leaked to the press, the Vice President intended to take questions about the charges directly from reporters. The letter's reference to a criminal investigation was enough to tarnish his name all by itself. The press conference was going to be broadcast live, and while television engineers connected large, bulky cables to their equally large, bulky cameras, we put the flags on the stage and the seal on the podium. By the time we finished, the room was overflowing with TV, radio, and newspaper reporters.

Nervous and klutzy, I cut my right hand on the edge of the podium and bled right about the same spot where the Vice President would have to put his speech. I wiped it up with the sleeve of my coat. Then I stuck my still-bleeding hand in my coat pocket. My dry cleaner must have thought that I'd been on a five-state killing spree.

While that was a lowlight, the highlight of my day was sitting in the audience next to a new friend, Jean Spencer, Ph.D., the Vice President's research director. Months before working for the Vice President of the United States ever crossed my mind, I read about Dr. Spencer's work in reorganizing Maryland's executive branch of government in one of my political science classes. Frankly, I was in awe of her and whenever I could, I'd drop by her office to chat. I'd always walk away knowing a lot about things I didn't know that I didn't know. She was very kind to me. Brilliant, with a self-effacing nature, she had a favorite Nixon story she liked to tell. One day she was waiting for the elevator on the ground floor of the EOB with several co-workers.

Somebody said something funny and she responded by bowing and saying, "All hail, Great Master!" At the same moment, a surprised President Nixon walked out of the elevator. He smiled sheepishly and kept walking.

Dr. Spencer later became the state's highest-ranking woman in education as deputy chancellor of the University of Maryland system. In 1993, she was inducted into the Maryland Women's Hall of Fame alongside Clara Barton, Harriet Tubman, St. Elizabeth Ann Seton, Billie Holiday, Eunice Kennedy Shriver, and a host of other stellar names. She fit that glittering group like a glove.

The Vice President made it clear to the people in the room that he had no intention of being destroyed by accusations that were being leaked to the media by people who were said to be close to the investigation. He denied the allegations, called them "damn lies," and answered the reporters' questions. Almost as soon as it was over, the Senate Office started to receive what would amount to more than a thousand encouraging telegrams.

The next day, an Associated Press report about the press conference summed up the problem that the leaks were causing: "The case has not yet been referred to a grand jury, nor have any charges been filed against the Vice President," the AP wrote. "The adverse publicity, however, is expected to damage, if not destroy, Agnew's chances for the Presidency in 1976, even if no criminal indictments come out of the investigation."

Over the next week or so, there was a new leak of highly confidential information from inside the investigation nearly every day and, as far as my friends and I were concerned, things were starting to stink. It looked like somebody was trying to deny the Vice President his right to have the investigation conducted in secret. Worse, it appeared that the same somebody wanted Agnew tried in the court of public opinion rather than a court of law.

In the absence of solid information, of course, the gossip mill took over.

There were suggestions that senior White House staffers, who reportedly received regular updates about major Justice Department investigations, were behind the leaks to take attention away from Watergate. Another story had it that Attorney General Elliott Richardson, who had opposed Agnew's nomination in 1968 and purportedly had his own presidential ambitions, wanted to get rid of Agnew either through resignation or incarceration. A related rumor had it that Richardson had agreed to kill evidence in the Watergate investigation in exchange for Nixon's agreement to appoint him as Vice President. There was also a claim that the Vice President couldn't be indicted unless he was first impeached and removed from office by Congress.

Frankly, with so much speculation coming from so many quarters, I was surprised that the lady who was worried about the Martians squishing her bread hadn't thrown in her two cents, too. It was beginning to look like the only thing constant about the whole affair was that it kept changing and getting more complicated.

On Tuesday, August 21, I was recruited to dash down to Room 474 again to help set up the stage for another live press conference. Two days earlier, *Time* magazine had released to reporters portions of a story entitled "Heading Toward an Indictment?", which was scheduled to appear in their August 27 edition. The piece said that "In the view of Justice Department officials in Washington, the case against Agnew is growing

DOWNSTAIRS AT THE WHITE HOUSE

steadily stronger, and an indictment appears inevitable" and that "at least three witnesses have told of delivering cash payoffs to Agnew. The evidence is so strong that the case must be taken to trial."

In an eight-minute speech, the Vice President lashed into the Justice Department for the continued news leaks, labeling them as a "clear and outrageous effort to influence the outcome of possible grand jury deliberations." The Vice President said that he had asked the Attorney General to conduct a formal investigation into the leaks, requesting that Richardson "compel sworn testimony to reveal the identity" of the people passing information.

The following day, Washington's leading newspapers, the *Post* and the *Star-News*, both published editorials that agreed with the Vice President's position. At the same time, President Nixon ordered the Attorney General to conduct a full, formal investigation of the leaks.

Back on the 5th floor of the EOB, we were nearly up to our waists in letters, postcards, and packages. Although there were a few nasty comments here and there, the vast majority of the messages were supportive. One postcard had a photo of a cat holding on for dear life to something like a chin-up bar. It said "Hang in There!" After we thanked the sender for her thoughtfulness, I put the postcard up on a cork board that was behind my desk. People sent in campaign buttons that said "President Agnew, '76", "Sock It to 'Em, Spiro!", "Spiro my Hero", and "The Spiro of '76!", among other things. I put those up next to the cat.

My favorite item, however, was a hand-painted Spiro Agnew hand puppet that looked a little like him. It was dressed in a little suit that looked better than the one I was wearing and sported a tiny metal button that said "Agnew for President" in equally tiny letters. It even had little black shoes. It was really an exquisite piece of work and, as far as I was concerned, was the Rolls Royce of hand puppets. Of course, I never put my hand in it and "talked" it to make people in the office laugh or anything like that.

Over the next few weeks, things started to look a little brighter.

The *Chicago Tribune* wrote that "the leaks concerning the Agnew probe are reprehensible. In the face of them, Mr. Agnew's candor in dealing with the scandal is all the more commendable."

Although a Gallup report showed that the Vice President's support among GOP voters for the 1976 presidential nomination had dropped by a third since the spring, he was still in a tie for the top spot with Ronald Reagan.

To add to the good news, highly respected columnists Rowland Evans and Robert Novak wrote shortly after Labor Day that "Vice President Agnew has bluntly informed President Nixon that, indicted or not, he will fight alone to end any effort to force his resignation."

That was a very big newsflash, particularly since we didn't know that the Vice President was being pressured to resign to begin with. For reasons that I suppose are understandable, more than a few people I knew assumed that White House employees had the scoop on every big story in the world. That, of course, was laughable. The truth about being "in the know" was that most of us at the bottom of the food chain weren't. Ever. We rarely knew more than what we read in the newspapers or saw on television unless we stumbled across something by accident or somebody said something they shouldn't have.

Speaking out of school was exactly what someone did on September 10, and it made me as angry as hell.

Late that afternoon, a fellow student who knew that I worked in the Vice President's office came up to me outside of the university library. A nasty little thing, she told me with a big smile that I was about to lose my job. She said that a member of her family worked for the Justice Department and had told her that "they had the goods" on Agnew and that the Vice President would have to resign.

"When Nixon goes," she said, "we can't have a crook take his place, can we?"

She laughed.

I didn't.

Instead, I told her that I envied people who had never met her. I may have said things about her stupid face, too.

Despite my sense that she was just a jackass looking for attention, I passed along what she said to one of the Vice President's senior staffers the next morning. I was thanked for the information and that was that.

Or so I thought.

As the calendar moved deeper into September, the news about the Vice President's situation, not to mention what was also going on with Watergate, was rapid-fire and a lot like riding a rollercoaster. If there was anything positive in the chaos, it was that I was getting an accelerated education about how the government and the press functioned, albeit in surprisingly wobbly and messy ways.

On September 20, there was very bad news. That morning's *Post* said that Vice President Agnew was "going to go in the next few weeks."

On September 22, the bad news turned worse and, to my horror, was almost exactly what I had been told. The *Post* reported that a plea bargain was being negotiated. It included "a possible Agnew resignation...coupled with a guilty plea to a relatively minor offense." Although the Vice President's attorneys said that the story was "without foundation," I had to wonder. Either the vile girl on campus knew exactly what she was talking about or she was the single best guesser on the face of the Earth.

On September 23, the news was better.

The *Post* said that the Vice President's attorneys would try to stop the U.S. Attorney from submitting evidence to the grand jury on the grounds that a sitting Vice President was immune from indictment, an issue that might have to be decided by the U.S. Supreme Court. They would also argue that the news leaks had made it impossible for him to get a fair trial. Moreover, the paper reported that a legal defense fund was being formed, commenting that it was the "strongest indication so far that the Vice President would resist all pressures to resign."

On September 25, the news wasn't just better, but surprising and exciting, too. At about four o'clock in the afternoon, the Vice President literally took his case to Congress.

In a meeting at the Capitol with Speaker Carl Albert and other House leaders that had been arranged only a few hours earlier, Agnew personally requested that the House of Representatives investigate the allegations against him. Moreover, he handed Albert a letter to that effect that raised a 150-year-old precedent for the House to involve itself in the matter. It stemmed from a case that appeared to be nearly identical to the problem that Agnew was facing.

In 1826, Vice President John C. Calhoun asked the House to investigate claims that he had received payoffs from a contractor while Secretary of War during the Monroe Administration. Calhoun's line of reasoning was simple: since the House was the only body that could impeach a Vice President for committing "high crimes and misdemeanors," it was the only body that could investigate charges of "high crimes and misdemeanors" made against him. The House leadership agreed, appointed a special committee, and eventually cleared Calhoun.

Vice President Agnew wanted the House to handle his situation the same way and for the same reasons. Some people suggested that his request was rooted in much more than constitutional issues. It was also politically smart. The Vice President stood a much better chance being judged by other politicians than the men and women from other walks of life who would serve on a grand jury.

Because September 25 was a Tuesday and I devoted Tuesdays to college work, I wasn't at the EOB that day. I'd spent the afternoon studying in the breathtaking surroundings of Main Reading Room at the Library of Congress which, as far as I was concerned, was the single best place to concentrate on anything. When I was done for the day, I walked towards a bus stop near the Botanical Garden on Independence Avenue by cutting across the Capitol grounds. As I got closer to the House side of the Capitol, I saw a horde of flashing lights, D.C. Police cars, Capitol Police, a black Fleetwood limousine, Secret Service agents, a Secret Service follow-up station wagon, TV cameras, and a lot of people just milling around.

Seeing the ruckus, I knew two things right away: the first was that it was none of my business. The second was that I was going to stick my nose right into it. I got close enough to the excitement to catch the eye of one of the Secret Service agents I knew. He waved me over, and I asked him what was going on.

"I don't know," he replied. He wasn't being helpful. Secret Service agents weren't supposed to be, of course, although it didn't stop me from asking.

Since whatever was going on was going on inside, I casually walked up the outside stairs and into the House wing of the Capitol. Despite my jeans, corduroy blazer, and acne largely screaming that I probably didn't belong there, I followed a chorus of loud voices to the hallway outside of the Speaker's office. It was jammed with people. Word that Agnew and Albert were meeting had spread across Capitol Hill like wildfire. The next day, I read that there may have been more Members of Congress spreading rumors in the hallway than working in the House Chamber.

Having a typically short teenage attention span, I found the milling around very boring, walked back down the stairs, and decided to stand around with the TV people since they were closest to the action.

When the Vice President came down the grand marble stairs, a network cameraman handed me a heavy case that was connected to the camera he was holding on his shoulder. He shouted "Come on!" and dragged me to the spot where the Vice President was telling reporters that he had no comment. When the cameraman was done filming, he turned around. He gave me a funny look which I thought meant that I wasn't who he was expecting to see.

I put down the case, which I later figured out contained a video tape recorder.

"What? Are you crazy?" he said. He was about 50 years old, overweight, red-faced, and sweating much more than was socially acceptable.

"Don't put it down, kid! Pick it up! We've got to go!" he yelled in my face. Confused, I picked up the case, followed him to his car, and put it in the back seat.

"You're fired," he said.

"But I don't work for you," I replied, terribly confused.

"Damn right you don't!" he shouted at me as he drove off.

For about a millionth of a second, the kid part of me felt bad that I had let him down. Then I realized that he had just conned me into carrying a 45-pound case all the way across the Capitol parking lot for free.

While I was busy getting fired from the network I didn't work for, the Vice President's letter was being read aloud on the floor of the House of Representatives. More than a few Members were said to be practically speechless. It wasn't exactly commonplace for a Republican Vice President to ask a Democratic Congress to help him out.

Speaker Albert, a Democrat, told reporters that he didn't know what he would do about Agnew's request. Republican House Minority Leader Gerald Ford, who would eventually succeed both Agnew and Nixon, said that the House should immediately grant Agnew's request. Democratic Majority Leader Tip O'Neill was strongly against it and in favor of letting the courts address the matter. A dark rumor floated around that the

Democrats wanted Agnew to remain in office under a cloud of suspicion, preventing Nixon from replacing him with a potential GOP presidential candidate who could pose a problem in 1976.

The next afternoon, Albert curtly told an overflow press conference that he had decided to leave the question of whether a Vice President could be indicted to the courts and rejected Agnew's request. House Judiciary Committee chairman Peter Rodino, who shared the same opinion, cited a different precedent from 1873 involving Vice President Schuyler Colfax. In that case, the House had decided that Colfax could not be impeached on bribery charges because the alleged crimes had been committed before he was Vice President.

Obviously, we were very disheartened by the news and even more so when we read that the charges were going to be taken before the grand jury. A lawyer friend said that there was no question that Agnew would be indicted whether there was suitable evidence or not. As he put it, the average grand jury would indict a ham sandwich just because they could.

Nevertheless, we were buoyed the next morning by a visit from the Vice President himself who came to thank everyone for their hard work in keeping up with the ever-increasing volume of mail. Although he looked pale and tired, he had a smile on his face and was very friendly. When he reached my desk, he asked me about each of the buttons and postcards I had on my corkboard and broke out in a big laugh when he saw the puppet. He also laughed that I was wearing a Spiro Agnew watch. After we shook hands and he started to walk away, he stopped, turned his head, and asked me how I doing in college. He even remembered what I was studying. That meant a lot to me.

Going forward in life, it gave me an appreciation for leaders who show respect for supporters and employees by remembering details about their lives. One of the more extraordinary examples I ever came across happened in 1997 during a conversation with former President Carter. Our brief chat turned to the topic of a career White House employee we both knew. My jaw dropped when the former Leader of the Free World, a man who had encountered tens of thousands of people around the globe and had not lived in the White House for 16 years, not only remembered our mutual acquaintance but the name of his wife, where he grew up, and how he came to be employed in the Executive Mansion. It blew my mind.

On Friday, September 28, Vice President and Mrs. Agnew left for Palm Springs, California for the weekend at the home of their friend, Frank Sinatra. Peter Malatesta, a member of the Vice President's staff and Bob Hope's nephew, had introduced them several years earlier. While the Vice President was flying west on Air Force Two, his lawyers were filing a motion in U.S. District Court to bar the grand jury from hearing additional evidence.

The next day, the Vice President delivered a nationally televised speech to a crowd of 2,700 who were attending a meeting of the National Federation of Republican Women in Los Angeles. When he walked into the convention hall, he was greeted by a three-minute standing ovation. He said that he was innocent and that he was being framed because he had refused to use his position as Vice President to stop a federal investigation of others in Maryland. He called the news leaks "malicious and outrageous." He said that he wouldn't resign. His rousing, defiant speech was interrupted by applause and cheering more than 30 times.

On Sunday, the *Washington Post* quoted the Justice Department as saying that a report to the Attorney General "indicated that all Department of Justice employees interviewed about the leaks swore under oath that they were not the source of published information concerning the Vice President."

Based on my personal experience, that may not have been true.

The following Friday, October 5, the Justice Department responded to the motion filed by Agnew's lawyers to stop the grand jury proceedings. They took the position that only a sitting President could not be indicted. They also said that they would continue to present evidence to the grand jury because the statute of limitations on some of the alleged crimes would run out on October 26. At that point, the Vice President and others could no longer be prosecuted.

The judge was to hear oral arguments on the constitutional issue on October 12.

In the meantime, the judge authorized the Vice President's lawyers to serve subpoenas on the Attorney General and reporters from the *Post*, the *Star-News*, *Time*, *Newsweek*, *CBS News*, the *New York Times*, and the *New York Daily News* to force them to reveal the sources of the leaks. Not surprisingly, the news organizations and the Justice Department immediately tried to quash the subpoenas.

Like many people, I'd occasionally experienced flashes of déjà vu and spooky moments. During the early morning hours of October 10, one of these came wrapped in a strange dream. I was in a big room standing next to a friend who was one of the secretaries. I turned my head to look at her. Her mouth was open as if she was in shock.

Then I woke up.

I'd switched my hours at the office for that Wednesday to attend a special lecture that morning. It ended up being cancelled. Instead of hanging around campus, I caught the bus and went to work. I got there just in time for my daily coffee and doughnut gala.

Around eleven o'clock, we received a memo instructing us to assemble in the Vice President's Conference Room at two that afternoon. The news went off like a shot. For reasons that still mystify me, several of us were convinced that the Vice President was going to tell us that the investigation was over, that he'd been vindicated, and that all was right with the world.

The Vice President's Conference Room was spacious and dignified. The massive conference table and chairs surrounding it were made of dark wood. Because all the seats were taken by the time we arrived, I stood with several other people along the left wall. Among the decorations on the opposite wall was a model of the Saturn V, the rocket that took American astronauts to the moon, and a very large, framed picture with the words "The Vice Presidents of the United States" across the top and the portraits of every Vice President since John Adams below it.

We waited. Then we waited some more. The friend who was in my dream came in the room and stood next to me on my right.

There was as much excitement blowing in the air as there was anxiety.

Then, in one big burst there was a flash of Army green. General Mike Dunn, the Vice President's military aide, briskly walked into the room. He threw some papers down at the head of the conference table.

"Our leader has just resigned his high office," he said.

I looked at my friend. Her mouth was open. She, like everyone else in the room, was in shock.

David Keene, the Vice President's chief political aide, hit the table with his fist.

"The Vice President should have told us himself," he said.

General Dunn told us that the Vice President was in a courtroom in Baltimore pleading no contest to a single charge of tax evasion in 1967. Dunn added that the White House would see to it that we'd get comparable jobs elsewhere in the government.

Everything had a weird buzzing to it, sort of like the way things feel in the aftermath of an auto accident. Somebody asked if we were supposed to answer the phones "Office of the Vice President" anymore. There were tears. Several people were angry. Some simply shrugged and walked away. A few others just stared.

The meeting lasted about three minutes.

When we got back upstairs, fear started to spill out. Although we'd been told that the White House would find us new jobs, no one knew what they would be or how long they would last. I was fine. I had enough money saved to make it for a while. My heart went out to my friends, particularly those with families to support. Not surprisingly, no one got any work done the rest of the afternoon. In fact, there was a question of what our work was anymore.

At around five o'clock, Jim asked if I'd help him deliver bundles of press releases about the resignation to the major newspapers, wire services, and television networks. We loaded up one of the White House cars and made our first stop at the National Press Club at 14th and F Street. I hopped out, grabbed one of the bundles, and walked into the lobby. I told the guard, an old guy with an enormous gut, that I was from the Vice President's office and politely explained what I was delivering.

He laughed and said something nasty about Vice President Agnew. Then he suggested that maybe I was a "crook," too. I told him that whatever I was, I at least didn't look like a pork roast with shoes.

Unfortunately, he wasn't the only jerk who felt compelled to express an unkind opinion that evening, and towards the end I stopped saying where I was from. Our last stop was at NBC Washington, which was near where I lived. It was about eight o'clock when Jim dropped me off. My landlord, who had a heart of gold, invited me upstairs for a beer. My mom and dad and a few friends called to be supportive. I nodded off with the TV on, slept through the national anthem and hours of static, and woke up before the station signed on for the day. I made a cup of coffee and watched the test pattern.

I was angry and stayed that way for a while. Although some of my colleagues leveled their frustrations at President Nixon, the Attorney General, Carl Albert, and the former Vice President himself, mine went in a different direction. As I saw it, legitimate critics had an important role to play in society. They were one thing. People with holier-than-thou attitudes were something else. None of the many people I heard spew sanctimony had any right to claim moral superiority over anyone about anything.

Working in the Vice President's office had a certain amount of sentiment attached to it. Although my job was very small and routine, I felt like I was a part of things. Even though working for a pop icon who was a heartbeat away from the Presidency clearly had cachet, it had nothing to do with feeling involved and appreciated. While I have been treated as well in other jobs, I have never been treated better than I was in the Vice President's office. Everybody knew me and I knew them. I had an immediate boss that I adored, and everyone was very friendly. One of the Vice President's daughters spent two weeks helping us with the mail. She was a class act. We went out to lunch, joked, talked, and got to know her. Every time there was an unhappy headline, we felt for her, her dad, her mom, and the rest of her family.

On Friday, October 12, President Nixon announced that he would nominate Gerald Ford to succeed Agnew as Vice President.

On October 15, Spiro Agnew addressed the nation on all three television networks. He reiterated his innocence, noting that the government's case was based on the statements of confessed criminals who had been granted immunity in exchange for their testimony against him. None of what they said had been substantiated and, worse, it had been "published and broadcast as fact." He said that he had resigned in the best interests of the nation and his family. He praised President Nixon and Vice President-designate Gerald Ford and thanked the American people for the honor they had bestowed on him by twice electing him Vice President. Then he said farewell.

The speech was dignified and optimistic.

Some people believed him. Some didn't. Some pointed to the 40 pages of evidence that the Justice Department had assembled against him.

For the next week or so, the former Vice President spent time in his EOB office organizing his papers for the National

Archives. Then, he and a few senior staff members moved across the street to 716 Jackson Place, a three-story brick townhouse adjacent to Lafayette Square.

It looked like the time had come for me to move on to a new chapter. Just like nearly everything else I experienced in life, it turned out to be pretty weird too.

American University students recruit campaign volunteers for Democratic presidential candidate George McGovern. Washington, D.C. November 1972 (Courtesy: American University Historical Photographs, American University Archives and Special Collections.)

President Nixon being greeted by school children at a campaign stop. Utica, Michigan. August 24, 1972 (Credit: The White House. Source: Richard Nixon Presidential Library/National Archives)

Bob Hope, backstage prior to performance at Camp Casey, South Korea. December 1972 (Credit: Bill Charles)

Police and Vietnam War protestors line Pennsylvania Avenue during the inaugural parade. Washington, D.C. January 20, 1973 (Keystone Pictures USA / Alamy)

DONALD M. STINSON

The Old Executive Office Building (now known as the Eisenhower Executive Office Building), Washington, D.C. Note the West Wing of the White House to the left. (Source: whitehouse.gov)

(L) to (R): Vice President Agnew, Prime Minister and Mrs. Giulio Andreotti of Italy, Frank Sinatra, Pat Nixon, President Nixon, and Judy Agnew. East Room, The White House. April 18, 1973 (Everett Collection, Inc / Alamy)

Former White House counsel John W. Dean III and his wife, Maureen, at the Senate Watergate Committee hearings. Russell Senate Office Building, Washington, D.C. June 29, 1973 (Everett Collection Inc / Alamy)

Vice President Agnew working at his desk in Room 274 of the Old Executive Office Building, Washington, D.C. (RBM Vintage Images / Alamy)

Demonstrators at the White House protesting the "Saturday Night Massacre." Washington, D.C. October 22, 1973. (Everett Collection/Alamy)

Ground floor of the White House Residence, facing west towards the Rose Garden and the Oval Office. Note the stairs to the State Floor at right. (Credit: White House Historical Association)

The author (far right) and friends shortly before President and Mrs. Nixon boarded Marine One for Andrews Air Force Base. Mrs. Nixon was leaving on a goodwill mission to South America. South Lawn, The White House. March 8, 1974 (Credit: The White House)

Julie Nixon Eisenhower and an unidentified, sweaty Easter Bunny at the annual Easter Egg Roll. South Lawn, The White House. April 15, 1974 (Credit: The White House. Source: National Archives)

President Nixon prepares to address the nation on television from the Oval Office regarding his release of the White House transcripts. The White House, April 29, 1974. (Credit: The White House. Source: Richard Nixon Presidential Library)

Congresswoman Barbara Jordan (D-Texas) and colleagues listen to testimony before the House Judiciary Committee relating to the impeachment of President Nixon. (Credit: U.S. House of Representatives Photography Office)

(L) to (R) Senator Hugh Scott (R-PA), Senator Barry Goldwater (R-AZ), and House Minority Leader John Rhodes (R-AZ) speak with reporters after meeting with President Nixon. The White House, August 7, 1974 (Source: National Archives)

President Nixon and Vice President Ford meet in the Oval Office to discuss Ford's impending ascension to the presidency. The White House. August 8, 1974 (Credit: The White House. Source: Richard Nixon Presidential Library/ National Archives)

Demonstrators in front of the White House during President Nixon's nationally-televised resignation speech. Lafayette Park, Washington, D.C. August 8, 1974 (Danita Delimont / Alamy)

President Nixon speaks to the White House staff in the last hours of his presidency. East Room, The White House. August 9, 1974. (L) to (R) David and Julie Eisenhower, President Nixon, Tricia and Ed Cox. Mrs. Nixon is standing behind the President to his left. (Credit: The White House. Source: Richard Nixon Presidential Library)

President and Mrs. Nixon bid farewell to Vice President and Mrs. Ford on the South Lawn of the White House. August 9, 1974. The photograph was taken from inside the presidential helicopter. (Credit: The White House. Source: Richard Nixon Presidential Library)

Chief Justice of the United States Warren Burger administers the oath of office to the Vice President Gerald Ford. making Ford the 38th President of the United States. Betty Ford holds a Jerusalem Bible under the new President's left hand. East Room, The White House. August 9, 1974 (Credit: The White House. Source: Gerald R. Ford Presidential Library)

President Ford with his golden retriever, Liberty, in the Oval Office. November 7, 1974 (Credit: The White House. Source: Gerald R. Ford Presidential Library)

Chapter Five

"I NEVER WANTED TO BE PRESIDENT"

Much to their credit, the White House Personnel Office wasted no time in helping us find new jobs. In fact, a higher-up invited me to his office for a chat just a few days after the Vice President resigned. While he was optimistic that they'd find work for me, he cautioned that the demand for part-timers in the Federal Government was low and that finding the right spot might take a little while.

I listened to him carefully and, with every bit of naiveté, misplaced self-confidence, and outright denial I possessed, walked away with the impression that my job search would be a piece of cake. After all, being sent to an interview by the White House had to be like being touched on the head with a magic wand. And, of course, I was also a Key Operator. I had no doubt that I was a hot property and was going to have more offers than I could handle.

October 1973 also brought a fuel crisis that created panic at gas pumps, heating oil shortages, and anxiety from sea to shining sea. In the middle of the month, the Organization of Arab Petroleum Exporting Countries, a group comprised of Saudi Arabia, Kuwait, Syria, Egypt, Libya, and other Middle Eastern nations, placed a petroleum embargo on the United States and its allies and raised the price of crude oil by 70%. The dual reduction in supply and increase in price was used as an economic weapon to retaliate against countries that had supported Israel in the Yom Kippur War against an Arab military alliance spearheaded by Syria and Egypt. The next month, the same exporters slashed their oil production by 25% to reduce the global supply and doubled the already jacked-up price of crude. In the United States, the average price of a gallon of gasoline rose from 39 cents to about 55 cents from 1973 to 1974, or $2.12 and $2.69 per gallon, respectively, in 2017 dollars.

At the beginning, service stations limited how much gas you could buy per visit. Then, the government set up rules for rationing using license plates. Vehicles with plates ending in even numbers could buy gas one day and those with odd numbers could buy gas the next. Signs saying "Sorry, Out of Gas!", "Pumps Closed", and "Gas for Regular Customers Only" were common. The lines of cars were often several city blocks long. Fights occasionally broke out between the attendants who pumped the gas for you and drivers who tried to get fuel on wrong-numbered days. The problems went far beyond local gas stations. The Secretary of the Interior suggested that people buy long johns to survive winter shortages of heating oil. Airlines cut back flights or eliminated them altogether. Even President Nixon got into the act in December. Eager to show the country that he, too, was conserving energy, Nixon left Air Force One in its hangar at Andrews Air Force Base and took a regularly scheduled United Airlines flight from Washington to Los Angeles to visit his home in San Clemente, California.

The crisis also offered opportunities for cottage industries to bloom. I saw entrepreneurs selling coffee and hot chocolate to people stuck in line. For a price, others would sit in your car while you got a sandwich or rent you a license plate with the right number on it. There were girls who stuffed pillows under their shirts to look pregnant and play on the sympathies of the mostly male gas attendants.

The best story I heard was about a guy who drenched his shirt with ketchup and drove into a gas station with the wrong day's number on his plate. The driver told the attendant that he'd been in a bad accident and needed gas to get to the hospital. Apparently, the pungent smell of tomato didn't tip off the worried attendant, who shouted for somebody to call an ambulance. When the Emergency Medical Services guys arrived, they thought that the driver had been shot and tried to get him to lie down on a stretcher. The driver turned violent and punched one of the EMS guys in the face. The gas station owner called the cops. When all was said and done, the driver, who must have looked like a tailgate party gone terribly wrong, was arrested for assault, spent the night in jail, and got a huge bill for the ambulance.

What he didn't get was gas. The good news, though, was that he didn't need it.

By the time he got back to his car, it had already been towed away.

In the meantime, I still had a job in the Office of the Vice President even though the Vice Presidency was vacant. My boss, God bless her, wanted to make sure that we left the office shipshape and substantially better than the Agnew staff was said to have found it on Inauguration Day in 1969. A friend said that it looked like Vice President Hubert Humphrey's people had simply walked out of the office, leaving mail, supplies, coffee cups, and other things behind as if they'd gone out to lunch and were coming right back. Somebody had even left a half-written letter in an electric typewriter, right next to the remains of an aggressively gnawed apple.

Along with my normal clerical duties, I was also put to work carrying things around. An Army sergeant who was assigned to the Vice-Presidential staff asked me to help him take some things to the Agnews' house in Maryland. To seal the deal, he threw in an offer to drop me off at the university on the way back. Considering how much I hated the fumes from the D.C. buses, it was an offer I couldn't refuse.

The Agnews' home, a 12-room Colonial fieldhouse built in 1938, was in the Kenwood section of Chevy Chase, a neighborhood filled with tall, beautiful trees and exquisitely manicured lawns. They had lived in the Sheraton Park Hotel before moving into the house in June 1973, the year before the Naval Observatory on Massachusetts Avenue was designated as the Vice-Presidential residence. The idea of an official home for Vice Presidents was intended to eliminate the high costs of equipment and construction necessary to secure their personal homes. In the Agnews' case, those costs totaled some $125,000, or roughly $700,000 in 2017 dollars. Gerald Ford was supposed to be the first Vice President to live in the house in 1974, but obviously moved into the White House instead. Ford's Vice President, Nelson Rockefeller, a member of one of America's wealthiest families, continued to live on his 25-acre estate on Foxhall Road in Washington. As a result, the 9,000-square-foot house at One Observatory Circle was largely used for entertaining until Vice President Walter Mondale and his family moved in in January 1977.

At the bottom of the Agnews' driveway was a small shelter for the Secret Service. An agent neither of us knew stopped us, looked at our identification, and eventually sent us up the fairly steep driveway. Outside of a back door in an extra-large turnaround area meant to accommodate limousines, the Navy stewards who had been assigned to the Vice President's home were packing up their things and loading them into a van. When my friend opened the trunk of our car, I was surprised to see the very large framed picture bearing the portraits of America's 39 Vice Presidents that I'd seen only days earlier in the conference room. As we carefully unloaded it, Mrs. Agnew came out to greet us. She looked at the picture, softly said, "The Vice Presidents of the United States," and blinked her eyes as if she was fighting back tears. She mustered up a smile, graciously thanked us for bringing the things from the office, and went back inside the house.

Mrs. Agnew was a sweet, lovely lady. Seeing her sad made us sad.

A week or ten days later, my fellow staffers and I received invitations to a farewell party at the Agnews' home on Saturday, November 3. Not only was it a big event for those of us who were invited, it was a big enough news item to rate a mention in *Newsweek* and the *Washington Post*.

Despite being on the edge of unemployment, I decided to make a desperately needed investment in new clothes. I'd worn a quarter-size hole in my best pair of pants and had ineptly tried to repair it with an iron-on patch that needed to be secured with scotch tape. I could feel and hear the tape crinkle when I walked. Worse, I was convinced that other people could hear it, too.

Wandering around 10th and F Streets after work one day near Woodward & Lothrop, one of Washington's major department stores, I came across a men's suit shop that was advertising a 50% off sale. I spent quite a while picking out a conservative navy blue suit and a red tie. The store manager, a gruff, unkempt guy with a clean-shaven face and a seriously weird-looking neck beard, measured me for alterations. Then, I took out my checkbook. The manager told me the price of the suit and the alterations, a total that was triple what I had expected.

I told him that I didn't understand how the bill could be so high.

He went nuts.

"You buy the suit! You buy the suit!" he screamed, jabbing his index finger in my chest.

I pointed at the sale sign hanging on the wall. It said, "All Suits 50% Off!" in gigantic red letters.

"This is a rip-off! I want this suit at 50% off!" I demanded, holding it up on its hanger with one hand while stupidly assuming that he'd do the right thing.

Then I noticed that there was something small scribbled at the very bottom of the sign in light pencil.

It said, "Except suits NOT."

"I'll cut you," he said in a low growl with a disturbing emphasis on the word "cut".

I threw the suit at him and ran. On the way out, I may have accidentally-on-purpose knocked a huge pile of neatly arranged, ugly ties to the floor.

Until I went to that shop, I never realized how violent the men's suits and furnishings business apparently could be. The next day I went to Woodward & Lothrop, better known as "Woodies", and steered very clear of suits. Instead, I bought a navy blazer, grey trousers, and a red-white-and-blue tie. Thankfully, the Woodies sales lady didn't threaten to slash my throat when I hesitated about buying the tie. She did give me kind of an annoyed look, though.

The next evening, I rolled up in front of the Agnews' house in my Pinto and found a place to park on the street. I got out of the car to close the passenger's side door which, like usual, had sprung open as I rounded a corner. Then, I got back in and just sat there. I remembered reading something about always being fashionably late to a party, but the article didn't say anything about how late fashionably late was. I might have been twiddling my thumbs there in the dark for God-knows-how-long had it not been for one of my co-workers and her husband knocking on my window. The three of us decided that 15 minutes after the time on the invitation was good enough. Even if it wasn't, I was hungry and my teenage stomach, which frequently dictated the decisions I made about everything, was telling me to go inside and get some groceries.

We collected other co-workers on our walk up the driveway and, when we all reached the house, a familiar Secret Service agent knocked on the front door. The door opened. Standing there in a receiving line were Mr. and Mrs. Agnew and two of their daughters. Mrs. Agnew took my hand into both of hers and thanked me for bringing out the items from the EOB. The former Vice President put his left hand on my shoulder and gave me a hearty handshake. I wanted to thank him for inviting me, but I didn't know how to address him. Was it still Mr. Vice President or now Mr. Agnew? I picked Sir. It didn't appear to present a problem.

Although I did the right thing in that instance, I'm quite sure that my mother wouldn't have approved of my manners when I quickly abandoned everyone and followed my nose to the buffet like a wolf. I was the first one to plunge into the food. I left a couple of ugly divots in the cheese, spilled some meat juice on the tablecloth, threw caution to the wind, and pressed on.

The house was beautiful. I had been in the kitchen with the stewards and Secret Service agents a couple of times but never in the living area.

To the right of the front door was a room with a stunning black Japanese room divider that particularly caught my eye. On the left was a formal living room. Along with the usual collection of sofas, tables, and chairs found in most American homes, there was a grand piano with a sculpture planted on the ledge above the keys. It was a bust of their family friend, Frank Sinatra.

Sitting on an ottoman in the crowded room was an extremely nice, exceptionally beautiful co-worker and her husband. She introduced me to him. At some point, I asked her quite seriously if she had a sister my age. She said that she didn't, but that the question was one of the nicest things anyone had ever asked her. She was smiling and I was smiling, but it was clear that her husband wasn't grooving on all the happiness. Then I realized that I had not paid as much attention to his crew cut and Marine Corps lapel pin as I should have. More importantly, I hadn't noticed the enameled .45 pistol on his tie clasp.

I went back to the buffet.

The party went on for a couple of hours and then, little by little, started to break up, led, like they almost always are, by people with babysitters. The article I read about arriving fashionably late at a party didn't say a word about when it was fashionable to leave a party. I was having such a good time that I decided to stay until someone either told me to go home or handed me a pillow and a blanket.

Had I tried to predict what was going to happen next, I couldn't have come up with it in a million years.

I found myself sitting across from Spiro Agnew.

On the floor.

Seated to the right of the Japanese room divider with five or six former senior staffers, he had a frosted mug of beer in his hand. He seemed to be very much at ease. I'd heard that the members of his Secret Service detail thought highly of him and regarded him as a regular type of guy who enjoyed playing cards with them on long flights. With that in mind, sitting on the floor probably wasn't that much out of character for him.

The former Vice President talked for quite a while about his career and what he hoped to do with his future, an apt topic since, at 54, he was still a young man. He talked about a variety of things from Vietnam, the economy, the impending oil embargo, and Richard Nixon to Watergate, writing his memoirs, and the Baltimore Colts' lousy 2-5 record.

It struck me that he didn't utter an unkind word about anybody or anything.

But he did say something that shocked me.

He said that he never really wanted to be President.

Sitting there sipping a beer, I didn't quite understand how anyone wouldn't want to be President of the United States. The honor of holding the highest office in the land alone seemed to me to be the loftiest of lofty goals, not a choice.

It took years for me to fully appreciate that conversation and the man who was at the center of it.

Every four years, a host of candidates walk across the American political stage in a quest to become President. A few have a chance of succeeding. Most, however, have better odds of being run over by a snow plow in Miami. Say what you will about how Spiro Agnew's political career ended and the charges lodged against him, but he was no pretender to the throne.

It's one thing to speak with someone who would like to be on a ticket that drew almost 80 million votes in two national elections. It's quite another to talk to someone who was. And won.

Spiro Agnew spent nearly five years within a heartbeat of becoming the Leader of the Free World.

Had the legal problems that forced his resignation never come to the fore, he would have almost certainly become President when Richard Nixon resigned. He might also have been elected President in his own right in 1976, whether Nixon had resigned or not.

As for me, I said very little that night other than to offer a minor opinion about the Colts. Despite my reputation as a chatterbox, I must admit that I was intimidated. The people I was sitting with were all very accomplished. I was nothing but a pile of flesh taking up room. Nonetheless, I wasn't treated that way and, in retrospect, I give myself credit for realizing how very unusual the moment was. I listened very carefully. I think I learned more about how the world works in that hour or two than I had learned in all my 18 years of life.

I remember Peter Malatesta saying something about he and Frank Sinatra planning to sell the house they shared in Washington. I also remember wondering if I'd heard what he said correctly. Conversations about Frank Sinatra weren't exactly part of my daily routine. The mention of Sinatra, of course, made me want to tell Peter all about my ice water incident in the East Room, which I didn't do thanks to a little voice in my head that was telling me to shut up.

My walk back down the driveway to my car was a sad one.

I didn't want the ride to end.

There was something else that happened that evening. The wife of my friend the Army sergeant told me a story about traveling on an airplane and passing the time by chatting with her seatmate. My friend's wife mentioned that her husband was in the Army and assigned to the Vice President's office. She added that his role was not the kind you'd read about in the paper. "It sounds fascinating," the lady replied. "Most people never do or see much of anything. It doesn't matter what your husband does in the White House. He's there. Just being there can be enough to change your life." I had never thought about it that way.

◆

By the Friday before the Agnews' party, I'd had three job interviews in three different departments within the executive branch. Jobs everywhere were tight at the time and I wanted to stay with the government if possible, both for stability and the opportunities it afforded me to make important contacts. I'd shined my nerdy, brown penny loafers, made sure my blazer and trousers were clean and pressed, and put a smile filled with eagerness, humility, and sincerity on my face for each meeting.

Curiously, all three interviews went almost the same way. It was almost as if the people I met with were reading from a script.

"The White House sent you?" the interviewers asked.

"Yes," I replied each time.

"You worked for Agnew?" they would ask.

"Yes, I did," I'd say.

"We don't have anything," the interviewers replied.

Every little thing about this was bizarre, including the fact the Personnel people had me come all the way downtown on the bus just to tell me that they didn't have a job opening. I was perplexed and freaking out a little about where this was all headed or, rather, not headed. Obviously, I hadn't considered the possibility that people might not enjoy having me shoved down their throat. I let the gentleman in White House Personnel know about it and, with a deep sigh, he said he'd look into the problem.

I was also concerned that when my job in the Vice President's office ended and I had to give up my EOB pass, I was going to lose touch with friends and the Personnel staffers who could help me get another job. Frankly, I was afraid that I was going to lose a lot of other connections, too. So, I did as much as I could with the time I had left.

At the top of my list was getting some high-powered help with a problem in an economics class.

I enjoyed college except for the occasional episodes when a professor was crushingly boring or went into a tirade against the Nixon White House and Watergate, two common situations on every college campus in those days. Since I was a political science major, I clearly understood that strong, diverse opinions came with the territory. I didn't have a problem with any of it if the instructor eventually came back to the subject matter.

One professor who taught an economics-related course un- fortunately overdid it. He launched into a 20-minute rant that punched every single hot button I had, political and otherwise. He did the same thing in the next class and virtually every one after that. He got so wrapped up in calling everyone at 1600 Penn- sylvania Avenue stupid that he couldn't remember where he'd left off in his lecture.

I went to see two very smart guys from CIEP with doctorates in economics. They were in their thirties and treated me like I was a little brother. Like big brothers, they had a great time peppering me with questions about what I was learning and telling me that I was a hopeless case. Over lunch, I told them how much of an aggravation my professor had become. Instead of commiserating with me, they burst out laughing.

"Why don't you just 'fix' him?" one of the guys asked. I had no idea what he was talking about.

"Ask him an absurdly complicated, brilliant question. That'll shut him up," he said.

That sounded easy to do, particularly since I'd been taking the class for an entire six weeks.

The guys were happy to help, of course, and crafted a ridiculously intricate question for me to pose about M1, the sum of money in a nation's economy in currency and bank deposits. In fact, they thought the question was so dazzling that we all went out to celebrate with the cash in my wallet. They told me to memorize the question so that it looked as if I knew what I was talking about which, clearly, I didn't.

Despite nervousness in my voice and a healthy concern that my big brothers had set me up, I asked the question the next time the professor jumped from economics to Watergate. The professor stared at me. He squinted his eyes a little and asked me to repeat the question.

Then he coughed.

Then he said he didn't know the answer to the question.

Then he asked me how I knew enough to ask the question.

Then I told him that while he was talking about Watergate, I read ahead.

And that was the end of that, except for having to buy my very smart friends lunch and tell them ad nauseum, ad infinitum how their question kicked the professor square in his rear end.

◆

I've often found that the more I convince myself that something will go horribly wrong, the better it turns out or, at least, seems to turn out. In high school, my friends and I used negative thinking when we took tests. If we persuaded ourselves that we'd flunked a difficult exam and then made, say, a B, we'd feel like we'd faked out the universe. Even though it was kind of stupid, it worked for us and I saw no reason to give it up when I got to college.

So, after fuming, pacing back and forth in anger, and absolutely, positively writing off any hope that the White House was going to help me get a job and deciding I'd be a failure for eternity and probably die, I got a call from a very nice lady in the Personnel Office at the beginning of December. She asked me if I was available to interview with the Department of Health, Education, and Welfare, today known as the Department of Health and Human Services. When I nearly yelled "Yes!" through my black rotary phone, the nice lady gave me the name of the man I was to speak with and strict instructions to be there at 10:30 on the dot the next morning.

All spiffed up once again in my blazer and penny loafers, I showed up about ten minutes early. A substitute receptionist in the Personnel Office told me to take a seat and that someone would be with me shortly. In the meantime, I was entertained by the noise the vinyl cushion on her chair made when she moved.

It sounded exactly like she was passing gas and, unfortunately, it didn't faze her a bit.

At 11:30 a.m., I was still sitting there after having asked the receptionist about a million times to check with the person I was supposed to see. At noon, she went to lunch with barely a word to me. At 12:30, I got up, moved around to get the feeling back in my legs, and started poking my head in office doors. After four or five tries, including one in which I walked in on a very nasty exchange between two middle-aged women who were calling each other "fatty pants," I came across a guy who was about 60 with his elbows on his desk and hands on his forehead as if he'd just had something go terribly wrong. I introduced myself. He asked me why I was two hours late and, ignoring my attempt to explain that their receptionist was an idiot, began to lecture me about punctuality.

Eventually, he told me about the job opening which, he said in as nasty a tone as possible, wasn't an opening at all but a job that had been created for me because the White House said they "had to."

"You're our little charity case," he said, looking at me over his glasses with obvious contempt.

I was furious. It wasn't my fault that I'd lost my job. The White House offered to help us. It wasn't like I'd asked anybody to pull strings for me. Without saying a word, I stood up and simply walked out of the office, exhibiting much more independence than my bank balance gave me a right to have.

Evidently this was not how my introduction to the Department of Health, Education, and Welfare was supposed to go because the old guy followed me down the hall and out to the street. He didn't help his case by shouting, "Come back here, boy!"

What a pupik.

Much to my surprise, the same lovely lady from White House Personnel called me at home the next morning. She said that she'd arranged for me to meet directly with the hiring manager for a group that was involved in a lot of cool, interesting things related to children and youth. As it turned out, the people in charge there were very nice, didn't insult me, and were more than willing to work with my college class schedule. I happily accepted the job. In retrospect, I can only imagine how delighted the White House must have been to finally get rid of me.

The fact that I had finally found reliable work, however, didn't stop me from trying to get a better job, and potentially screw everything up, in the meantime.

Since I wasn't scheduled to start at HEW until December 10, I decided to see if I could weasel my way into a job on the new staff Vice President-designate Ford would be hiring. So, on Friday afternoon, December 6, just hours before Gerald Ford, Minority Leader of the House of Representatives, became Gerald Ford, 40th Vice President of the United States, I strolled into the Capitol with my resume, a smile, and an oversupply of unsupported optimism.

After melting into a thick crowd of people who looked like they knew what they were doing, I was waved through security and followed the horde into a large room with dark wood paneling near the Minority Leader's office. Towards the back and to the right sat Robert Hartmann, one of Ford's senior aides, whom I recognized from my trips to Capitol Hill. Had I known that he had a reputation for being prickly, I might not have approached him. Since I was ignorant, I walked right over and tried to politely interrupt a conversation he was having with another gentleman.

Both men ignored me. I tried to politely interrupt again. When that failed, too, I fake-sneezed. I cleared my throat. I coughed.

Failing miserably to get his attention, I used a ploy I'd read about in a magazine. I walked over to a coffee pot, poured some hot Joe into a Styrofoam cup, and sauntered directly into his line of sight.

"Here's your coffee, sir," I said.

"Thank you," he replied, somewhat inattentively. He must have had damn good peripheral vision because he took it in his hand without even a tiny look in my direction.

Then he quickly tilted his head towards me.

"Who are you?" he asked, looking at me with an appropriate amount of wariness.

For me, the opportunity to answer that question was like a dream come true. I immediately introduced myself while handing him a crisp copy of my resume. I told him that I wanted a job with Vice President Ford.

I was nervous and could feel my right knee wobble. I hated it.

"I'll look at it later," he said as he looked away. He folded the resume in half and stuck it in the side pocket of his jacket.

"Well, sir, I'm standing right here. I'd like to talk about it with you right now," I said with a disastrous combination of resolve and arrogance, trusting that my experience with opening mail was bigger than anything he could possibly have on his mind.

Believe it or not, that was a mistake.

"Okay! Enough!" Hartmann said angrily as he and the guy he was talking to suddenly stood up and walked away.

Words would not come out of my mouth. I just stood there.

"Thank you, sir," I finally said, nearly shouting because he was already on the other side of the room.

If that wasn't bad enough, I saw what I assumed to be my resume on the floor. Disappointed in myself, I left it there.

A week or so later, my mail contained a letter from the Vice President's office. I assumed that the envelope contained one of the millions of pieces of paper that were sent out when you left the U.S. Government. In fact, I didn't even open it for a few days. When I did, I saw that it was a handwritten note from a lady on Ford's staff.

The letter said that she had received my resume from Robert Hartmann.

I was shocked. Apparently, I was wrong about what was on the floor that day. Although I didn't get a job on the new Vice President's staff, his gesture was incredibly kind and much appreciated. Mr. Hartmann, who nine months later would write the famous line, "My fellow Americans, our long national nightmare is over" that President Ford delivered in his inaugural address about the end of the Nixon Presidency, turned out to be a much nicer man than I deserved to meet.

The following Monday I reported to HEW as planned. For starters, I had my picture taken and, after waiting for the Polaroid to develop and dry, was presented with an ID badge that said I was assigned to the Office of the Secretary. It didn't mean anything of importance, but it looked cool.

Even though I missed the White House and my friends, I liked my new job and felt very welcomed. Happily, the clerical work I was given to do was generally quite interesting. In fact, I had the feeling that the professional staff went out of their way to find projects for me that I might learn something from. They even graciously invited me to join them at a couple of events on

Capitol Hill, including a Senate subcommittee meeting. I found it all fascinating.

Unfortunately, my happy mood began to wane by the end of my second week. That was when I crossed paths with a woman from another department who spent her days pushing around a large, decrepit-looking gray cart that was perpetually overloaded with office supplies. It must have weighed 300 pounds.

On the Friday afternoon before Christmas, I was sitting at a secretarial desk with my attention focused on a project that was due the first week of January. The office was virtually empty and very quiet. Except for the cries for mercy that the wobbly wheels on her cart made, I'd have never noticed that she was headed my way. Without introducing herself, she bluntly asked me if it was true that I'd worked in the White House. When I said that I had, she told me in a hulky, coarse voice that I was stupid-looking. Not that I was terribly surprised by anything she said at that point, but she went on to describe a slew of axes she had to grind with several Presidents with an emotional fury that rivaled the shower scene in *Psycho*. Among them was Herbert Hoover, who she incorrectly assumed was a member of the Hoover family of vacuum-cleaner fame.

"He didn't care about the Depression," she said. "He always had a job making sweepers."

I could have corrected her, but I was scared.

She also went on to say things about the private conduct of other famous Americans that were so mind-blowingly obscene that I had to look them up in a medical text to see if they were even possible. Amazingly, all but one were.

With no clue where any of this was going except downhill, I smiled, wished her a Merry Christmas, stood up, and walked away.

There was a very sharp pain in my right leg when she rammed me from behind with the cart, explaining that she didn't want me to forget her over the holidays. One wise guy I told about the incident suggested that she probably liked me and was showing it the way a kindergartener would. Instead of chasing me across a playground, she preferred assault with a deadly weapon.

As entertaining as that was, violence was only a slice of her vibrant personality. I later heard through the grapevine that she went into the ladies' room every day at noon, locked herself inside a toilet stall, slumped against the back wall, and snoozed for an hour. Cozying up on, in, or around a commode seemed so natural for her that the vision of it didn't even make me blink.

The good news was that I stopped limping by Christmas Eve. The bad news was she was nothing compared to what was in the offing when I returned in January.

Back in the dark ages before electronic banking and automatic deposits, employees received paper checks that we took to a bank and deposited, cashed, or in the cases of some of my older male friends, immediately turned over to their wives. Because I started in mid-December, I didn't expect to get paid until January and managed my collapsing bank account accordingly.

Imagine my surprise, then, when there was no check for me on the first pay day of 1974. I asked the nice lady in charge of distributing the checks if she'd investigate to see if mine had been lost or sent to the wrong place.

Sporting a helpful-looking smile on her face in front of her co-workers, the lady said that I shouldn't worry about it. She said she'd call a friend in Payroll right away to find out where it was. When I was finally able to chase down the nice lady two days later, she said that she'd forgotten all about it and then strongly suggested that I call the Payroll Department myself since, after all, it was my check and she had better things to do. Then she went back to painting her nails and smoking a cigarette at her desk.

I went to my boss who couldn't have been more helpful. He called the Payroll Department right away and found out that they had no record of me as an employee. When my boss told them that there had to be a record because I already had a security badge, they said that that was impossible. To resolve the problem, they said that I would have to present myself to the Personnel Department and prove who I was. If I did, and my boss would sign the hiring paperwork again, my file could be corrected in a few days and I could get paid a few days after that.

I presented myself to Personnel that afternoon with my driver's license and my university ID at the ready. I also had my HEW ID. I handed the lady who was vetting me the HEW badge first. Of course, she said that it was perfectly sufficient to prove my identity and status as an active employee.

A week passed. The only money I got was a dime somebody dropped on the floor. Because my boss was out of town, I decided to visit the Payroll Department myself.

The office was an endless line of drab green metal file cabinets adjacent to endless rows of drab green metal desks. I explained my situation to the first welcoming face I saw, who sent me to find a specific gentleman who purportedly could help. I eventually found him, and although he was curt and crusty, he seemed interested in the problem and excited about unraveling the mystery. He got up, walked over to the files, and returned with my paperwork about ten minutes later.

"What's your Social Security number?" he asked.

I handed him my HEW security badge. As strange as it may seem today, the badge had my nine-digit number printed right on the front of it.

"Is that the right number?" he asked, pointing at the badge.

I nodded.

He grinned as he showed me that the Social Security number on my paperwork had been entered incorrectly—so incorrectly, in fact, that it might as well have been pecked out with a sledgehammer.

"Can you just change it and give me a check?" I asked, trying to look as pathetic and destitute as possible. He told me that my file would have to be processed again. The way it sounded to my impatient ears, I had the impression that processing was going to take six months.

"What's the fastest way to get paid?" I asked.

The gentleman laughed.

"Besides filing the paperwork again?" he asked. "You'd have to quit. Then we'd have to cut you a check."

It only took a moment for my mind to weigh the upsides of being patient against the downsides of acting on impulse.

Impulse won.

I went back to my little desk, wrote a resignation letter, and left it on my boss's desk. Although he tried to change my mind when he came back, I politely declined. A week later, a check for the entire amount owed me arrived in the mail. I promptly went to the American Security & Trust Bank branch closest to the university and cashed it.

Maybe the man in Payroll was just kidding me about quitting, or maybe I heard it all wrong. Both were certainly possible since the wires between my ears and my brain were known to occasionally have loose connections. Nevertheless, I was dumb about the whole thing. In the end, if the United States Government would have gotten my Social Security number right, I'd have eventually been paid, and I wouldn't have been faced with unemployment again.

Even though quitting my job would turn out to be one of the best stupid things I ever did, it was only because I was insanely lucky. Good luck is a great asset, but it's not exactly something you can count on.

With money in my pocket and some extra time, I decided to celebrate by getting the door fixed on my Pinto and treating myself to the $2.50 open-faced Reuben sandwich, fries, and beer combo at The Tavern every day until the buildup of sauerkraut, hops, and barley in my system started to ruin my social standing.

I also treated a few friends to lunch. Among them was my pal Dr. Spencer, who by then was a Special Assistant to Presidential Counselor Anne Armstrong in the White House Office of Women's Programs and one of the few Agnew staffers who were retained by the Nixon Administration. I loved to visit Dr. Spencer and her office mate, Jill Ruckelshaus. Together, they beat a lot of the "male chauvinist pig" out of me. Mrs. Ruckelshaus, a brilliant, vivacious woman with a Harvard master's degree was also the wife of the Deputy U.S. Attorney General who resigned in the "Saturday Night Massacre." She was sometimes called "the Gloria Steinem of the Republican Party," a reference to the famous feminist movement leader and co-founder of *Ms.* magazine. In the 1980s, Jill Ruckelshaus' name was bandied about as a potential vice-presidential nominee. There were more than a few people, including me, who would have voted for her for president.

I told Dr. Spencer my story. She suggested that I visit with White House Personnel to see if there were any openings and, after lunch, she escorted me to their office with her EOB pass. Before leaving me at the door to the Personnel Office, she suggested that I remind them that I already had FBI security clearance and knew my way around the complex. That, she thought, had to be of value to somebody.

Even with great advice in my pocket, I hesitated to walk in. I was terrified that if I said or did even one little thing wrong, I would murder any chance to get another job in the White House. Ever. I was so nervous that I had a little hitch in my chest every time I took a breath. Just to make matters worse, I was also sweating so badly that I could feel the moisture soaking through my socks. I fished through my pockets in a panic to find a handkerchief to mop up the perspiration on my forehead and dry my clammy hands. Not finding one, I blotted my forehead with my tie and wiped my hands on my overcoat. It was a good thing that wide ties were the fashion then, because at about 4 3/4" wide, it made a pretty good towel.

Then, I buttoned up my jacket to hide the sweat stains on the lower part of the tie and walked through the door. I prayed that I was the only one who could hear the faint squishing sound in my shoes.

To say that the people in Personnel were surprised to see me standing in their office unannounced wouldn't quite cover it. There was dead silence. They just looked at me and then at one another.

I was a moist mess.

I swallowed hard and launched into what I was sure was going to be a painfully long explanation about why I was there and, more to the point, why I was already looking for another job. Afraid, I suppose, that I wasn't going to be understood, I did exactly what a lot of Americans do when they try to explain something to someone who doesn't speak English. I got louder, as if that was going to help. Today, my jittery, noisy behavior would almost guarantee a quick, and possibly painful, removal from the building by armed security; in 1974, however, I was entertainment. In what almost certainly had to be a billion-to-one shot, the nice, impeccably dressed man who had been so helpful to me came out of his office to see what all the noise was about. In a two-billion-to-one shot, he smiled, shook my hand, and asked me into his office.

When he made the mistake of asking me how I was doing, I told him my tale of woe. Everything was cool until I got to the part of the story where I quit. Then, the jovial expression on his face turned into a wince. He told me that I'd made a terrible mistake by resigning, that I hadn't thought the problem through, and that, at the very least, I should have called him for advice. Every word was uttered in a kind, fatherly way but with just a sharp enough point to get my attention.

Just when experience told me that he was going to really, truly, let me have it with both barrels, I stunned myself by interrupting and shamelessly asking if there were any White House job openings.

My inappropriateness even made me wince.

In a three-billion-to-one shot, he said there were, but only one I would qualify for.

It was a job as a White House messenger.

If there had been a lottery way back then, that was the day I should have bought a ticket. It was just like a very special Saturday I'd had two years earlier in high school. In the morning, I put 25 cents into a soft drink machine that proceeded to dispense a Coke and 20 bucks in quarters. In the afternoon, the mail brought an acceptance letter to college. In the evening, I was invited to a party with the cool kids.

Like lightning, I immediately followed Dr. Spencer's suggestion and pitched the value of my active security clearance and my knowledge of the White House and EOB. I told him that the taxpayers wouldn't have to spend an extra penny for me to work there. Although I wasn't sure what a White House messenger did, it had to be better than being battered by a violent toilet napper with a heavy cart.

The gentleman looked at me from across the desk with a little bit of a frown. He took a deep breath and asked me if I had time to meet with the head of the Messenger Service that day. Even if I hadn't, I would have. An energetic "yes" came out of my mouth along with an embarrassing mist of spit that was probably caused by talking so fast that I didn't bother to swallow.

Thirty minutes later, I was sitting in front of the head of the Messenger Service in the basement of the West Wing. As one might imagine, the interview was not terribly involved. Mostly, the boss wanted to know if I would show up on time and do what I was told. That was easy to agree to, even for me.

Despite being ready to go to work right that minute, there was obligatory paperwork to be filled out, followed by a discussion about benefits that included the government's pension program. With retirement nearly 50 years in the future, I confess that I snoozed through the details.

What did get my full attention, however, was being told that I had to pay a visit to the FBI.

That afternoon, the Federal Bureau of Investigation took my fingerprints in their office in the EOB, rolling my fingers across an ink pad and, one by one, pressing them on a card. After washing my hands, I picked up my overcoat and told the agent that I'd see him around. He replied that we wouldn't be seeing each other around anywhere until I met with another agent in an adjacent room.

The second I walked through the door, I knew exactly what was next. I'd seen them used on my favorite TV police shows.

Nobody told me that I had to take a lie detector test, though.

Sitting near the doorway was a machine with a lot of knobs, needles, and gauges. The FBI examiner invited me to take a seat next to the contraption and told me to relax, which was about the last thing I was ready to do. Scenes from old black-and-white crime movies danced in my head, the ones with a murder suspect shouting "I didn't do it, I tell ya!" as a calm, pipe-smoking examiner watches the needles on the lie detector jump around like a hot tamale.

Without any of the Hollywood drama, the examiner, clearly an Aqua Velva aftershave man, connected me to devices meant to measure my breathing, pulse, perspiration, and blood pressure. He explained that my body would react in one pattern if I was trying to be deceptive and a different one if I wasn't. In clearly one of the most interesting parts of my visit, he also explained that despite the name, lie detectors don't reveal if a person is lying; rather, they sense if a person is being deceitful. Surprisingly, lying and deceiving are not the same thing. Telling a lie is only one of several types of deception. Deception also includes things like stretching the truth, hiding important information, making the truth sound better than it is, and creating distractions.

Out of nowhere he asked me if I'd "always had problems working with other people." He quickly added that I could only answer "yes" or "no".

I felt a little paranoid.

If I said "yes", it meant that I had never gotten along with others. If I said "no", it meant that I'd had a problem in the past. Neither was true. It was like the classic loaded question, "Have you stopped beating your wife?" If you answered "yes", it meant that you had beaten her but stopped. If you answered "no", it meant that you were still beating her. Either way you were guilty.

I decided not to answer.

The examiner chuckled. I probably wasn't the first person he had done this to. He told me that I chose the right answer.

The examiner then asked me a real test question that was also supposed to be answered either "yes" or "no". Nervous, I responded in sort of a rambling sentence that made him roll his eyes and understandably lose a little patience with me.

Eventually, we got around to establishing my identity and, within a day or two, I was in front of a camera having my picture taken for a pass with the letters WHS on the bottom for White House Staff. I didn't think that I'd ever stop smiling. It came with a clip for attaching it to your jacket and a chain if you preferred wearing it around your neck. It even had cool wording on the back that said it was the property of the U.S. Secret Service.

It was the kind of thing that could give you a big head.

Mine grew to about the size of Texas.

According to the White House employee manual, the job of the Messenger Service was to "provide general messenger service for collection and distribution of mail, packages, and messages to and from offices within the White House and the Old Executive Office Building." It also said that the office was open seven days a week, and that employees were on duty each evening "until after the President retires."

There were three offices, one in the basement of the EOB, one in the basement of the West Wing, and the other, where I was assigned, in the basement of the East Wing adjacent to vending machines, a men's room, a hand-operated elevator, the Executive Protective Service command post, and two large, serious-looking gray metal doors that warned that they were for "Authorized Personnel Only." To the right of the entrance to our cubbyhole was a gray metal desk with a black rotary phone and a black secretarial chair and, to the left, three more desks and chairs. In the very back was a hole in the wall with a mess of plaster, wood, and general construction litter inside it. We had a single window that looked out on cement stairs that led up to the South Lawn.

There was a rumor that the room had played a role during the Cuban Missile Crisis in 1962. I'd find out later that there was a startling reason to believe that it could have been true, but no one knew for sure.

The East Wing was originally built by President Theodore Roosevelt in 1902 to provide an entrance for visitors and a large coatroom to accommodate guests attending White House social affairs. At the start of the Second World War, it was significantly expanded into a two-story building with offices, a visitor's lobby, a movie theater, a colonnade, and a large foyer that opens into the ground floor of the White House Residence.

Although it's well known that the East Wing has tradition-
ally, and primarily, housed the First Lady's staff, few know that it's
played an important role in our national security.

In 1942, the construction of the building itself concealed the
fact that workmen were also digging a very large, very deep hole
that might have proven crucial to the survival of our government
in wartime. Digging the hole was the first step in building a bomb-
proof underground bunker that could be used to secure President
Franklin Roosevelt and his chief aides in the event of an enemy
attack. Although I didn't know it at the time, a more contempo-
rary version of the bunker was what was behind the gray metal
doors marked "Authorized Personnel Only." The existence of the
facility, known as the Presidential Emergency Operations Center,
is no longer a secret. During the terrorist attacks on September 11,
2001, Vice President Cheney, Condoleezza Rice, the President's
National Security Advisor, and others were evacuated there. Had
President Bush been in Washington that morning, he might have
been escorted to that location as well. In 1974, however, it was either still a secret or somebody just enjoyed pulling my leg. When
I asked an EPS officer what was behind the doors, he told me that
there were hundreds of crates of grapefruit. I was very impressed
with how seriously President Nixon took his citrus.

One of the first things I discovered about the Messenger Service was that it was staffed by some very interesting people with a
cornucopia of interesting tales. Several had been with the White
House for 20 years or more, which meant that they started during
the Truman or Eisenhower Administrations. I'm pretty sure there
were one or two who had even worked for FDR.

One of the more unusual stories came from a gentleman who
had been employed for many years at the LBJ Ranch in Texas. He

and his wife were called to the White House shortly after Lyndon Johnson became President in 1963 and even lived on the third floor for a period. While that was extraordinary all by itself, it was even more surprising to learn that he knew firsthand what it was like to be in the President's shoes.

Literally.

Because he and President Johnson had the same size feet, the Commander-in-Chief gave him the responsibility for breaking in his new shoes. At the end of LBJ's term, he transferred to the Messenger Service so that he and his family could remain in Washington. The punch line, at least as I remember it, was that Johnson continued to send his new shoes to my friend by mail for a year or so after he left the Presidency. I vividly remember him telling me that story as we walked together on the colonnade between the West Wing and the Residence one day. I also remember my embarrassment when I realized that I had started to laugh at the story just as President Nixon came walking toward us.

Several of the gentlemen I worked with were also White House butlers. One of them, Norwood Williams, gave me a very memorable tour on my first day of work in part by telling me about his first day of work.

Norwood joined the White House as a butler during the Truman Administration working under White House maître d'hôtel Alonzo Fields who had served under Presidents Hoover, Roosevelt, Truman, and Eisenhower. Fields had Norwood join him to serve breakfast to the President.

The introduction alone proved to be a bumpy start.

"I'm so very happy to meet you, Mr. Truman," Norwood said, noticing that Fields looked disturbed as soon as the words came out of his mouth. When breakfast was over, Fields took Norwood into the butler's pantry.

"Don't you ever say that again!" Fields said tersely. "It's not Mr. Truman. It's Mr. President. It's always Mr. President."

Right off the bat, I felt better about my own mistakes.

One thing I quickly found out was that if you knew Norwood, you knew almost everybody. Starting with the East Wing, he introduced me to a variety of people, all of whom were very welcoming. We called on the First Lady's Press Office, the Calligraphy Office, the Social Office, the Social Secretary's Office, the East Wing receptionist, the Visitor's Office, and the offices where the Assistants to the President for Legislative Affairs were housed. Then we walked down the East Colonnade, passing Jacqueline Kennedy's Garden, entering the foyer and the Center Hall on the ground floor of the Residence.

I had been in the Center Hall before. But that day, standing there in silence under the vaulted ceiling, surrounded by marble, with the busts of Washington, Jefferson, Franklin, and Lincoln and the rich red carpet stretching out in front of me, I was speechless.

Norwood pointed out the Library, the Vermeil Room, the Curator's Office, and the China Room. When we reached the Diplomatic Reception Room, where President Franklin Roosevelt had made his famous "Fireside Chat" radio broadcasts, I stopped. My parents had told me how they and millions of other Americans had huddled around radios in the 1930s and 1940s to listen to FDR speak about the New Deal, World War II, and other matters of national importance. I couldn't believe that I was standing there. We moved on to the Map Room, so named because FDR hung maps inside to keep abreast of the war, the kitchen where I picked up a couple of cookies, way back into the florist's shop, to the President's doctor's office, and the Housekeeper's Office. He also showed me the elevators to the State Floor and the First Family's residence, which would later create a situation that I remain a tad mortified about to this day.

Because I already knew my way around the West Wing, we turned around and started walking back to our office. In the vaulted archway, however, Norwood made a quick left turn up the Center Hall's marble stairs to the first floor where the East Room, the Blue Room, the Green Room, the Red Room, the State Dining Room, and the Family Dining Room are located. Near the Family Dining Room, we walked through a set of double doors with what struck me as larger-than-average windows into the Chief Usher's Office.

The Chief Usher has the enormous task of running 1600 Pennsylvania Avenue which, when you think about it, is the equivalent of a home, an office, a museum, an event venue, and a 5-star hotel all in one place. The job includes overseeing a staff that runs the gamut from housekeepers, launderers, gardeners, and chefs to butlers, elevator operators, carpenters, plumbers, electricians, and florists to carry out responsibilities for everything from housekeeping, maintenance, historical preservation, event logistics, and even redecorating. It's a job only for the stout of heart.

Four men were standing in the office.

Norwood introduced me to Rex Scouten, who had been the Chief Usher since 1969 and whom he had known for many years. Scouten first came to the White House in 1949 as a Secret Service agent assigned to President Truman and accompanied Truman on his famous trip to Wake Island that preceded Truman's firing of General Douglas McArthur. Later, he was assigned to protect

Vice President Nixon. By the time he retired in 1997, Scouten had served under ten presidents.

With Scouten was Preston Bruce, the White House doorman, a handsome, white-haired, mustachioed gentleman dressed impeccably in a black suit, white shirt, and white bow tie who looked as if he'd been ordered up from Central Casting. I remembered him from my visit to the East Room to see Sinatra. Bruce received invited guests and formally introduced them to the President and members of the First Family. During the Kennedy Administration, he regularly retrieved a tiny, barefoot John F. Kennedy, Jr. who would run through the White House and pop into his father's office.

There was John Ficklin, the White House maître d', who had started there as an assistant butler when FDR was President and would remain into Ronald Reagan's Presidency. In 1963, Jacqueline Kennedy personally requested that he serve along with her brothers as an usher at President Kennedy's funeral.

Last, but far from least, was butler Gene Allen, who started towards the end of Truman's Presidency and would later rise to become maître d' himself. His career was the inspiration for the 2013 movie *Lee Daniels' The Butler*, although as at least one critic noted, all Eugene Allen and Cecil Gaines, the main character, had in common was that they were both long-time, African-American White House butlers.

Each of these men had an elegance that spoke through their exceptional manners, poise, and serious approach to their duties. Mr. Allen, who, surprisingly, would remember my name when I'd run into him from time to time, called me Mr. Stinson. I called him Mr. Allen. I would have called Norwood Mr. Williams if he hadn't told me not to.

Among other things they shared was an evident affection for President Truman and his family, whom they described as being very thoughtful, nice, regular people. On the other hand, I never heard a single word of criticism about any member of the other First Families they had served.

Most of the men I worked with were African-American. Growing up in the South, I have a vague memory of "White Only" and "Colored Only" signs on water fountains and restrooms, some of which were sadly still hanging in the early 1960s, and a sharper memory of African-American men and women sitting in the backs of buses. Sad to say, but more than a few of the kids I went to school with in Atlanta's lily-white Buckhead neighborhood in the mid-to-late 1960s came from homes that were less than accepting of people of color. I can't quite forget seeing a family's African-American maid having to take her lunch outside to eat on a very cold, icy day because in that household, as the kid's mother said, "They don't want to eat with us." What the mother really meant, of course, was that she didn't want the maid to eat with her.

My family was far from that. My father successfully fought for equal pay for African-Americans doing the same jobs as whites which, in the 1960s and 1970s, was no small task. My mother helped many of the same ladies who were forced to eat outside sign up for Social Security, something their employers never cared to consider. Nevertheless, we were far from being a politically active family; we were, however, a family with very strong views about right and wrong. My father, who had grown up in North Carolina during the Depression, gave me something to think about regarding racism that has lasted a lifetime.

"If all you've got going for you is the color of your skin," he said, "you've got yourself a big damn problem."

That said, the truth of the matter is that if I ever thought about the fact that being a white kid made me a minority in the Messenger Service at the time I started there, I didn't think about it very long.

Negativity only raised its ugly head once.

The guys made puking noises when I tried to bust a move I saw on *Soul Train*. Their failure to appreciate my artistic interpretation of "Jungle Boogie" is still a mystery to me. That moment of heartbreak aside, I can't remember a single instance when the people I worked with at 1600 Pennsylvania weren't extremely polite and respectful to one another. That was the case even when things were hurried and tense. Today's world could take some much-needed lessons from those men and women about how to radiate grace and dignity.

Among the items that shot to the top of my to-do list in the wake of Norwood's tour was finding a way to spend quality time in the White House kitchen. My teenage metabolism kept me in a permanent state of hunger, and I would eagerly eat almost anything that looked like food. In fact, just about the only thing that I couldn't get down my gullet was the combination of lima beans and canned salmon loaf, a meal my mother made that I came to regard as the electric chair of childhood dinners. No matter how big of a pile of mashed potatoes was on my plate, it was never enough to hide the lima beans.

The cookie I wolfed down in the kitchen that day with Norwood was so delicious in every conceivable way that I nearly cried and gave my imagination a glimpse of how wonderful everything else would taste. Norwood suggested that I stop by the kitchen now and again to see if there were leftovers. Believe me, nobody had to make that suggestion twice.

Actually, there were four kitchens in the White House proper at that time including three in the Residence that came under the supervision of the Executive Chef and one in the West Wing run by the Navy. There was a small kitchen on the second floor that offered the First Family a convenient way to make their own meals and snacks. When Gerald Ford became President, the kitchen drew unusual media attention because the new President made his own breakfast, a toasted English muffin, every morning. I visited it once or twice to help a friend who oversaw the pantry. Frankly, I remember being a little disappointed. Instead of something very ornate and presidential-looking, it was quite plain. There was a toaster, a drip coffee maker, a small breakfast table, a butcher-block island, standard appliances including a four-burner gas stove, and very '70s-ish fluorescent lighting. For all intents and purposes, the President of the United States could have been eating at my nana's house.

The third floor had a small kitchen that Franklin Roosevelt had added, and in the West Wing there was a kitchen attached to the Navy Mess where senior staff members often ate. The granddaddy of them all, and the focus of my attention, was on the ground floor of the Residence. That kitchen was used primarily for State Dinners, other large events, and meals for the First Family. I think it was the cleanest kitchen and, in fact, maybe the cleanest anything that I'd ever seen. Everything literally sparkled and shined. I remember a myriad of ladles, whisks, colanders, and strainers hanging from overhead racks near stainless steel prep tables, large mysterious-looking drawers, and shelves that had pans in probably a hundred different sizes. It was the kitchen that produced the largest dinner in White House history on May 24, 1973 in honor of 600 American Prisoners of War who had been held captive by North Vietnam. To make it even more challenging, the dinner wasn't even served inside the White House. The entire evening was conducted under an enormous tent on the South Lawn.

It was a kitchen's kitchen.

Along with their incredible culinary creations, the White House's food inventory management was also remarkable. Every egg, every piece of bread, every everything had to be accounted for. That's because food used for official government purposes, like hosting foreign heads of state, is paid for by U.S. taxpayers. The First Family, on the other hand, pays for their meals and those of guests and is presented with an itemized bill every month.

Even though I couldn't get to the kitchen as often as I would have liked, I managed to cruise through it enough to learn a little about cooking. I also got to taste a few things like duchess potatoes, a dreamy version of mashed potatoes made special by the addition of magical ingredients known only to the chefs. Sometimes roast sirloin ends, not suitable for serving at a formal dinner, ended up in the kitchen, too, in search of someone to eat them.

My absolute, hands-down favorite, however, was steamship round, presented as a large, glossy roast with an aroma like Christmas. On one occasion, one of the chefs cut a small piece of leftover roast and wrapped it in tin foil for me to take home. I put it in my briefcase and caught my regular 6:00 p.m. bus back to campus. Somewhere along Massachusetts Avenue, hunger got the best of me and I opened the foil. When the other passengers caught a whiff of it, I was sure that I could hear their salivary glands start to slosh. I moved fast. It only took three bites get it safely in my stomach.

Among the people I frequently saw on trips to and from the East Wing basement was a gentleman by the name of Fred Jefferson, better known as Jeff. He turned out to be one of the most fascinating people I ever met.

Several of us were sitting in the Messenger's Office early one morning when Jeff walked in, took a chair across from me, and lit up a smoke. Clearly a very nice, friendly man, he and I started chatting about the kind of basic things that help people get to know one another. We discovered that we were both from Georgia. I told him about my family. He told me about his. Then I asked him how long he had been in the White House and how he had arrived there.

With ashes occasionally falling from his cigarette onto his suit jacket, he very matter-of-factly related that he had started out as a chauffeur to golfer Bobby Jones. Jones, an Atlanta lawyer, was one of the most important personalities in the history of the game. Founder of the Augusta National Golf Club, co-founder of the Master's Tournament, and the winner of the British Open, the U.S. Open, and the British and U.S. Amateur Championships, all in 1930, he occasionally played golf with a highly regarded Army officer named Dwight David Eisenhower. Jeff drove both men around town. When World War II began, Jones asked Ike to look after Jeff who was about to join the military.

When Eisenhower became Supreme Commander of the Allied Expeditionary Forces in Europe, he took Jeff with him as an aide. When Ike accepted the Presidency of Columbia University after the war, he had Jeff assigned to the Pentagon. When Eisenhower became President, he brought Jeff to the White House as an aide to the First Lady, a butler, and a jack-of-all-trades. He would take Mamie Eisenhower her mail every morning and sit with her as she told him how she wanted the appropriate staff to answer certain letters. When President Eisenhower's term ended in January 1961, Jeff remained with the White House staff. He retired during President Carter's term.

If there was one thing that Jeff had to show for his 21 years in the White House, it was great stories.

Knowing that I was hopelessly addicted to American history, he'd come by the office from time to time and tell me to follow him. Whenever we got where we were going, he'd stop and launch into a story about something interesting that he'd witnessed in that very location. Some were serious and others odd and funny.

Jeff pointed out a spot in the Rose Garden one day where he said that LBJ had unleashed his infamous "Johnson Treatment" on a U.S. Senator before a vote on the 1964 Civil Rights Act. Said to be effective in persuading people to his side, "The Johnson Treatment" was reportedly a nose-to-nose, high-velocity talking-to that delivered a storm of ridicule, criticism, blame, praise, threats, and promises all in one big, hairy fireball.

Another day, Jeff showed me a piece of the Oval Office floor that had to be replaced because it was badly pitted. Apparently, President Eisenhower didn't always take off his golf shoes after visiting his putting green on the South Lawn.

Jeff also took me to the East Room to point out where President Kennedy's casket and his military honor guard had been positioned. He told me that honor guards were supposed to stand with their backs to the casket to literally guard the remains of the fallen leader. Jeff said that Mrs. Kennedy asked them to turn around and face the casket. She didn't want President Kennedy to feel alone.

On another occasion, we only walked about six feet from the Messenger's Office doorway. Jeff pointed to a spot where President Kennedy and his brother, Attorney General Robert Kennedy, had stopped to talk during one of the thirteen days in October 1962 when the world came to the brink of nuclear annihilation. It gave me shivers. Jeff thought that the Messenger's Office had been used by a military communications team that was prepared to move inside the East Wing's nuclear-blast-proof bunker on a moment's notice. Two decades later in Moscow, I would share a bottle of vodka with a man who had worked inside the Kremlin that terrifying October. We talked about the Cuban Missile Crisis. He explained to me that the United States and the Soviet Union came much closer to mutually assured destruction than the world ever knew. It gave me shivers all over again.

Jeff was a fine man and a good friend. He was also loyal to the First Families he had served and protective of their reputations. When a story claiming that Ike had an affair with a woman in the British Army during the war came up in conversation one day, Jeff exploded. "I was with the General all the time!" he shouted. "It wasn't possible!"

Jeff made it a point to tell me in a fatherly way to remember that "duty always comes first, second, and third. Fun comes fourth if you can squeeze it in." Apparently, he followed his own advice to the point that it took the President of the United States himself to alter Jeff's course.

In an oral history produced by the Ford Presidential Library, Maria Downs, President Ford's White House Social Secretary, said that "Jeff was like family with us. He drove for us, but he'd also get things ready for parties. He helped me with whatever came up. He was kind of a man for all seasons. One of the nights that Jeff was butlering a private party, I forget what the occasion was, but it was also during the World Series, and President Ford wanted to get away to go watch the game. Jeff looked in on him to see if there was anything he wanted before he left and the President said, 'Yes, sit down and watch the game with me.' And Jeff said he felt kind of funny and tried to leave several times. The President would say, 'Sit down, you're finished,' he said, 'sit down and enjoy the game.' So, Jeff stayed, but only as long as he felt he could."

Over the next several months, Jeff introduced me to the First Lady, David Eisenhower, her son-in-law, and Julie Nixon Eisenhower, her daughter. The Eisenhowers first met in 1956 at the Republican National Convention where Julie's father and David's grandfather were being nominated for the presidential ticket. They were married in New York in December 1968 at the Marble Collegiate Church on Fifth Avenue. The bride's father was President-elect of the United States at the time. Interestingly, the church's history with American First Families extends to Donald Trump, who married his first wife, Ivana, there in 1977.

Jeff also introduced me to a lot of wonderful long-time employees in the Residence, including a housekeeper I was later told had claimed to have seen President and Mrs. Lincoln sitting in the Lincoln Bedroom. Regrettably, I never saw President Lincoln myself or followed up with the housekeeper about her story; however, she was by no means alone in her claim. Several distinguished people, including First Lady Grace Coolidge, Queen Wilhelmina of the Netherlands, and Winston Churchill, who was only wearing a cigar at the time, had also reported seeing Honest Abe. Eleanor Roosevelt and Lady Bird Johnson's Press Secretary said that they had felt Lincoln's presence. Even a White House Social Secretary during the Clinton Administration said that "a large percentage of people who work here won't go in the Lincoln Bedroom."

That might well be true. Based on what I heard, Franklin Roosevelt's valet and Eleanor Roosevelt's secretary ran screaming from the room on different occasions. Both had seen President Lincoln pulling on his boots.

Over the years, others have claimed to have heard or seen President Andrew Jackson, David Burnes, who sold the land the White House is built on to the Federal Government, President Lincoln's son Willie, who died of typhoid fever, a British soldier from the War of 1812, and a Union soldier from the Civil War. In 1974, a friend told me about a Secret Service agent who was so startled by a ghost while guarding President Nixon's bedroom door one night that he drew his gun. He claimed that it was the specter of John F. Kennedy. As far as I know, however, nothing about the story was ever substantiated.

Jeff also recommended me for a job.

For better or worse, it would put me on a collision course with a legion of sweaty, sticky-fingered children so high on sugar that they could barely walk in a straight line.

And a murder.

Chapter Six

"GOOD MORNING, MR. PRESIDENT"

There was a freight elevator in the East Wing that made me laugh every time I got on it.

Manually operated with a gray outer door that opened vertically in the center, it had a folding metal inner door and an old-time lever control that moved the elevator up and down. There was nothing mechanically funny about it.

What amused me was a story about the elevator and President Johnson.

Jeff told me that LBJ would occasionally ditch his security detail late at night and mosey around the White House. Sometimes he was very quiet. Sometimes not.

More than once, according to the versions of the stories I heard, the Secret Service found him in the main kitchen swearing and throwing things out of refrigerators in a desperate search for his favorite tapioca pudding,

On another occasion, the President wandered into the Carpenter's Shop in the wee hours of the morning, saw lights on, and turned them off.

"What idiot did that?" asked an annoyed carpenter who was working on a project.

"This idiot!" said the President of the United States as he switched the lights back on. People joked that it took three days for the carpenter to get the color back in his face.

Then there was the freight elevator.

Rumor had it that the President meandered into the East Wing at two o'clock or so in the morning and came across the elevator. With curiosity getting the better of him, he opened the doors, stepped in, and pulled the lever. The elevator rose but came to an abrupt stop halfway between the first and second floors. Mad as a hornet, the President pulled the lever again, this time so hard that he dislodged it from the control box. Realizing that he was stuck, he started yelling at the top of his lungs. It took Secret Service agents and a White House engineer about 30 minutes to get the furious Commander in Chief out safely.

The elevator came in particularly handy one afternoon when I needed to deliver a heavy package to Helen McCain Smith, the First Lady's Press Secretary, whose office was on the second floor. When I walked in, I saw an elegantly turned out lady sitting behind a desk in the corner office. I asked her where I should put the package. She answered me in the most exquisite British accent I'd ever heard, a surprising development since we were in the White House, not 10 Downing Street.

Then there was another bolt out of the blue. She looked up from her desk and asked me, "Are you Don?"

When I told her that I was, she introduced herself as Helen Smith and said that she had wanted to speak with me.

I immediately panicked, thinking that I had done something wrong. As my paranoia ran amuck, Mrs. Smith explained in a featherlike voice what sounded like a great opportunity.

A young woman in her office was going to be on leave for at least a month. Mrs. Smith said that she was looking for someone to help with various duties on a temporary basis. She asked me about my research skills which, I was happy to report, were being well honed in college. Finally, Mrs. Smith told me that Jeff had recommended me and that it had already been cleared with my bosses if I was interested.

Having no idea what a Press Office did, what Mrs. Smith wanted me to research, or, for that matter, exactly who Mrs. Smith was other than a very elegant lady, I of course said yes. On the verge of turning 19, I was sure that I could handle whatever they threw at me with ease. The plan was that half of my hours would be devoted to the Messenger Service and half to the First Lady's Press Office until the young lady went on leave. Then, all of my hours would be allocated to the Press Office.

That was on Thursday. On Friday, March 8, I got a call from Mrs. Smith. She told me to drop whatever I was doing and come to the Diplomatic Reception Room right away. Although I wasn't exactly sure why my presence was being requested, I knew that the First Lady was leaving on a goodwill mission to South America to attend the inaugurations of presidents in Venezuela and Brazil. Fifty people, including Vernon Walters, the Deputy Director of the CIA, and the President's personal physician, Major General Walter Tkach, were scheduled to accompany her on the 9,000-mile trip.

It was a big event. Behind the scenes, though, there was an even bigger backstory that I knew nothing about.

Sixteen years earlier, in April 1958, a motorcade carrying then-Vice-President and Mrs. Nixon had been attacked by hundreds of anti-American demonstrators in Caracas furious with the Cold War policies of the Eisenhower Administration. The angry crowd threw rocks at Nixon's limousine, broke the car's windows with pipes, spat on it, kicked it, and tried to flip it over on its roof. Inside the automobile, Secret Service agents covered Mr. and Mrs. Nixon with their bodies to protect them from shattering glass and drew their weapons. It took the help of Venezuelan troops to remove the protestors and get the motorcade safely to the U.S. Embassy. Ike immediately sent 1,000 troops to the region in the event that the Nixons had to be rescued.

Mrs. Nixon said that she was not afraid to visit Venezuela again. Perhaps, but the memory of her last experience surely had to be in the back of her mind.

Inside the Diplomatic Reception Room, it was like a Black Friday sale at Walmart. Jeff was there along with what looked like every member of the First Lady's staff. Everybody was trying to get through the door at once. I, of course, was the last to walk onto the South Lawn where Marine One was sitting only a short distance away. There were 20 or so people standing in an uneven line facing newspaper and White House photographers and holding signs that said things like, "Adios, Ambassador Nixon," and "We Love You!" They were also applauding.

Not having a clue about where to go, I inelegantly walked right in front of Mrs. Nixon and to the very end of the line where I took a spot next to the lady holding the "We Love You!" sign. When I turned around, I noticed that I was not the last one out.

President Nixon was about ten feet behind me.

He walked all the way down the line greeting everyone. When he came to me, we shook hands. Just as he was about to walk away, he turned around, looked at me, and said something that I couldn't hear. Having become older and wiser, I decided not to say "What?" or "Excuse me?" and just let it go. Then the President walked to the middle of the line and joined the First Lady. After the photos were taken, President and Mrs. Nixon boarded Marine One for a quick trip to Andrews Air Force Base. From there they were scheduled to fly on Air Force One to Florida where they would spend the weekend before Mrs. Nixon departed.

It didn't take long for me to figure out what the President said.

After Marine One's powerful engines took it airborne and the presidential party traveled east past the Washington Monument, I turned to walk back into the White House. I tripped on something and nearly fell flat on my face.

I'm pretty sure that the President was trying to tell me that my shoelace was untied.

In the days following, I dogged one of the White House photographers for copies of the shots he took to the point that he was about to slug me. He eventually gave me a nice 8x10 mounted on a board that the President and First Lady signed. That, however, wasn't the end of it. A wire service photo showing President Nixon speaking to me appeared in several newspapers across the country. I was not happy about how it came out, though.

President Nixon was in the picture.

The lady holding the "We Love You!" sign was in the picture.

I, however, was not in the picture. I had been cropped out.

◆

Within a week or two, I was working in the Press Office my full 20 hours a week. My first assignment, beyond answering the telephones and filing, was to work on a speech that a member of the First Family was to deliver at the dedication of a dam. My job was to find a joke that would be appropriate for the audience and the occasion. I jumped into the project with gusto. I was psyched.

It's hard to remember how much time I put into my research, which, of course, required flipping through the pages of piles of joke books for hours on end. The nice people at the Library of Congress even helped me. In the end, the only thing I could tell Mrs. Smith was that there were no dam jokes that were even funny, much less suitable. There were interesting facts and figures about dams. There were jokes about fish, flooding, water, and reservoirs. There were puns about dams. But no good dam jokes. The best one I found was "What do fish say when they swim into a wall? Dam." It was the kind of remark that needed to be followed by a rim shot. One person suggested that since beavers build dams, beaver jokes might be appropriate. I couldn't tell if they were trying to help me or pave a path to the unemployment office. As far as I know, no one ever gave the dam speech.

For most of the time I was employed by the U.S. Government, Watergate rarely entered my world other than through newspapers, television, protesters, and angry professors. Now, in the East Wing, that was changing. It took me a while to realize just how small the world inside of the White House was, at least for the people who were political appointees and served "at the pleasure of the President."

Different from members of the Federal Civil Service, who were protected from partisan politics and couldn't be arbitrarily fired, political appointees could be history in a New York minute. Because many of them had been involved in the President's campaigns or came from the same social circles, they knew one another. With more than 30 people either pleading guilty or going to trial in the Watergate affair, it made sense that some of the people I was acquainted with knew some of the people charged with perjury and obstruction of justice. More than once, I came across tearful co-workers talking about people that I had read about in that morning's paper. They were worried about their friends going to prison and the effects that might have on their friends' families. It was very understandable.

From what I gathered, the already somber mood in the White House had grown noticeably darker after February 6, 1974 when Congress gave the House Judiciary Committee permission to consider impeachment charges against the President. It grew darker again after March 1 when a grand jury indicted seven of President Nixon's former aides. Little by little, the wider effects of stress and anxiety over the possibility that the President might have to leave office were becoming more noticeable, even to someone with as little life experience as I had. In fact, had I been acquainted with Elisabeth Kübler-Ross' model of the five stages of grief (denial, anger, bargaining, depression, and acceptance) at the time, I'd have much better understood what was going on around me.

There was enough denial to fill Lake Superior. Despite increasing evidence to the contrary, I knew more than a few people who had convinced themselves that Watergate would blow over. One lady in particular not only believed that it would go away but worked passionately to convert others to that view. She told everyone who would listen that President Nixon would defeat his accusers by bypassing the news media and speaking directly to the American people. He was just waiting for the best time to do it. Once the President could explain that Watergate was nothing more than a lie created by his opponents, America would back him to the hilt and everything would be fine. Remarkably, she attracted disciples. It was the first time that I'd ever come face to face with people who openly rejected reality. I found them scary.

There was unmistakable anger over the existence of the scandal in the first place. The anger led to sadness and outright despair. Most of the rage that I was exposed to was directed at the press, judges, prosecutors, and former White House and Nixon campaign aides. Curiously, virtually none of it was aimed at President Nixon. A few people were even furious with the private security guard who called the cops on the Watergate burglars. That was just weird. I was surprised that they didn't toss in the Framers of the Constitution while they were at it.

In some corners, though, there was also acceptance. Those individuals remained optimistic but grasped the reality that Watergate might not end well. They quietly prepared themselves for whatever was on the way. By and large, they seemed to be the happiest.

Watergate was a swamp that had something gross in it for everyone. More than a few friends worried about being reassigned or losing their jobs in a change of administration. There were regular whispers in the hallways about who was hitting the booze a little too hard and who had the most Valium on hand. Some folks were eating their emotions and gaining weight. Others were letting their emotions eat them. They were losing weight.

At least in the First Lady's case, the stress and anxiety were said to be relieved by exercise. Several times a week, Mrs. Nixon would take a late-night walk along Pennsylvania Avenue accompanied by the Secret Service and sometimes, as I heard, by her daughter, Julie. Before she left the White House, Mrs. Nixon would put a scarf over her hair to avoid being recognized. She also did that whenever she went shopping. Most people wouldn't think that a simple scarf would be much of a disguise. They'd be wrong about that.

As I was walked through the Center Hall towards the East Wing one rainy afternoon, I saw somebody standing near the elevator to the First Family's living quarters.

I waved. The person waved back.

"Hi, kiddo!" a pleasant, feminine voice said.

"Hi, kiddo!" I replied.

The next morning, I got my head handed to me by a usually cheerful authority figure.

"How dare you talk like that to the First Lady!" the authority figure said in a sharp voice that was nowhere near cheerful.

I had no idea what we were talking about and said so. Then it dawned on me that the mysterious "Hi, kiddo!" came from Mrs. Nixon. I was mortified. I thought she was one of the housekeepers. I wrote a note of apology to the First Lady, explained my honest mistake to Mrs. Smith, and asked if she would be kind enough to forward my note to Mrs. Nixon.

A day or two later, I was feeling pretty good about the fact that I hadn't been fired when Mrs. Smith called me into her office and, without a word, simply handed me the phone. I said hello. The person on the other end introduced herself. She said that my note was lovely but quite unnecessary and apologized to me for being turned in by someone who thought they were doing the right thing. We chatted a little more. She asked me about my family. When our conversation ended, she said "See you later, kiddo."

You could have picked me up off the floor.

On the occasions when I ran into Mrs. Nixon after that, she'd always ask me how I was doing and seemed truly interested in the answer. That was no small thing to me and no small thing for her to do, particularly as the Watergate scandal raged around her. Mrs. Nixon was a very thoughtful, gracious lady. The world makes all too few of them.

◆

Believing that I had outgrown brightly colored eggs, chocolate bunnies, plastic grass, and jelly beans, I didn't pay much attention to the conversations in the East Wing about the annual White House Easter Egg Roll. What little I heard, however, led me to believe that anything involving eggs, grass, and a swarm of shrieking rug rats had to be the party equivalent of the Hindenburg disaster and probably wasn't well attended anyway. On top of that, the whole mess sounded like a "girl" thing. I wanted no part of it and concluded that my best bet was to avoid the gaze of anyone who could highjack me. If nothing else, the "out of sight, out of mind" tactic seemed worth a shot.

Naturally, I was wrong about everything, including the value of avoiding eye contact. It didn't work. Instead, my boss sold my soul to the Easter Bunny in the blink of an eye.

Thanks to the lady who ran the event with great efficiency and enthusiasm that made my quiet protest seem un-American, I learned that the Easter Egg Roll had a surprisingly interesting history. I was astonished to discover that the event was a Washington tradition that stretched back to the early 1800s and that 14,000 people had walked through the White House gates to join the fun in 1973 alone. It had its own march, "Easter Monday on the White House Lawn," which John Phillip Sousa composed in 1928. Moreover, except for interludes brought on by bad weather, construction, and war, the White House Easter Egg Roll had been held on the South Lawn on every Easter Monday since 1878. That year, President Rutherford B. Hayes opened the White House grounds to families that had been barred from rolling eggs on the west lawn of the Capitol after ruining the grounds in 1876. The damage was so bad, in fact, that Hayes' predecessor, Ulysses S. Grant, joined Congress in making it illegal to use the Capitol grounds as a play area.

That, however, wasn't the only instance in which the event had been the subject of controversy up to that time.

The first was mostly amusing. Since the Easter Egg Roll is for children, adults have always had to be escorted into the event by a boy or girl, usually under the age of 13. Not surprisingly, there were more than a few late 19th and early 20th century child-less adults who wanted to picnic or otherwise wander around the White House lawn anyway. It created a cottage business for enterprising children who rented themselves for a quarter or an ice cream cone to walk through the gate with their new "parents." There were complaints that the practice was undignified. A 1910 newspaper report made a derogatory reference to the kids as "street urchins."

The second wasn't amusing at all. In 1953, new First Lady Mamie Eisenhower looked out across the South Lawn and saw hundreds of African-American children watching the Easter festivities from behind the White House fence. African-American families had never been officially welcome to attend the event.

The good news was that an outraged Mrs. Eisenhower saw to it that everyone was included the following year.

Now knowing something about what I had been involuntarily volunteered to participate in, I was starting to feel better about it. We even had a meeting in the Family Theater where, as a friend told me, President Nixon watched *Patton,* starring George C. Scott, three times in a single day. Despite being a little rankled that there wasn't any popcorn to eat, the gathering opened my eyes to the logistics and the staggering number of details involved in an event that usually drew 10,000 to 15,000 people. Considering that I had never organized much more than a family birthday party, I was more than a little taken aback by it all. Someone with a nearly encyclopedic knowledge of the event asked what would happen if there was a repeat of the legendary Easter Egg Roll of 1941 that brought 53,000 people, the majority of them adults, to the White House gates. The silence in the room was deafening. I guess no one wanted to even think about that.

We were told that Mrs. Nixon would be spending Easter in Florida with the President and that Julie Eisenhower would be the host for the event. Last, but far from least, we were informed that we'd be making history. In addition to an egg decorating contest, we were going to hold the very first official Easter Egg Roll race. Along with giving every child a cool "Certificate of Participation," Mrs. Nixon also wanted to give away as many prizes as possible. I was assigned to a team responsible for getting kids lined up for races, handing them long-handled spoons for egg rolling, and handing a prize to every child who rolled his or her egg across the finish line from 10:00 a.m. until noon or later, if necessary. We'd be open until two in the afternoon. From my perspective, it sounded like a piece of cake. I was even looking forward to it.

The 18,000 people who walked through the White House gates that Monday found a lively, cheerful, brightly colored world of Easter eggs, balloons, and costumes waiting for them on the other side. It reminded me of a carnival. There was live music from "The President's Own" United States Marine Corps Band and an Italian bandwagon, games, clowns, jugglers, and life-size Warner Bros. cartoon characters wandering the grounds with the Easter Bunny. As if all of that wasn't brilliant enough, it was all happening under a spectacularly clear blue sky and temperatures in the seventies.

Everything was simply wonderful until it wasn't. Regrettably, no one told me that the races were restricted to children eight and under. I don't know how old I expected them to be, but I wasn't prepared for a slew of tiny barbarians with the collective attention span of a gnat.

By 10:30, Porky Pig was getting on my nerves and I wanted to strangle a kid with God-knows-what on his hands who decided to use me as a towel. I had nothing personal against the world-famous pig, but he was constantly wandering into my race area and causing a problem. The moment he showed up, the kids bolted from my neatly organized lines to give him a hug and pose for pictures. The kid with the filthy hands never even said a word to me. He simply came up from behind and left a blackish-brown smear, complete with his fingerprints, that nearly encircled the knee on the right leg of my pants. I guess that was as high as he could reach. His mother looked at me, shrugged her shoulders, and just walked away. I'm still looking for him.

By 11:00, I needed to sit in a time-out chair.

The good news was that most of the children were adorable. One tiny moppet put her egg down at the starting line, sat on it, and then burst into tears because she couldn't find it. Another crossed the finish line, picked up her egg, kissed it, and thanked it for being "a good egg."

The kids were even cute in the midst of what they thought was a murder scene.

A star-crossed little guy in a bow tie and suspenders picked up what might have been the only colorful Easter egg on the South Lawn that day that hadn't been hard-boiled. Intent on crossing the finish line, he hit the egg a little too hard with his long-handled spoon and completely freaked when yolk started leaking out.

He started screaming, "I killed it! I killed it!" at the top of his lungs. That created a chain effect that sent other kids who had witnessed the tragedy into hysterics, too. It took the Easter Bunny, Bugs Bunny, and Porky Pig as a group to get everyone calmed down.

The children with behavior problems, on the other hand, were monsters. My first impulse was to tie them up en masse. While not necessarily a bad idea, I concluded that it wasn't realistic if I expected to keep my job. So, I gritted my teeth and did my best to be accommodating and diplomatic around the little hellions.

At the end of the day, I was proud of myself.

I kept my cool when a pickle-faced kid with a leaky nose demanded a piggy-back ride and kicked me in the shins when I politely told him "no". Instead of stringing him up by his heels, I got him to go away with a bribe and a whispered threat about a monster following him home. I even kept a smile on my face when a five-year-old boy wantonly smashed a hard-boiled egg on the forehead of an adorable little girl in a chiffon dress and patent leather shoes. Fortunately for me, the incident settled itself. The girl punched the boy in the head, pulled off his shoes, sprinted to the White House fence, and threw them in the street. The pint-size bully ran away in tears.

None of that, however, could compare with my run-ins with others whose open hostility, seething anger, and threats of physical violence made them very scary.

Mothers can be like that, you know.

One literally got in my face and, with spittle flying everywhere, told me that her three-year-old daughter would have finished her race if she'd had a better egg and accused me of incompetence because I didn't notice that it wasn't entirely oval. She demanded in no uncertain terms that the tot, who was by then rolling around in the grass playing with a bug, be allowed to rerun the race. Of course, I graciously put her little darling back in the action. It was an Easter Egg Roll for God's sake, not the Olympic Games.

An even meaner mommy was furious that the prize we gave race winners, a gold ballpoint pen stamped with President Nixon's signature, was the same one we gave the winners of our egg decorating contest. Since her daughter had won both, the mother insisted that we provide a different prize. I told her that we didn't have other prizes. Her face turned an ugly, alarming red and she called me a liar. As she walked away in a huff, she shot me the bird and, in a hoarse, breathy voice that sounded like a hippopotamus with the croup, told me to watch my back.

Not unduly rattled by the mother imitating Don Corleone, I was ready to move on. It was noon, and I was hungry and excited about picking up a Pepsi and a hot dog and enjoying a quiet lunch under the sun in Lafayette Park. Before I turned over the reins of power to a friendly clown, a couple of news photographers showed up and started taking pictures. One asked me to stand next to the clown. I was very excited a few weeks later when I heard that newspaper clippings from the Easter Egg Roll had arrived. Most of the shots were of Julie Eisenhower holding hands with kids and posing for pictures with cartoon characters. There was, however, a sole UPI photo that showed the Egg Roll in progress and had been published in several papers around the country. Kids were there. The clown was there. I was nowhere. I had been cropped out again.

On my way back to the East Wing, I saw the cool lady in charge of the Easter Festival, the "Bunny Boss" as some of us called her, standing near the starting line for the egg races. She waved at me and I waved back. Then I noticed that her wave had an insistent quality to it and that it was more of a "come here" kind of motion. I walked over. She looked me over from head to toe. Then she told me that there was a problem.

The Easter Bunny wasn't feeling well. She was very overheated.

Frankly, that's a sentence that you just don't hear every day. In fact, you could live an entire lifetime without any one ever telling you that. I felt badly for the cute fellow East Wing staffer who was inside the suit. Although I had never been a mascot or a cartoon character, the fur on the outside clearly gave the impression that the suit was uncomfortably warm inside. With the head on, it could only be worse, particularly on a warm day. Just looking at the suit gave me pre-perspiration.

I have to say that I was probably not anybody's first choice to be the "backup" bunny. I was an unknown quantity as an Easter Bunny, and there was probably a clue that my patience was un-ravelling when my first words to the "Bunny Boss" were "I can't wait to get out of here." The growing look of horror on my face when I realized what was about to happen likely made a poor impression, too.

I was handed the head and the body and given strict instructions to hurry because the children couldn't see a disassembled Easter Bunny. Frankly, I thought about sending a few of the little miscreants into long-term psychotherapy by kicking the bunny head around like a soccer ball. Instead, I moved on, trying to find a place to change and deciding if I was going to strip down to my skivvies or put the bunny body on over my clothes.

I don't remember exactly which men's room I ran to, but whichever one I picked couldn't have been a worse choice. Standing inside were two Executive Protective Service officers I knew. They took one look at me and doubled over in such loud, hysterical laughter that I thought they were going to bring up their intestines. I was so embarrassed that I stopped thinking and pulled the suit up over my clothing as fast as I could. Trust me when I say that it didn't help when I put the head on, assuming, I guess, that it was somehow going to disguise me. When I looked out through the black screen that was either inside the bunny's nose or mouth, I could see that one of the officers was lying on his stomach making whooping noises and banging his fist on the floor.

Then it got even worse.

I had to take it off the head because the ears were too tall for me to get through the men's room door.

To put it politely, the suit was a lot more than just warm. I felt like I was trudging across a desert in an alpaca turtleneck. I waddled off to the South Lawn, trying to keep the head from wobbling as sweat, already excessive because of an inherited thyroid problem, literally poured down my face and into my eyes. I was also trying to keep my balance in bunny feet that were unwieldy and making my feet sweat so badly that I was convinced that I could hear splashing noises.

If I'd drowned that day I wouldn't have been a bit surprised.

I was besieged by kids the moment I appeared on the scene. Most of the little ones just wanted to shake hands, take a photo, and tug at my fur, all of which was perfectly fine. On the other hand, at least one kid slapped me in the rear end and another, sitting high on his father's shoulders, decided to grab my ears. That hurt because the head slid and I got popped in the nose. A couple of others asked me to hop, which was utterly out of the question considering that the weight of the head was making me sway backwards and I was getting nauseous. The little heathens smelled like refugees from a salmonella festival that was cooking up rotten eggs and spoiled chocolate.

To top it all off, I heard a kid scream that he had a jellybean stuck in his nose. I have no idea how that was resolved, but I'll bet that it wasn't a joy for anybody.

Shortly thereafter, I was tapped on the shoulder and relieved of my duties. At least for me, it was a cause for celebration. I think that I was the Easter Bunny for a grand total of about 15 minutes, if that. Even though I didn't speak when I was "suited up," I have a feeling that my hand gestures, although certainly not obscene, were probably grouchy-looking enough to get me benched.

Of course, that wasn't the end of it. Smart-alecks left carrots on my desk and asked me if things were "hippity-hoppity." They'd tell me stupid bunny jokes. If I even looked in the direction of an EPS officer, even ones I didn't know, they'd break out laughing. It went on for months.

In fact, the only thing that brought it to an end was when the President released transcripts of the Watergate tapes a few weeks later.

That changed everybody's conversations.

◆

A few days after the Easter Egg Roll, I was back in my old job as a White House messenger. The lady who had been out on leave from the First Lady's Press Office was back at work and I was happy for her and, frankly, for me, too. Although I thoroughly enjoyed working for Mrs. Smith, I missed being able to visit with friends and cruise the White House complex. Not being a complete dummy, my first priority was to get back in the good graces of the kitchen staff since there were probably leftovers from a Latin-American foreign Ministers' dinner the night before.

I stopped in the West Wing basement to see Milton Pitts, the President's barber, who joked that he would cut my longish hair down to a crew cut for free, and introduced myself to the stenographers who were said to be transcribing the Watergate tapes and typing the now-historic phrase "expletive deleted" for the first time. I also bumped into the U.S. Marshal who had just served President Nixon's attorney with a subpoena from the House Judiciary Committee for the actual tapes, including the infamous "Smoking Gun" conversation that later proved to be President Nixon's undoing.

Last, but far from least, I was back to giving unauthorized tours of the Oval Office by the end of the week.

The White House employee's guide strictly stated that members of the White House staff were "not to take guests to the area of the President's Office and the Cabinet Room" without the permission of the White House Visitors Office. Since that seemed cumbersome and paved the way for someone to tell me "no", I simply, but unwisely, ignored it. When one of my childhood friends and his college buddies came through Washington on a backpacking trip, I brought them in through the East Wing and took them straight to the Oval Office door. On a couple of occasions, I was ridiculously brazen and had friends meet me at the northwest gate on Pennsylvania Avenue. From there, I escorted them up the driveway to the West Wing entrance that was, and still is, often shown on television and in movies.

I took people on tours frequently and got to be reasonably good at relating details about the desk, the furniture, the flags, the color scheme, and the history of the office, if I do say so myself. I even knew that the rug was the first one in the Oval Office with the presidential seal woven into it.

Unfortunately, I deluded myself into believing that I could always tell when the President was in and when he wasn't based on the presence of two of the largest human beings God ever made in front of the door. I was very lucky that I didn't get fired, particularly after one occasion when two guests, a young married couple I knew from college, and I nearly came face to face with a troubled-looking President Nixon as he and we both walked towards the Oval Office.

More than a little surprised to bump into the most powerful man in the world, the husband made a weird squealing noise. He followed that by "cutting the cheese" as loudly and indelicately as possible.

All I could do was stand there and pray that God would take me.

The reaction of the President's Secret Service agents was as forceful and rightfully unforgiving as you would expect it to be. An EPS officer thoughtfully said goodbye to my friends for me and escorted the couple out of the building so that the agents could take me to the woodshed for bringing them inside the West Wing. Why the matter never went further than that, I'll never know for sure; however, after the agents were done raking me over the coals, they started laughing. One of the guys waved a hand in front of his face and suggested that my guest had been a threat to national security.

Although I honestly tried to keep a lower profile after that, it didn't last long.

One sunny late-April morning while there was still dew on the grass, I decided to meet up with a group of American University students who were taking a special, eight o'clock guided tour of the White House conducted by the EPS. I was in a hurry and, rather than walking through the Residence to find my friends, I elected to create my own shortcut to the North Portico, the front door of the White House that faces Pennsylvania Avenue, where their tour would end. I walked out through the Visitors Foyer in the East Wing into the courtyard and up a flight of stairs to the lawn. From there I marched towards the North Portico. I noticed that there were three or four EPS officers running in my direction, and I looked over my shoulder to see what they were chasing. I didn't realize that it was me until they had me surrounded. I had apparently set off a multitude of silent alarms, one right after the next. Obviously, my shortcut idea wasn't a very good one. Before they let me go, one of the aggravated officers wanted to provide me with just enough humiliation to dissuade me from trying to cross the lawn again.

"No problem," he shouted. "It's just the Easter Bunny."

Around the same time, I had just finished reading a memoir entitled *Six Months at the White House with Abraham Lincoln.* Published in 1867, the book was written by Francis Carpenter, an artist who lived in the White House while painting *First Reading of the Emancipation Proclamation of President Lincoln,* an oil that still today hangs in the United States Capitol. In the book, Carpenter quoted the 16th President as saying:

"I do the very best I know how—the very best I can; and I mean to keep doing so until the end. If the end brings me out all right, what is said against me won't amount to anything. If the end brings me out wrong, ten angels swearing I was right would make no difference."

I really liked that. As I frequently did with quotes I found inspiring, I wrote it down on a sheet of yellow legal paper. I put it in the left breast pocket of my blazer where I also kept my aviator-style reading glasses in a bulky hardcover case. Since the blazer was a staple of my wardrobe and I rarely cleaned out the pockets, the paper was still in my coat when I walked across West Executive Avenue from the EOB to the West Wing one afternoon a week later. Just as I reached the EPS officer's desk in the basement lobby, there was a minor commotion as Secret Service agents filled the area.

I could see that the President was coming my way.

I thought that Lincoln's quote might cheer him up.

As he approached, I reached in my breast pocket and said something on the order of, "Mr. President, this is for you."

Faster than you can say "dummy", one of the agents was directly in front of me with his hand firmly gripping my wrist. When he realized that the bulky thing in my jacket was an eyeglass case and not a weapon, he let go. He took the handwritten quote and said he would give it to the President. After having yet another run-in with the Secret Service, I was too worried about keeping my job to give the quote another thought.

Believe it or not, my plan to hand President Nixon a note wasn't quite as irrational as it may seem. I thought that the President knew me. Although I doubted that he remembered the incident with my shoelaces, I was sure that he remembered a conversation that we'd had about Teddy Roosevelt.

I had heard that President Nixon walked along the West Colonnade from the Residence to the Oval Office at about eight o'clock every morning. On days when I didn't have morning class-es, I'd get up extra early to catch the bus in time to make it to the Colonnade a few minutes before the President did. I didn't make it there on the dot every day and neither did he; occasionally, however, there would be several days in a row when everything went like clockwork.

I would say "Good morning, Mr. President." He'd say "Good morning" back to me or flash a smile. The exchange would un-questionably make my day.

One chilly April morning, I left the ugly brown briefcase I used for toting schoolwork at home and took only one book to work with me., It was Theodore Roosevelt's autobiography. There must have been something identifiable on the cover because it caught the President's eye. He stopped and asked me if I was enjoying the book. Struggling to get my voice to work, I told him that I was.

For the next few minutes, I stood spellbound as the President of the United States spoke to me about Teddy Roosevelt.

It was surrealistic. I could even smell the President's aftershave.

The President covered a lot of ground in a short time, and one comment he made about Roosevelt and Winston Churchill sharply increased my interest in studying history. The President noted that these two giants of the 20th century were both prolific writers who also authored distinguished historical works. In Roosevelt's case, it was *The Winning of the West,* a sweeping, four-volume chronicle of America's expansion west of the Alleghenies. Churchill penned *History of the English-Speaking Peoples,* an equally sweeping history of Great Britain from the time of the Romans to the first days of World War I. The President believed that their writings helped them gain an unparalleled understanding of their nations' personalities. Moreover, their study of the past gave them almost uncanny foresight into the future.

It would be fun to think that the President actually wanted to speak with me about Roosevelt; the truth, I'm afraid, was that I was the only thing with a pulse standing in front of him that morning, and he decided to let his mind wander briefly when he saw the book. Nonetheless, I wouldn't trade those few minutes for the world.

I've had the good fortune to speak with more than my fair share of Presidents and, except for one, my impressions of them were relatively the same. President Ford was fatherly and instantly likeable. President Carter was gracious and humble. Ronald Reagan would have been impossible not to like. George H.W. Bush made me feel like a long-lost friend, and George W. Bush was as personable as he was surprising. At a crowded dinner in Washington, President Bush and I chatted about a mutual friend who I knew was in the room but couldn't find. "If I see him," the President said, "I'll tell him you're looking for him." Later, my friend and I finally located one another and I mentioned that I'd been searching for him high and low. "I know," he replied. "The President told me."

Richard Nixon struck me differently.

I found the President to be more polite and reserved than friendly and more ill at ease with me than I was with him. Nevertheless, he didn't come across at all like the cold, aloof character he was held to be. In fact, there was something exceptionally imposing, even gravitating, about President Nixon. Just listening to him was exhilarating, like punching the accelerator on a Lamborghini. Perhaps I felt that way because I was very young and hadn't yet learned to demystify the people and things we think are larger than life. Perhaps it was because, Watergate aside, he had a brilliant mind. Perhaps it was some of both. Whatever it was, I have yet to ever find that kind of voltage in anyone else.

On April 29, I saw the President again as he crossed the West Wing basement on his way to his office in the EOB. This time, I stayed far away. With talk of his impeachment growing daily, he had asked the television networks for time to address the nation that night. The story was that he would announce the release of some 1,200 pages of edited transcripts of the taped conversations about Watergate that had been subpoenaed by the Judiciary Committee. I remember thinking that it was odd that the President had paper tucked into his shirt collar and thought that he might have cut the dickens out of himself shaving. It never dawned on me that he'd just had TV make-up applied to his face.

I went home that night and turned on my black-and-white TV. The President's speech ran well over 30 minutes. He said that he had nothing to hide, that he'd had no advance knowledge of the Watergate break-in or of the cover-up. Eventually, he pointed to a pile of loose-leaf notebooks stacked on a table to his left. On the covers were the presidential seal and "Submission of Recorded Presidential Conversations to the Committee on the Judiciary of the House of Representatives by President Richard Nixon." Having tripped over a pile of the books awkwardly left outside of the Roosevelt Room earlier that day, I was already more familiar with them than I wanted to be.

The President told the country that the entire story of his involvement in Watergate was there, even though the transcripts did not contain everything that was on the tapes. Nonetheless, he insisted that they contained everything that the Judiciary Committee had requested and invited the leaders of the Committee to listen to the tapes at the White House and compare their accuracy against the transcripts. The President also said that he would make the materials public. He warned about the potential fallout that could be caused in the international community by a presidential impeachment and trial by the Senate. He attacked the media for treating allegations of wrongdoing as if they were true. He told the nation that he placed his trust in the basic fairness of the American people to judge his truthfulness.

At the very end, he said:

"As for myself, I intend to go forward, to the best of my ability, with the work that you elected me to do. I shall do so in a spirit perhaps best summed up a century ago by another President when he was being subjected to unmerciful attack. Abraham Lincoln said:

'I do the very best I know how—the very best I can; and I mean to keep doing so until the end. If the end brings me out all right, what is said against me won't amount to anything. If the end brings me out wrong, ten angels swearing I was right would make no difference.'

Thank you and good evening."

It was probably a coincidence. But I kind of hope it wasn't.

◆

Although calls for the President's impeachment had been getting progressively louder for more than a year, the mood among my White House friends brightened after the speech that night.

People's spirits rose again on April 30 when the President's attorney, James St. Clair, asserted that there was nothing in the transcripts to suggest that Nixon had obstructed justice.

They rose a third time on May 3 when President Nixon addressed a crowd of more than 10,000 cheering Republicans in Phoenix. He said that he had done everything necessary to prove his innocence in the Watergate matter. He said that it was time for the country to move on.

Then, just as things were looking up, they made a swan dive into hell.

On May 7, St. Clair told reporters that the President had decided not to turn over the tapes subpoenaed by the House Judiciary Committee and the special Watergate prosecutor. Furthermore, the President had decided that he would "respectfully decline to comply" with any further subpoenas and would take his fight to the Supreme Court if necessary.

On May 8, House Republican Leader John Rhodes said that President Nixon should consider resigning if a lack of public confidence prevented him from performing his duties. The chairman of the House Republican Conference, John Anderson of Illinois, said that the country would be better off if Nixon left office.

On May 9, the House Judiciary Committee opened its first hearing into the possible impeachment of the President. On the same day, the *Chicago Tribune* called for the President's impeachment or resignation in an editorial.

On May 10, the *Los Angeles Times*, the *Kansas City Times*, and the *Cleveland Plain Dealer* echoed the *Tribune*'s sentiments on their own editorial pages. Later in the day, an aide to a GOP Senator told a reporter that he had information from a reliable source that the President would resign on Sunday. The unexpected cancellation of a Cabinet meeting added extra fuel to the fire. The story wasn't true, of course, but it made a lot of White House people edgy.

By Friday afternoon, snarky remarks were flying everywhere, some of them wrapped inside some of the worst knock-knock jokes I'd ever heard, like "Knock-knock. Who's there? Hanover. Hanover who? Hanover the tapes or we'll impeach you." Mercifully, somebody came up with "What did the President know and when did he forget it?" a clever twist on the famous "What did the President know and when did he know it?" line from the Senate Watergate hearings. Somebody else came up with what I thought was the funniest one: "Why are there so many 'expletives deleted' in the Watergate transcripts? Because calling people 'poo-poo heads' doesn't sound presidential."

One of the transcriptionists told me that she clearly heard my voice on one of the tapes. I knew that that wasn't possible, but I worried about it anyway.

For many Americans, the transcripts failed to live up to their expectations of the Presidency. Some were shocked by the President's use of profanity and seemed more interested in washing his mouth out with soap than determining if he had committed a crime. Some thought that the transcripts proved Nixon's innocence, while others believed that they showed a man with a moral blind spot who was guilty as hell. Senate Republican Leader Hugh Scott referred to the transcripts as "a shabby, disgusting, immoral performance" by all involved. A lot of people were astonished that the President had made the transcripts public in the first place. Even Bob Hope said that he thought that releasing the transcripts was a "big mistake."

Partly because of all of that, perhaps, the transcripts were such a hot commodity across the country that nearly a million copies had been sold by May 8. Some 50 U.S. newspapers printed them in their entirety and sold tens of thousands of copies for 50 cents apiece. *The White House Transcripts*, an 886-page paperback sold by Bantam Books for $2.50, or about $12.25 today, and *The Presidential Transcripts*, a 736-page Dell Publishing book that went for $2.45, were sold out in book stores within days. It was crazy. I remember seeing a two-block-long line across the street from the EOB that stretched from the book store at the corner of Pennsylvania Avenue down 17th Street towards the Corcoran Gallery of Art. A bookseller was reported as saying that the only book she remembered selling as fast was *The Joy of Sex*.

◆

Somebody had to work in the Messenger's Office on Saturdays. That wasn't a problem as far as I was concerned; in fact, I was often willing to swap with the other guys because Saturdays were usually quiet and gave me the opportunity to get paid while I studied. Better yet, when the tours were over for the day, I'd take a book to the Library and read for a while. The room was stately, brilliantly conducive to thought, and much more enjoyable since I wasn't being thrown out the same way I had been in the past. I knew most of the EPS officers, or they knew me from my Easter adventures, and when they said "get the hell out of there, you idiot" there was now an air of civility about it.

Saturday, May 11 turned out to be unexpectedly violent.

While delivering mail in the East Wing, I was surprised to see a cluster of staffers there. When I asked them what they were doing, they told me that they had come to support Julie and David Eisenhower, who were going to hold a press conference about Watergate in "the garden."

I finished what I was doing and went out to join them. I walked through the Residence and out to the Rose Garden, adjacent to the Oval Office. I was startled to see that there was no crowd. One of the EPS officers laughed, shook his head, and told me that I was, of course, in the wrong garden. Evidently, I had never noticed the large crowd of reporters gathered right outside the window along the East Colonnade in Jacqueline Kennedy's Garden.

This time, at least, I had a half-decent excuse for screwing up. I was walking down the Colonnade in a roped-off area that barely separated me from a sea of tourists. A woman whose body was twice the size of the madras muumuu she was wearing grabbed my left arm, jerked me towards her, and pulled my face so close to hers that I could see her tonsils.

"Are you anybody important?" she roared. Her breath was so bad that my eyes rolled back in my head. It was dank and stale like mold.

I shouted "No!" and had to force her fingers loose to get my arm back. I felt like a raccoon trying to pry the lid off a garbage can.

It took two officers to throw her out and three weeks to get the odor out of my nose.

In the wake of my escapade on the North Lawn, I retraced my steps to the East Wing rather than risk my luck cutting across the yard to the East Garden. Rows of chairs had been set up on the grass and, not seeing any of my friends around, I took a seat in the second row. The weather that day was spectacular with a temperature of about 75 degrees, perfectly clear skies, and bright sunshine. Every tree and plant that was supposed to bloom was blooming, and the smells were intoxicating. A gentleman who looked familiar sat down next to me and started writing in a notebook.

After sneaking a couple of sideways peeks to try to put a name with the face, it dawned on me that he was Robert Pierpoint of CBS News. He was a legend who had originally been hired by Edward R. Murrow to cover the Korean War. By the time I met him, he was a well-known figure on *The CBS Evening News with Walter Cronkite*. He had covered Ike, JFK, LBJ, and Nixon and was in the presidential motorcade in Dallas on November 22, 1963. He filed live reports from Parkland Hospital. In 1970, he covered the Pentagon Papers story. In 1983, his CBS Radio report about the Korean War cease-fire in 1953 was played in the final television episode of *M*A*S*H*.

Seven months earlier during a Nixon press conference, Pierpoint stunned other reporters by asking the President, "What is it about the television coverage of you in these past weeks and months that has so aroused your anger?"

"Don't get the impression that you've aroused my anger," Nixon replied. "You see, one can only be angry with those he respects."

A chill reportedly shot through the room.

Despite a host of denials by the White House, Nixon's remark was said to have been aimed directly at the CBS reporter.

I started to feel uneasy sitting next to Pierpoint, but not because I hadn't been around renowned reporters before. It was quite the opposite, in fact. Whenever I was in a hurry to get back to the East Wing, I regularly cut through the press room, and it wasn't terribly unusual for me to cross paths with Tom Brokaw, Dan Rather, Connie Chung, Tom Jarriel, and others. I remember having the impression that Tom Brokaw had very large thumbs, a thought that probably sounded just as weird then as it does now.

What made me anxious about my proximity to Robert Pierpoint had to do with a phone call I fielded from him while I was working for Mrs. Smith. I was the only one in the office, and he was not happy that none of the people who could speak for the First Family were available. I offered to take a message and asked him how to spell his name. That didn't make him particularly happy either. Then, I had to ask him to hold because my pen ran out of ink. Probably sounding remarkably like the town idiot, I wrote out his message. After making me read back what I had written, he asked my name and, instead of just hanging up like I did on sleepy press secretary Ron Ziegler a year earlier, I gave it to him.

"New at this, Don?" Pierpoint asked me. I said that I was.

"Just take a breath," he told me. "Everything will be fine."

Even in the face of his understanding, I was positive that he was going to tell Mrs. Smith that I was a dunce. I kept worrying about it even though nothing ever happened.

Seated in the East Garden, Mr. Pierpoint looked at me and asked me who I was. In almost the same breath, he said that the seats were reserved for the working press. I didn't tell him my name this time. Fearful that he might remember me, I simply stood up and walked to the very back of the crowd and stayed there. It was just a plain, dumb teenager kind of reaction. Nevertheless, I often think about Bob Pierpoint whenever I get exasperated with someone who's stumbling their way through a new job. I hope that I'm as considerate to them as he was to me.

Julie, 25, casually dressed in a polka-dot blouse and skirt, and David, 26, in a dark polo shirt and khakis, stood under a white pergola and answered reporters' questions for about 35 minutes. When asked if her father would resign, Julie said without hesitation that he would not. Moreover, he planned "to take this constitutionally down to the wire" if necessary. She added that, far from the picture being painted of him as a broken man, the President was in good spirits, good health, and not consumed by Watergate. David said that his father-in-law had decided to release the tapes to "remove the taint of criminality from the White House."

Pierpoint was called on to ask a question.

"Mrs. Eisenhower, may I say first of all that I feel I have to apologize for addressing these questions to you, since in our system we do not hold the sins of the fathers against the following generations, and we don't have a monarchy in which you are going to inherit power," he said. "I am not quite sure why you are here to answer these questions."

There was a collective gasp followed by complete silence.

"Mr. Pierpoint, I am going to try to control myself in answering the question because it really does wound me," Julie replied. "If the media has a hang-up and an obsession about resignation and feels they must be reassured from members of the family that my father is not going to resign, I feel as a daughter that it's my obligation to come out here and say 'No, he's not going to resign.'"

The Eisenhowers showed remarkable grace under fire that day. On the way back into the East Wing, a friendly voice in the crowd suggested that they should both run for President at some time in the future. A different voice said that they'd probably had enough of politics to last a lifetime. Another said he was confident that hell would freeze over before they ever ran for public office.

About a week later, a friend brought by a White House photo that had been taken that day showing the crowd at the press conference. Although I was only about a quarter of the size of a pencil eraser, I was thrilled to see myself standing in the back row. A couple of decades later, I noticed that one of the men in the picture looked unusually familiar although I wasn't sure why. I finally figured it out while watching a movie one night. I had known the guy in the picture in passing. He was Ben Stein. Long before he uttered the immortal words, "Bueller? Bueller?" in a brilliantly tedious monotone in *Ferris Bueller's Day Off*, Ben Stein was a speechwriter for President Nixon. He had also been an adjunct professor at American University.

On May 22, President Nixon notified the House Judiciary Committee that he would refuse to obey any further subpoenas. The chairman of the Committee, New Jersey Democrat Peter Rodino, said that he considered the President's response to be "a very grave matter."

The same week, I was sent to the East Gate to meet a messenger who had come to deliver the upcoming issue of a magazine that had just begun publishing in March. It was called *People*. Mrs. Nixon was on the cover that week.

On May 24, Leon Jaworski, the Watergate Special Prosecutor in the Department of Justice who succeeded Archibald Cox, asked the Supreme Court to decide if President Nixon had the right to defy a judicial order to produce evidence on the grounds of executive privilege.

On May 31, the Supreme Court agreed to make an expedited decision and laid out a timetable to deliver a ruling in July. The case was given the formal name of *United States v. Richard Milhous Nixon, President of the United States, et al.* Most news reports simply called it *U.S. v. Nixon.*

On June 6, James St. Clair confirmed that a federal grand jury had voted 19-0 in February to name Nixon an unindicted co-conspirator in obstructing the investigation of the Watergate burglary. Nixon was not indicted because it was not clear if a sitting President could indeed be indicted under the Constitution.

As Yogi Berra said, it was feeling "like déjà vu all over again."

Vice President Agnew had said that he wouldn't quit either.

Since I was the only one in my tiny circle who had lost his job in one history-making resignation, some people assumed that I knew what would happen to their jobs if there was another, bigger one. Particularly, and very understandably, concerned were folks like me whose jobs weren't in the Civil Service system. The fact that all I could say was that I lost my job and had to get another one made me unpopular for a while. I know that they wanted to hear something warm and comforting, but the truth wasn't it.

Piled on top of that was a woman I barely knew who would have fit right in at the Salem Witch Trials. I'm certain that she saw me as bad luck in the flesh because she grabbed the petite gold cross around her neck whenever she saw me. She didn't do that with other people. I took it as a joke until President Nixon resigned and she bought a larger cross.

◆

By the time summer was in full swing, I'd come to appreciate my knack for stumbling onto people and things that were at least a little offbeat if not completely outrageous. I asked a friend why she thought I ran into so many funny things so often. She said it was because I was weird. A nicer friend said it was because I had a habit of going places where interesting things had a chance to happen. I went with that friend's analysis, although the first one was probably more accurate.

This much I know, however: looking back, I'm very glad that I didn't have the kind of perpetual distractions that permeate society today. If I'd been constantly looking at a phone, I'd have surely missed a lot of memorable things.

I might not have witnessed a rare chain reaction of air sickness on a turbulent flight to Boston. A kid upchucked his strawberry milkshake over the seat in front of him, hitting a man squarely in the head. The lady sitting next to the man was so grossed out by it that she blew chunks between the seats in front of her. Then, the man who was originally vomited on vomited. As the guy sitting next to me pointed out, "That's just not something you see every day."

I might not have had the President's doctor examine my ears near the Oval Office. On my way to the West Wing one afternoon, I bumped into Major General Tkach, the President's physician. He said something to me. My right ear was clogged from a cold and I couldn't hear him. General Tkach said something else, and I cupped my ear like a 90-year-old to try to make it out. He motioned me to him and inspected both of my ears right on the West Colonnade. He shook his head and directed me to a military doctor in the EOB. The doctor, who couldn't have been nicer, diagnosed my problem as a big, old heap of earwax. After he cleaned out both ears, he explained that he'd used a water flosser to remove the wax. He'd modified the motor for use inside ears himself. The next time I saw General Tkach, he simply looked at me and said, "Wash your ears better, young man."

I might not have seen a twin mattress being thrown out of a seventh-story apartment window onto the sidewalk, quickly followed by two chairs, a mini-fridge, and a black telephone that unfortunately didn't survive the fall. According to police, they also unfortunately didn't belong to the guy tossing them out of the window.

I might not have noticed when a young couple walked into a hospital emergency room where I was waiting for a friend one night. The man had a large knife stuck in his left thigh that the woman had apparently put there on purpose. She was crying and apologizing to him profusely when the man said something that must have pissed her off. She proceeded to rip the knife out of his left thigh and use it to stab him in his right thigh. I learned a lot about knife wounds and gushing blood that night. It wasn't pretty, but it was educational.

Most importantly, I might have never had a conversation with a man who worked in a small office in an executive department that I visited from time to time.

Taped to the wall behind his desk had to be a hundred snapshots taken on every vacation he'd taken in the 20-odd years he had worked for the Federal Government. When the pictures piqued my interest one day, he took me on a half-hour tour of America from sea to shining sea and the hundred or so places in between that he and his wife had visited. I told him that his collection was very impressive. He suggested that his photos were a wonderful example of how I could live my life, too. Slog through 49 weeks of work every year, he said, and look forward to the two or three weeks when you can see and do something new. He and his wife had already planned when and where they would vacation for several years past his retirement.

He was a very nice man and, in retrospect, I know that he was generously offering me advice that had served him well. Nonetheless, his description of life had the word "boring" scrawled across it in big, red crayon as far as I was concerned and, by the time I got back to the office, I was quite sure that I had no interest in "slogging" through anything. I was coming to understand what my mother meant when she said that "good medicine for some is poison for others." The fact that what worked for him didn't work for me didn't make him bad or make me good. It just made us different.

The most productive outcome of the conversation was that it helped me give a name to what I wanted to be. I decided that I wanted to be "interesting," a word that I discovered can be a synonym for "intriguing" for some people, "strange" for others, and "Norman Bates", depending on the topic. I also learned the hard way that I could tumble into the "strange" category and even graze "Norman Bates" if I wasn't careful.

If you want to be interesting, as a wise person told me, you have to be interested in lots of different things that create ear-catching conversation. The good news was that I was very curious and read a lot. The bad news was that I sometimes didn't think before I spoke.

There was a medical museum at Walter Reed Army Hospital that displayed all sorts of curiosities from legs with elephantiasis to a section of President Garfield's spine that had been struck by an assassin's bullet in 1881. Mark, who later became a doctor, and I liked it so much that I even took him there for his birthday.

What I discovered was that not everyone shared the same joy I found in medical specimens floating in jars of formaldehyde. The sentence, "You wouldn't believe the diseased eyeball I saw at the medical museum" will not make you "interesting" at a wine and cheese mixer. Trust me.

◆

On Monday, June 10, with Watergate growing hotter by the hour, President and Mrs. Nixon boarded Marine One on the South Lawn to begin a 14,000-mile trip to Egypt, Saudi Arabia, Syria, Israel, and Jordan. The White House billed the trip as a peace mission designed to demonstrate the friendship between the United States and Arab nations, two of which, Syria and Egypt, had previously been under the influence of the Soviet Union. Nevertheless, the trip was criticized by both Democrats and Republicans who saw it as an attempt to distract the American public as Congress wrestled with the possibility of impeaching the President. There were also said to be deep concerns about providing the President with adequate security in that part of world, despite the promised deployment of some 10,000 police and military guards by the host countries.

I stood on the South Lawn that morning with a group of several hundred to wish the Nixons bon voyage, including a very large contingent from the National Citizens Committee for Fairness to the Presidency, a pro-Nixon group. The President had spoken to more than a thousand members of the Committee the previous day at a $50-a-plate luncheon at the Shoreham Hotel where a bevy of anti-impeachment and anti-press speeches inflamed members of the audience who reportedly climbed up on chairs, yelled, and shook their fists at reporters in the room. The Committee was headed by a New England rabbi named Baruch Korff. Korff joined Jesuit priest Rev. John McLaughlin, a Deputy Special Assistant to the President sometimes called "the Watergate priest," as one of "The President's Holy Men." McLaughlin later hosted television's "The McLaughlin Group" for more than 20 years.

As a white-gloved Marine closed the helicopter's forward door from the inside, a friend said something to me very quietly that I was sure I hadn't heard correctly.

"The President isn't coming back," she said.

Considering the impeachment hearings, I told her that I could understand that.

She gave me a funny look. I know that she wanted to say something else but couldn't compete with the whooping noise of Marine One's rotating blades.

"No," she said when we could hear again. "I don't think he's coming back at all. Ever."

"What?" I asked, not following her in the least.

"Lots of problems here," she replied.

If she intended to explain what she meant, the words were lost when the departure ceremony came to an end and we were separated in the crowd. I had other things inviting my attention, and the conversation didn't cross my mind again.

At least for a while.

Walking through the West Wing later that same day, one of the secretaries I was friendly with waved me over to her desk. She was on the phone and whispered something like "listen to this" and had me put my ear up to part of the receiver. I was amazed. The sound was so crystal clear that I wouldn't have been surprised if the person speaking had been inside my ear. My friend wrote "Wow!" on a White House notepad and pointed to it. I smiled and, with no clue what any of this was about, started to walk away. She grabbed my hand and held me there as she finished the call.

"Can you believe that?" she asked. "That call was from Air Force One. And they're over Europe."

That was a very, very big deal, and not just because it involved Air Force One.

For mere mortals, making a telephone call from the United States to a party overseas in those days could be an annoyingly slow process. First, you had to dial "0" for a local operator. That operator would then connect you to a U.S. long-distance operator. That long-distance operator would, in turn, call a long-distance operator in the country you wanted to reach. Then, that long-distance operator would call a local operator who would connect the call to the party you wanted to speak with. The sound was often very faint, and there were weird echoes and pauses. A friend likened it to yelling into a toilet paper roll. On top of that, it cost an arm and a leg.

The next big surprise arrived on Wednesday. In a stroke of luck, I was in the First Lady's Press Office when Mrs. Smith called from Cairo where she said she had a remarkable view of the 4,500-year-old Pyramids of Giza. That was mind-blowing to me. At that point, I don't recall ever having met an Egyptian or even knowing an American who had traveled there. In the pre-internet, pre-CNN age, chatting on the phone with someone near the banks of the Nile was even cooler than the call from Air Force One.

Apparently, the President's reception in Egypt's capital had been far more than simply stunning. Standing side by side in an open limousine in 90-degree heat, Presidents Nixon and Anwar

Sadat passed cheering crowds waving American flags and carrying signs that read "God Bless Nixon" in English. A giant banner strung overhead across a street said "We Trust Nixon." Egyptian officials estimated the crowd on the seven-mile motorcade route from the airport at a staggering two million people.

The next day, Presidents Nixon and Sadat rode 130 miles in an open train car from Cairo to Alexandria, waving and smiling to a crowd along the route that Egyptian officials estimated at more than three million. The Associated Press reported that the train was forced to slow down at points "because of crowds surging onto the tracks."

Watching the coverage on television that night, I was shocked to see just how thick the crowds were and how close they were to Nixon and Sadat with only spotty security in between. It looked to me like an assassination waiting to happen. Then it dawned on me what my friend had been trying to say. When I read the next morning that terrorists had killed three people in Israel in protest over Nixon's Middle East visit, it sent a formidable chill down my spine. Seven years later, in October 1981, President Sadat would be assassinated by members of an Egyptian terrorist group during an army parade.

On June 15, more or less in the middle of the President's travels, *All the President's Men*, written by *Washington Post* reporters Bob Woodward and Carl Bernstein about their investigation of Watergate from June 1972 to March 1974, was published by Simon and Shuster. It had the eye-popping price tag of $8.95, or roughly $44.00 today. Within a week, it was at the top of the *New York Times* bestsellers list for nonfiction and remained on the list for six months.

There were people in the White House who rushed out to buy the book just to see whose names were in it. There were others I knew of who nervously checked to make sure that their names weren't in it, whether they had any reason to be mentioned or not. There was even a guy who might have had a reason to be mentioned and was very disappointed that he wasn't. He told a friend of a friend that he had missed his shot at immortality.

The line at the bookstore on 17th Street was just as long as it had been for the presidential transcripts paperback. Displayed near *All the President's Men* was another book on the bestsellers list. Written by Peter Benchley, it had the curiously scary title *Jaws*.

Somehow it was fitting.

On June 25, President Nixon left the White House again, this time for a meeting in Brussels with members of NATO and one in Moscow to discuss nuclear weapons controls with Soviet leader Brezhnev. We trotted out on the South Lawn to wave goodbye again. The President said, "I wish you could all go along with us."

It would have been very hard to blame him for leaving town again. He was infinitely more popular in other parts of the world than he was at home. On Inauguration Day 1973, 68% of Americans approved of the job President Nixon was doing, according to the Gallup Poll. That week in June, the number was on its way down to 24%.

As bad as that was, there was something worse.

The chances of altering the course of his Presidency were between zero and none.

Chapter Seven

"YOU'RE NOT THAT STUPID"

In my opinion, the Supreme Court is the most unexpectedly impressive building in the Nation's Capital.

I say that because many of the people I took on walking tours of Capitol Hill over the years said that they were surprised by the building's beauty and dignity, an impression that seemingly fell short of the mark in photographs but grew very strong as they crossed the football-field-size plaza in front of the Court. I don't think that I ever saw anyone, regardless of their citizenship, not pause in awe to read the inscription on the building's neoclassical-style façade.

It says "Equal Justice Under Law."

As the highest court in the land and the leader of the judicial branch of government, the Supreme Court serves as a vital check on the power of Congress and the President. It holds the final word on whether laws and executive orders violate the U.S. Constitution. It is a critically important institution in our system of government with exceptionally solemn responsibilities.

With that in mind, it's fun to note that the Supreme Court Building and the land it sits on have an interesting and somewhat checkered history. It is no slacker in a city that puts irony on display as widely as white marble.

Built during the Great Depression, the Supreme Court contains marble quarried from different locations in the United States. The columns inside the courtroom, however, are made of ivory buff and golden marble that the architect desperately wanted from Siena, Italy. To ensure that he received the quality of marble he expected, the architect enlisted the assistance of the Italian Government, notably Fascist dictator Benito Mussolini himself. Mussolini, who had established a tyrannical police state in Italy that eliminated press freedoms, promoted angry xenophobia, and unleashed extreme violence against his opponents, was hardly an admirer of our constitutional republic. In fact, Mussolini and his pal, Adolf Hitler, declared war on the United States in 1941. In the end, of course, things didn't work out so well for Mussolini. At the close of World War II, he was shot by his enemies and his body was hung upside down on a meat hook from the roof of a gas station. It was not his best day.

The grounds of the Supreme Court may have once been a hotbed of prostitution.

The Court was built on land previously occupied by a temporary U.S. Capitol Building constructed in 1814 after British troops burned the White House and the Capitol. The Old Brick Capitol, as it was later called, housed the Senate, the House of Representatives, and the Supreme Court until the original Capitol was rebuilt in 1819. According to folklore I gathered from a local historian who sounded like he knew what he was talking about, the Old Brick Capitol was purportedly surrounded day and night by working girls on the lookout for lonely Congressmen. If that's true, it made the area one of the city's premiere meeting places for the world's two oldest professions, both of which were legal at the time out of respect for their similarities.

Last, but not least, the grounds have a connection to the assassination of President Abraham Lincoln. During the Civil War, the Old Brick Capitol was converted into a prison. John Ford, the owner of Ford's Theater, Dr. Samuel Mudd, and boarding house owner Mary Surratt, among others, were held there as suspected collaborators with Lincoln's assassin, John Wilkes Booth. Ford was exonerated and released. Dr. Mudd was convicted and was sent to prison in the Dry Tortugas where he admirably served as a physician during an outbreak of yellow fever. He was eventually pardoned by President Andrew Johnson. Mrs. Surratt was convicted of treason and hanged. On the plus side, she went down in history as the first woman executed by the U.S. Government. Believe it or not, the Washington, D.C. boarding house where Mrs. Surratt met with Booth and other conspirators still stands at 604 H Street, Northwest. It's currently a Chinese restaurant.

On the warm, sunny morning of July 24, 1974, on the same plot of earth where the Old Brick Capitol stood, the question of how the Court would decide *U.S. v. Nixon* was about to be put to rest. At approximately 11:00 a.m. Chief Justice of the United States Warren Burger read aloud what still stands today as one of the most consequential rulings in American history. *U.S. v. Nixon* set a precedent for limiting the power of the President of the United States.

It's important to note that President Nixon had never clearly promised that he would comply with the Court's decision if it was not in his favor. His attorney, James St. Clair, had only said that the case was presented to the Court for its "guidance and judgment with respect to the law." The President, St. Clair said, had his own responsibilities as a co-equal branch of government under the Constitution. In other words, Nixon believed that he was not necessarily subject to the will of the courts.

The possibility that the President and the Supreme Court might have a head-on collision was particularly unnerving considering Nixon's deteriorating position with Congress and the American public. There was another unsettling consideration. Because the Constitution doesn't provide the judiciary with its own police power, courts depend on the executive branch to see that its decisions are executed. No one was quite sure what would happen if the President just said "no."

A friend who worked in the Senate and had sprinted to the Supreme Court plaza the moment he heard that the decision would be read called me around 11:45 to let me know that the vote was 8-0 against Nixon. He had to go back to his office to find an open line because reporters had all of the nearby pay phones tied up.

The ninth member of the Court, Justice William Rehnquist, a Nixon appointee who had also served as Assistant Attorney General, had recused himself to avoid any conflict of interest.

In short, the decision meant that the President had to turn over the tapes and other materials that had been subpoenaed for use in the Watergate cover-up trial of Nixon associates that was slated to begin in September.

The Court rejected the President's argument that he had the constitutional authority to determine whether he turned over confidential communications or not, stating that although the President had a legitimate claim to executive privilege, it did not include an "absolute, unqualified immunity from the judicial process under all circumstances." Those circumstances included withholding evidence in a criminal trial, particularly when no military or diplomatic secrets were involved. Moreover, the Court ruled that it, not the President, had the last word in deciding constitutional matters.

After eight hours of discussion at the Western White House in California, the President responded through his attorney at 7:00 p.m. eastern time that night that he was disappointed in the decision but would comply "in all respects."

That was good news.

◆

As far as I was concerned, the nine black-robed justices of the Supreme Court had a "not fun" look about them, sort of like the old, grouchy men in American suburbs who yell at anyone that comes within spitting distance of their manicured lawns. Even worse, perhaps, they seemed like the kind of guys who were only comfortable at tax audits and funerals.

Like so many other authority figures in my teenage years, I saw them as one-dimensional. Under the circumstances, my wet-behind-the-ears self was very surprised to learn that Supreme Court justices are people too. I got a preview of that the first time I went to see a case argued before the Court in 1973. As an attorney made what may have been the single most important argument of his life, the justices frequently interrupted him with questions and comments while sort of bouncing back and forth in their stately, high-backed leather chairs. Years later, I asked a friend who worked at the Supreme Court why they did those things.

Her response was priceless. "Sometimes they just get bored."

Because of a friendship I was very fortunate to make in the White House, I had the incredible opportunity to spend a little time with Justice Harry Blackmun. He shocked me by turning out to be the opposite of what I imagined. He was very personable and down-to-earth and certainly didn't fit any of my pre-conceived notions about judges. There's a story about a lunch counter that Justice Blackmun frequented near Capitol Hill that speaks volumes about his lack of pretense. One day, a friendly gentleman sat down next to him and introduced himself to Blackmun.

"I'm Harry. Nice to meet you," Blackmun replied.

"What do you do for a living, Harry?" the man asked.

"Oh," Justice Blackmun responded, "I work for the government."

That's how everyone at the lunch counter knew him. He was just Harry who worked for the government. In fact, he was just Harry who worked for the government who also, believe it or not, drove himself to work and back in a blue Volkswagen Beetle and had breakfast in the cafeteria every morning with his law clerks.

I remember that we talked mostly about baseball. Justice Blackmun, who had grown up in St. Paul, was a big Minnesota Twins fan. There was an account that he and Justice Potter Stewart would pass notes to one another in Court with scores brought to them by their clerks. On October 10, 1973, Justice Stewart was famously said to have passed Blackmun a note that said, "Agnew just resigned. Mets 2, Reds 0."

Justice Blackmun's distinguished judicial career spanned 35 years, including eleven on the U.S. Court of Appeals for the Eighth Circuit and nearly a quarter of a century as a member of the U.S. Supreme Court. Appointed to the Court by Richard Nixon, his influence was felt on a wide variety of issues ranging from the death penalty and privacy rights to upholding Major League Baseball's exclusion from anti-trust laws. He voted against the President's position in *U.S. v. Nixon*. It is no small thing to note that he also wrote the Court's 7-2 majority opinion in a case called *Jane Roe, et al. v. Henry Wade, District Attorney of Dallas County.*

It's more commonly known as *Roe v. Wade.*

I've often thought of Justice Blackmun over the years, particularly whenever I've run into people whose high opinions of themselves aren't supported by reality. It's nice to remember that there are people in the world like Harry Blackmun, a real, very significant somebody who never acted like he was.

On Thursday, July 25, the House Judiciary Committee met until nearly 10:00 p.m. to conclude the first round of its deliberations over impeachment, which included 15 minutes for each of the 38 committee members, 21 Democrats and 17 Republicans, to present an argument on the matter. The impeachment debates were televised on a rotating basis by the three networks, NBC, CBS, and ABC, and a few friends and I tried to catch what little we could of them during the work day on a black-and-white TV in the press room. What I missed during the day I watched after work courtesy of PBS, which videotaped the sessions and aired them in the evenings. It was handled just like the Senate Watergate hearings the year before.

I can't recall if I saw Barbara Jordan, a 38-year-old African-American freshman Member of Congress from Houston, Texas, deliver her remarks live or on tape that day. What I do remember, however, was being thunderstruck by her eloquence. To say that Congresswoman Jordan's speech was moving would be to do it a grave disservice. It is widely acknowledged as one of the most extraordinary speeches of the 20th century.

"Earlier today, we heard the beginning of the Preamble to the Constitution of the United States: 'We, the people.' It's a very eloquent beginning. But when that document was completed on the seventeenth of September in 1787, I was not included in that 'We, the people.' I felt somehow for many years that George Washington and Alexander Hamilton just left me out by mistake," she began in a solemn, authoritative voice, placing herself inside the narrative as both an African-American and a woman.

"But through the process of amendment, interpretation, and court decision I have finally been included in 'We, the people.'"

She spoke passionately about the Constitution. "Today I am an inquisitor. I believe hyperbole would not be fictional and would not overstate the solemnness that I feel right now. My faith in the Constitution is whole, it is complete, it is total, and I am not going to sit here and be an idle spectator to the diminution, the subversion, the destruction of the Constitution," she said in a voice that resonated with passion.

I was watching the speech with friends.

The phone rang.

No one answered it.

There weren't any volunteers to take their eyes off of the screen.

She proceeded to frame the question before the Committee: "A President is impeachable if he attempts to subvert the Constitution," she said, quoting James Madison. "Has the President committed offenses, and planned, and directed, and acquiesced in a course of conduct which the Constitution will not tolerate? That's the question. We know that. We know the question. We should now forthwith proceed to answer the question. It is reason, and not passion, which must guide our deliberations, guide our debate, and guide our decision."

At the end of Ms. Jordan's 13-minute speech, one of the guys in our group shook his head and said loudly, "Nobody could recover from that."

For a nation that had all but lost its trust in its institutions that summer, Barbara Jordan's explanation of the Constitution was spellbinding. At the Congresswoman's funeral in 1996, former Texas Governor Ann Richards said of Jordan, "There was simply something about her that made you proud to be a part of the country that produced her."

At 7:05 p.m. EDT on Saturday, July 27, the House Judiciary Committee voted 27-11 to recommend the impeachment of the President for obstruction of justice to the full House of Representatives. Representative Edward Mezvinsky (D-Iowa), whose son would marry former First Daughter Chelsea Clinton in 2010, cast the vote that formed a majority. There was no joy in it. Several Members, Republicans and Democrats alike, had tears in their eyes during and after the vote. Next to war, it was a matter as grim and serious as anything the government touches.

On Monday night, July 29, the Judiciary Committee voted 28-10 in favor of a second article of impeachment for abuse of power. The next day, a third article of impeachment charging the President with contempt of Congress was approved 21-17. On August 1, the House leadership announced that the impeachment debate would be televised and begin on or about August 19. A vote was expected by August 31.

◆

Since the beginning of summer, the number of tourists filing through the White House had seemed to be getting larger by the day. If it was more than just my perception, it was probably because of the country's fascination with all things Watergate. A friend quipped that people were trying to get in before Nixon closed the doors and locked himself inside.

In those days, touring the White House was a whole lot less complicated than it is today. Unless visitors had a ticket provided by a Member of Congress to a special, early morning guided tour conducted by the Executive Protective Service, they simply got in line for a self-guided tour. Unfortunately, the line that summer frequently wrapped from the visitor's gate on East Executive Avenue halfway around the entirety of the White House grounds. When they eventually reached the door to the East Wing after God-knows-how-long, they just walked in.

There were no metal detectors or bag checks or pat downs at the White House in 1974. Believe it or not, I walked right past the President many mornings carrying a briefcase that no one ever x-rayed or asked me to open. There weren't any dress codes for tourists, either. Visitors were expected to conduct themselves with decorum, a nice thought that didn't always work out so well.

One morning, two men screamed something unintelligible, scared the bejesus out of the other tourists, and threw animal blood on the drapes in the East Room. They were quickly arrested.

Another day, three men yelled something, opened a door that led to the basement of the Residence, and ran down the stairs. I guess their plan was to take over the White House. I heard that the EPS walked up to the door, locked it, and started to laugh. The men were caught on a stairway between the door they had opened and a heavily fortified steel door that they probably couldn't have opened with a nuclear warhead. I heard that after a while the men begged to be let out.

Soon after that, a woman who followed me behind a very large, red room divider that separated the public tour area from the ground floor offices in the Residence, the elevator to the First Family's private quarters, and the path to the West Wing. I was simply walking along, doing what I did every day when the tours were active. When I reached the divider, I walked through a hidden opening in the center. I didn't notice that the woman was literally at my heels. The EPS officer sitting on the other side immediately stood up and blocked her from going any further.

"What's back here?" she asked, craning her neck. Her voice had all the charm of a fingernail scraping a blackboard.

"This is where we keep Abraham Lincoln," the officer shot back.

The lady, who was both horror-stricken and extremely gullible, put her hand over her mouth in the I-just-stumbled-across-a-dead-body kind of way that you see in movies, turned, and sprinted back to the tour.

There were also more than a few stories about the oddities people had brought in with them, including a wall telephone, a family member's ashes, and a 24-inch taxidermied alligator.

Perhaps the funniest one I ever heard, though, had to do with a reception the First Lady held for a women's group.

The guests were queued up in the Entrance Hall on the State Floor to shake hands with Mrs. Nixon as they departed. One of the ladies had apparently stopped at a drug store before the event and brought the toilet paper, toothpaste, and jar of face cream she purchased with her in a paper bag. Just before she reached Mrs. Nixon, the bag broke and the face cream jar, which was made of glass, hit the floor, broke into a million pieces, and spewed face cream all over the place. The woman acted like it never happened, shook hands with the First Lady, and walked out of the White House.

In 1974, Americans were only a handful of years removed from a time when families wore their Sunday best to go shopping in downtown department stores. That often meant a suit, or at least a tie, for boys and a dress and white gloves for little girls. In the early 1960s, before my buddies and I decided that girls had cooties and had to be avoided at all costs, little girls even wore pretty dresses to boys' rough-and-tumble birthday parties. My dad always wore a suit to work. My mom always wore a dress. In 1974, it would have been hard to imagine a world in which college students wore pajamas to school and airline passengers dressed like they were going to colonoscopy appointments.

Not everyone in those days was expected to be dressed up all the time, of course, and the tourists who endured Washington's hellish summer heat had the best excuses of all. There were standards, though, and very few people ever threw common decency out of the window just to make themselves more comfortable. Thankfully, it would be a quarter of a century before that actually happened and exposed underwear, entirely too much bare flesh, and the burning-tar-like aroma of Chinese sneakers became a regular part of the American landscape.

It was just my luck that I didn't have to wait 25 years to get a peek at that part of the future. I walked right into a couple who were way ahead of their time.

About a week before President Nixon resigned on August 9, I was walking through a throng of tourists in the East Colonnade when I got a whiff of something awful muscling its way down the hallway. Frankly, the word "awful" didn't begin to cover it. It was hideous. It smelled like somebody had mixed diesel fuel and decomposing potatoes together in a big vat and threw in a moldy pork chop for good measure.

Relieved after sniffing around to make sure that I wasn't the source, I tried to figure out what was.

It took no time at all.

On the left side of the hallway was a horde of fearful-looking visitors who looked like they had closed ranks for protection. On the right side, at least eight or nine feet away, was what they were trying to shield themselves from. The stink was coming from a middle-aged couple who, not surprisingly, were walking along all by themselves.

Then came the strange part.

Despite their alarming aroma, the man and the woman both had perfectly coiffed hair. The man was clean-shaven and the woman was wearing makeup. They even had nice smiles.

As if they weren't attracting enough attention to themselves, the woman was wearing a sleeveless dress. Although that wasn't particularly special by itself, the royal blue bikini she was wearing over the dress was. Parts of the dress were stuck in the bikini, making some areas of her anatomy disturbingly lumpy. An eight-inch-wide hole had been cut in the back that extended from about two inches below the collar to two inches above the hem. The man was decked out in style, too. He was in blue shorts and a white belt that were so tight that his rear end looked like he had two raccoons inside fighting for their lives. His white T-shirt was cut so that his shoulders, neck, and armpits were exposed, although most, but not all, of his stomach was covered. The capper was that the pants had a horizontal slit in the back just below the waistline.

What kept both of them cool unfortunately made everyone else around them woozy. The holes they cut to let air in also let their odor out.

The couple walked through the public rooms of the White House and eventually left, still with enough room between them and the rest of the visitors to fit a battleship. Everyone had let them go ahead. It was like they had taken their own private tour. As far as I was concerned, they were the single weirdest, oddest, least expected, most aberrant thing on the entire planet.

"That's nothing new," one of the older EPS officers said later, referring to the couple's disgusting odor.

I was sure that he was pulling my leg.

"No, really," he added with a shrug. "There's somebody like that every summer. Just think how much better your vacation in D.C. would be if you never had to wait in line."

◆

There had been a certain madness in the air for some time, but after the impeachment vote the severity seemed to jump up a couple of notches. The number of anti-Nixon demonstrators congregating in front of the White House and across the street in Lafayette Park was growing and getting louder every day. Sometimes you could barely see the demonstrators' faces because of all the signs they were carrying. "Impeach Nixon" was probably the most popular. "Jail to the Chief!" was big, as was "Resign Now!" There was a guy in a Nixon Halloween mask and a black-and-white-striped prison uniform with a "Honk for Impeachment" sign who got a big reaction from motorists on Pennsylvania Avenue and even made his way into a well-known photo. There was also an exceptionally well-endowed woman with "Impeach Nixon" across the front of her skintight T-shirt and the name of a strip club on the back. She got a much bigger reaction. When she walked along the White House fence, the crowd parted like Moses crossing the Red Sea.

Unable to resist the show, five or six of us wandered through the crowd one evening minus our coats and ties. Probably because of the sometimes widely different views I saw between younger and older adults about Vietnam, I expected that the tourist families that were overrunning Washington that August would stay far away from the impeachment demonstrators.

I was wrong about that. Everybody was lumped in together.

Tourists and protesters were posing for snapshots with one another and chatting like they were at a neighborhood barbecue. I saw a family in Lafayette Park sitting cross-legged on the grass with a picnic dinner. They were having fried chicken. A three-year-old was wiggling around in his father's arms shouting, "Impeach him, daddy! Impeach him!" There were card games going on. There was also the smell of weed. Lots and lots and lots of weed. Although I didn't see it, I heard that some guy and his friends sat down with their backs against the White House fence and lit up a bong while hashing out the implications of the full House having to impeach Nixon before the Senate could vote on conviction.

It was as much a party as it was a protest that President Nixon was still in the White House. It reminded me of Madame Defarge in Dickens' *A Tale of Two Cities* who worked on her knitting during the public beheadings of the French Revolution. I didn't like the circus atmosphere a bit until a friend suggested that there might be another way to look at it.

This wasn't like Vietnam, she argued. It wasn't about an un-popular war that cost 58,000 American lives. Nor was it like the French Revolution. We weren't overthrowing the government. This was about fixing the government, and there probably weren't any wide differences in what people in the crowd thought needed to happen. According to a Gallup poll conducted two weeks ear-lier, 51% of the public was in favor of impeachment. Only 30% were against it. Whether everyone's behavior was fitting, however, was another matter.

I listened carefully, but I must admit that my view changed slightly a day or so later. Walking into the White House through the East Gate, somebody hit me in the middle of my back with a rock. Obviously, not everybody was singing "Kumbaya".

◆

The week of August 5, which would be Richard Nixon's last as President, started out strangely even for me. In fact, it was a race from the ridiculous to the sublime and back again right off the bat.

As if Mondays weren't lousy enough, a fistfight broke out on the normally quiet bus I took to work every day. That morning, two old geezers got into an argument about homeowner's insurance. One man said something nasty about an insurance company he was doing business with. Another man who happened to work for the insurance company in question overheard it. Tempers flared. One man told the other to do something very painful. Violence ensued. A lunch box was crushed in the melee. The next day, both men boarded the bus with black eyes and the fetor of immaturity.

Young and innocent, I never knew that insurance could inflame such passion.

That was the first unexpected thing that happened.

The second had substantially more gravity.

The regular daily White House press briefing had been postponed until the afternoon.

That wasn't something that I'd normally even notice, much less pay attention to, but the buzz was that it might portend something big. The President had spent most of Sunday at Camp David with General Haig, Ron Ziegler, his Watergate attorney, James St. Clair, and speechwriters Ray Price and Pat Buchanan. They hadn't returned to the White House until about ten o'clock that Monday morning. Even though Deputy Press Secretary Gerald Warren kept denying it, the Camp David meeting was fueling hot rumors that the President was going to resign. There had also been an article in that morning's *Washington Post* that claimed that the tapes the Supreme Court had ordered Nixon to turn over, but which he had not yet surrendered, contained stuff so bad that it would make all hell break loose.

I had no intention of missing the chance to hear about this imbroglio in person. However, I had to clear a couple of hurdles first. Even though my White House pass gave me open access to the briefing room, it didn't give me license to be there during the actual briefings. Besides that, I'd heard that White House reporters were a might prickly about having rubberneckers around. So, I had no choice other than to cook up a plan. I'd been told that I had a talent for identifying obvious answers to very simple questions. Although I wasn't quite sure how that was meant, I was hoping that the person who said it was right.

The first thing I did was slyly call the Press Secretary's office and ask what time the briefing was going to be held. The answer was "around 3:30." That was quickly followed by an answer to a question I didn't ask. The voice on the other end of the line added, "after the market closes." In August 1974, the New York Stock Exchange closed at 3:30 p.m. instead of 4:00 p.m. as it does today. Although I knew very little about the stock market, I knew enough to assume that the White House didn't want to rattle Wall Street with bad news. The Dow Jones Industrial Average ended the day with a gain of 1%.

A few minutes before the briefing started, I walked into the press room and walked across the small stage and through the door on the far side that leads to an outside area where members of the press corps frequently mingled. Figuring that I was going to have to blend in to avoid being thrown out, I waited for the reporters to start walking in. When they did, I fell in line behind them. The room, which was quite a bit smaller in real life than it appeared on TV, was so overrun with humanity that no one noticed me. People were sitting on everything they could find, up to and including the floor. I just stood in the back with my mouth uncharacteristically shut.

Except for the clicking and whirring sounds of cameras, you could have heard a pin drop when Gerald Warren walked up to the podium. He read a two-page statement from the President in which Nixon admitted to having withheld evidence from the Court, the House Judiciary Committee, and even his own lawyer that tied him to a criminal conspiracy to obstruct justice. The statement rather surprisingly asserted the President's opinion that "a House vote of impeachment is, as a practical matter, virtually a foregone conclusion and that the issue will therefore go to trial in the Senate" but that he was "firmly convinced that the record, in its entirety, does not justify the extreme step of impeachment and removal of a President."

The evidence included what became known as the "smoking gun," a June 23, 1972 recording that confirmed the President's knowledge of the Watergate cover-up and his participation in a plan to obstruct justice. Nixon plotted with then-White-House-Chief-of-Staff H.R. Haldeman to use the CIA to thwart the FBI's Watergate investigation. The CIA would scam the FBI by telling them that the Watergate break-in was linked to national security issues. The CIA would then use that lie to convince the FBI to either drop its inquiry entirely or as a pretext to get inside the investigation and stop its progress. For a variety of reasons, Nixon expected the CIA director to fully cooperate in the sham. It didn't work out that way. In the end, the CIA correctly told the FBI that there were no national security issues at play and the FBI continued its investigation.

The disclosure of the June 23 conversation wiped out most of the remaining support Nixon had in Congress. Even the Republican members of the House Judiciary Committee who had voted against impeachment only days earlier told reporters that they had changed their minds.

The moment the briefing ended, the press room went nuts. It was like letting third-graders out for recess in the snow. People started trampling over one another to get transcripts of the newly released tapes and copies of the President's statement. One guy stepped on my right foot in the commotion and wouldn't get off despite my attempts to push him away. I finally had to punch him in the back to get his attention. Another guy used me as a blocking dummy so that he could make a path for himself through the crowd. I'm pretty sure that even UPI Bureau Chief Helen Thomas elbowed me in the ruckus.

Not unexpectedly, the events of the day spread quickly through the rest of the White House. The good news, if there was any, was that there seemed to be less distress in the air this time. That was true even among the people who had a lot personally invested in the Nixon Presidency. By that time, I think, everyone had become at least a little numb to the seemingly endless supply of Watergate surprises and the rumble of copiers that were spitting out resumes.

There were those, however, who really didn't care what happened one way or another as long as they still had jobs when the dust cleared.

There were even a few souls inside the White House who took glee in the scandal.

One of the civil servants in the Residence took every opportunity to recite Sir Walter Scott's famous verse, "Oh what a tangled web we weave / When first we practice to deceive!" with a dramatic punch to anyone who would listen. I knew another guy who regularly hummed Chuck Berry's "Don't Lie to Me" in the West Wing and occasionally sang the words. I was shocked. Maybe I was wrong, but 1600 Pennsylvania Avenue didn't exactly strike me as the best place for a White House employee to be dissing the President. If not respectful to the President, it certainly wasn't respectful to the Presidency.

On Tuesday morning, the President called a meeting of the Cabinet.

The rumor mill went into overdrive with speculation that something big was about to happen, which got a sort of a "duh" reaction under the circumstances. I would have liked to have hung around outside to see the expressions on the Cabinet members' faces as they left the meeting that day. A West Wing secretary told me that, with a few exceptions, the President's Cabinet would have been the world's worst poker players. You could tell if things were good or bad just by looking at how tight their jaws were clenched. I heard later that those who saw the Cabinet officers after the hour-and-a-half session were not comforted. The President had told them that he was not going to resign and that he would face trial in the Senate.

I missed the scene with the Cabinet because I was agog over something else.

Fred Jefferson had walked into our little office, put his hand on my shoulder, and told me to come with him. He didn't say another word until we walked into the Residence, took the stairs up to the State Floor, and walked to the north-facing windows in the East Room.

He told me to look outside and listen.

"Cacophony" was the only word I knew that captured the deafening jumble of headache-inducing noises I heard coming from Pennsylvania Avenue. It was all the worst parts of a pile driver, a jackhammer, and a middle-schooler starting violin lessons. Drivers were yelling and blasting their horns in response to signs and bumper stickers, some of which looked like they'd been changed from "Honk for Impeachment" to "Honk to Resign" and "Honk if You Think He's Guilty." Some motorists were so unrelenting that the D.C. police pulled them over and issued five-dollar fines. It was loud, annoying, aggravating, endless, and only going to get worse because rush hour was a long way off. If any of the honkers wondered if their anger and frustration could be heard inside the White House, I can assure them that they didn't go unnoticed.

When I asked Jeff why he'd brought me to the East Room to hear the infernal racket outside, he gave me a simple answer.

"Because you're going to remember this for the rest of your life."

Obviously, he was right.

Before too long, yet another rumor raised its head inside my little corner of the world. It was weird but potentially huge. The President wasn't going to go to trial in the Senate and he wasn't going to resign.

He was going to pardon himself and stay in office.

Not only had that possibility failed to occur to me, I wasn't completely sure how pardons worked in the first place. There had been talk about the possibility of Gerald Ford pardoning Nixon if Ford became President, but not about Nixon pardoning himself. When my friends and I didn't hear anything more about it, we simply let the matter go.

Nevertheless, when college resumed in the fall I asked one of my professors if a President could indeed pardon himself and remain in office.

The response was fascinating. The Constitution gives the President the power to issue a pardon to anyone for a federal crime before or after an indictment or conviction. There are, however, a few restrictions. The President cannot issue a pardon before a crime has been committed, he cannot pardon anything other than a federal crime, and he cannot pardon anyone who is being, or has been, impeached by Congress. At least in theory, a President could pardon himself for federal crimes he knew he committed as long as he did it before he was impeached. That said, however, the issue had never been tested and, until then, no one would know for sure if a President could do it until a President tried to do it.

In the final analysis, my professor's answer was "maybe". As I was learning, that was the answer to a lot of things in life.

The rest of Tuesday couldn't have gone downhill faster if it had been strapped to a Titan rocket. On Capitol Hill, Republican Senators met to agree on the best way to tell the President that the time for his resignation had come. The group included John Tower of Texas and Barry Goldwater of Arizona, the bedrock of Nixon's support in the Senate. The "smoking gun" revelations had made impeachment and conviction a "safe vote" for most Republicans concerned about a backlash from GOP leaders and the voters at home. That was very bad news for the President.

Also on Tuesday, Republican Congressman Robert Michel of Illinois, an ardent Nixon supporter, answered a reporter's question about who he might like to see as "President" Ford's Vice President. A day earlier, the mere notion of a GOP leader speaking openly about Ford taking Nixon's place would have been unthinkable.

Even more, and maybe worse, unnamed sources told the *Washington Post* that the White House was looking like *The Caine Mutiny,* with Nixon in Humphrey Bogart's role as the paranoid Captain Queeg. The 1954 movie tells the story of Queeg, the mentally unstable captain of a U.S. Navy ship during World War II. Unable to make critical decisions as a typhoon pummels his ship, Queeg is removed from the helm by his first officer to save the ship and crew. True or not, the comparison to the Oval Office was greeted with something less than delight.

And then, in what seemed to me like spectacular weirdness under the circumstances, the Dow gained 1.5% on Tuesday. I'd have thought that in the aftermath of so much negative political news the stock market would have dropped. Au contraire. In fact, the Dow closed with a 3% gain on Wednesday. At least one opinion had it that the market rose because investors believed that a new President would be able to concentrate on the nation's economic problems.

All in all, it appeared to me that the Nixon Administration ended that day. The resignation train had left the station and the only remaining issue was the transition of power from Nixon to Ford.

Other than seeing Ron Zeigler on the West Colonnade with a pipe in his mouth and looking terribly gaunt, I didn't come across anything first-hand that day other than the honking horns on Pennsylvania Avenue.

The next three days, however, would be very different. Before the week was out, I would meet America's new President in as awkward a fashion as possible.

In 1962, the Kennedy Administration declared war on thousands of purple-and-green-plumed starlings that took up residence every evening in the trees around the White House. Starlings are not popular birds for a variety of reasons, including their penchant for leaving disgusting marks on everything. That practice pushed the National Park Service to get rid of the birds. To do that, they put loudspeakers in the trees and broadcast a recorded starling distress call meant to keep the little critters away. Sometimes it worked and sometimes it didn't, and the system was still in place in 1974.

Wednesday must have been the day the starlings realized they were being scammed and decided to get even. As I walked through the West Executive Avenue gate a little before eight o'clock, two of them dive bombed me and, by the looks of things, let loose everything they had on the right sleeve of my oyster-colored poplin suit jacket. Disgusted out of my mind, I turned right into the EOB rather than left into the West Wing. Thankfully, one of the sainted ladies in the cafeteria took pity on me, got a bottle of soda water, and helped me try to get rid of the mess. Although I spent the rest of the day enduring laughter and brilliant comments about the still-visible stain like, "Why don't you clean that?", all was not lost. It turned out to be good luck in a way. When I walked out of the cafeteria, I bumped into one of the folks who ran the unofficial White House rumor mill. After glancing at my coat and giving me an understandably sickened look, he whispered, "What's General Haig doing over here?"

That was worth a couple of raised eyebrows. The White House Chief of Staff was not a man most of us at the bottom of the organizational chart saw very often and very rarely outside of the West Wing. My rumor buddy said that Haig had walked up the stairs to the second floor, but he didn't know where he went.

Maybe it was the shock from the starling bombing, but neither one of us came up with the obvious answer.

More than a few people have suggested, rather presumptively, in fact, that I absolutely, positively, must have known everything that was happening in Nixon's last days since we were in such proximity to the action. The truth, of course, was that most of what any of us knew outside of rumors traveled about 30 paces from the Oval Office to the Press Office, another ten paces to reporters, then to radio, TV, and newspaper outlets, and back to us. Nine times out of ten, we learned more during the day from the *Washington Post,* the *Washington Star-News,* and *WTOP* news radio than we did passing through the West Wing. So, after my pal and I failed to figure out that the most likely place for General Haig to have gone was the Vice President's office, I heard all about it on the radio. As everyone found out later, Haig had requested to see Ford that morning. He told Ford that he needed to prepare to assume the Presidency. The meeting was said to have had President Nixon's blessing.

Although I hadn't met Vice President Ford, I'd heard through the grapevine that he was a very fine man. The word was that whether you liked or disliked his stand on an issue, it was very hard not to like Gerald Ford. People I knew who had known him as the House Minority Leader said that he was approachable, truthful, and thoughtful, traits that no doubt contributed to his having made an unusually small number of enemies during more than 25 years in politics. He was a University of Michigan and Yale Law School graduate, an Eagle Scout, and, after a college football career at Michigan, received NFL offers from the Green Bay Packers and Detroit Lions. He had been overwhelmingly confirmed as Vice President by the House and Senate.

He sounded like a pretty good guy to me.

The Vice President had faithfully and very publicly defended the President against impeachment from the very beginning. After Monday's events, he said that while he had not yet reviewed the transcripts of the newly released tapes, he continued to believe that the President was innocent of any impeachable offenses. He did, however, suspend further discussion of the impeachment issue and further defense of Nixon. Despite his loyalty to the President, he had to disassociate himself from the President's troubles if he had any hope of maintaining his own credibility.

Another report arrived soon after. The *Detroit Free Press* reported that Ford's top aides had started preparing materials for him about important personnel and policy matters in anticipation that he would assume the Presidency much sooner than later.

And then there was another. This one, from the *Providence Journal-Bulletin* and the Mutual Broadcasting System, said that the President had made an irrevocable decision to resign. The paper described its source as someone in a small circle of people, including Vice President Ford, who were informed of the decision that morning. The White House wouldn't confirm the story, but neither would they deny it.

And then there was yet another blockbuster report from *Washington Post* reporters Woodward and Bernstein that may have explained why it took so long for the President to announce that he would comply with the Supreme Court's decision in *U.S. v. Nixon*. According to a White House attorney, the President had intended to defy the Court and not turn over the tapes. Had James St. Clair and other staff not convinced him otherwise, America would have had a constitutional crisis even bigger than the one it was already facing.

With explosive stories like these coming in one after another, I expected the White House to be whirring with activity early that day. Instead, at least from my vantage point, it looked and felt as empty as an elementary school on Christmas Eve. Things were so slow following my regular after-lunch Zero bar and Pepsi that instead of needing a good run up and down the stairs, I nearly fell asleep at my desk.

Things heated up a little in the early afternoon.

A rumor, later reported by UPI, circulated that David Eisenhower and Ed Cox, the President's sons-in-law, were in the West Wing. Cox was an attorney in New York and Eisenhower was a law student at George Washington University. That revelation fueled more talk that something was about to happen. I never met Ed Cox, but I played a baseball board game with David once or twice. I remember that the game was very heavy on statistics and that David excelled at playing it. He was a very nice, very smart guy and I felt sorry for what he and his family were going through.

Around 5:30 p.m. I had just finished dropping something off in the West Wing when I saw Senator Goldwater walking down the corridor with Senate Minority Leader Hugh Scott and House Minority Leader John Rhodes of Arizona. Then they disappeared, presumably into the Oval Office.

I walked to the area outside of the Oval Office where Rosemary Woods, the President's personal secretary, had an office in the hope of seeing something. Miss Woods was very sweet. There was a bowl on a table near her desk that was filled with matchbooks with "Richard Nixon" and an embossed drawing of the White House on the front and the presidential seal on the back. We had a little joke about my enthusiasm for anything emblazoned with the presidential seal, which were rarities in those days. Whenever I happened by, she'd feign a scornful look, raise her index finger, and tell me "only one" before I even got close to the matchbooks. Then, she'd smile. There was no smiling that afternoon, sadly. Having some sense of propriety, I gave her a little wave and kept walking.

Thirty minutes later, I called it a day and decided to walk through the White House, cross West Executive Avenue, and exit through the 17th Street side of the EOB. That path would put me a pretty good distance away from the demonstrators, most of whom were assembled directly in front of the White House. I wasn't worried about the people perambulating Pennsylvania

Avenue. I just didn't want to get held up in the crowd and miss my bus. It was, after all, fried shrimp night at my favorite hole-in-the-wall in Tenley Circle.

My walk through the West Wing was remarkably well-timed. I saw Senator Scott standing outside of the Oval Office door. Congressman Rhodes was in between Scott and Senator Goldwater. All three looked a little green around the gills. As it turned out, they had been summoned by the President to report on the political environment in the House and Senate. The news they shared with Nixon was not good. Goldwater was later quoted as calling the situation "very gloomy." At best, there were only 12 or 15 Senators willing to even consider acquittal, and Nixon needed 34 to remain in office. The men discussed options with the President that included a Senate trial and resignation, but not the use of the 25th Amendment, which would have allowed Nixon to step down temporarily during a trial and made Ford the Acting President.

I guess as far as Nixon was concerned it was all or nothing.

Hoping that Senator Scott might remember me, I waved to him.

Much to my surprise, he smiled, pointed his finger at me in recognition, and chuckled. Senator Goldwater smiled and gave me a little salute. That made my day and then some.

As they walked out, I continued down the corridor towards the West Wing staircase. I felt something go tap-tap on my coat sleeve. I turned to see General Haig holding a White House envelope.

"Take this to your boss," Haig said. That was confusing. It seemed like everybody was my boss.

"To whom, sir?" I asked, fighting back a whole lot of uneasiness. I regrettably slurred the "s" in "sir" and sprayed a little saliva his way.

"Senator Scott," the General shot back.

"I work for the White House, sir," I replied, pointing to the White House pass clipped on my jacket pocket.

"Then go faster," he said.

I dropped a book I was holding on a couch in the corridor and took off through the lobby. When I reached the driveway, I saw Senator Scott and company preparing to hold a press conference in front of a sea of reporters. I handed Senator Scott the envelope. The lights from the television cameras were nearly blinding, so I walked into the crowd behind them to hear what they had to say. At some point, I looked at my watch. Realizing that I was running very late, I turned around and walked as fast as I could back into the West Wing to retrieve my book and go home.

That wasn't to be, at least not immediately.

While I was leaning over to pick up the book, someone said something to me. While I was listening to what they said, one of the West Wing secretaries handed me a manila envelope with a red tag taped to it that meant "Expedite."

She told me to take it to the President.

That had never happened before.

I didn't give things to the President. I gave things to people who gave them to other people who gave them to the President.

In the wake of her spine-tingling words, I took on a hell-or-high-water determination to fulfill my mission. It was about 6:30. As I walked down the corridor, I saw that the Oval Office door was open and assumed that the President had gone to the family living quarters. I marched across the West Colonnade towards the Residence.

Just about the time I reached the Palm Room, my blood ran cold.

Did she really say President?

That's what I thought she'd said.

Then again, other words could sound like "President" depending how carefully you were listening and how the word was said. "Pleasant" could sound like "President." So could "Residence." Pronunciation made all the difference. A girl I knew from Boston told me that her mother was "foddy." I thought it was an insult until she explained that she was saying "forty."

I looked at the envelope. There was no name or destination on it. The more I eyeballed it, the faster the train inside my head traveled from moderate anxiety to full-blown, eye-bugging terror. I was starting to feel my heart beat in my ears.

I had no idea what to do, but I knew that breaking the seal and looking inside the envelope wasn't it. That was a one-way ticket to getting fired. Then again, failing to get the envelope to the right place could have had the same outcome.

So, I ran.

I literally ran back towards the West Wing to locate the secretary who had handed me the envelope. Unable to find her and seeing no other options, I marched back to the Residence and up to the EPS officer seated by the stairs to the State Floor.

"I've been instructed to deliver this directly to the President," I told him.

Skeptical is not a big enough word to describe the look on the officer's face. He just looked at me while he picked up the phone to call someone.

In less than a minute, a mountainous Secret Service agent was looming in front of me. He was so tall, in fact, that I had to look straight up about a foot to make eye contact.

I repeated that I was supposed to give the envelope to the President.

The agent laughed.

Then he said "No".

Then he put out his hand to take the envelope.

"I really have to take this to the President," I said.

"Well, you're not going to," he replied.

Reluctantly, I handed it to him. Then I went home. As I walked through the West Wing, the door to the Oval Office was closed and agents were posted in front of the door. A few years would pass until I learned that President Nixon had been inside working on his resignation speech.

I barely slept a wink that night. I was scared that I was going to get canned. The next morning, I found the lady who started the whole rigmarole. I told her that I had done my best, but that the Secret Service hadn't let me pass.

"Pass?" she asked. "Pass to go where?"

"To give the envelope to the President," I said. "That's what you told me to do."

Given the dumbfounded look on her face, I could have just as easily said that I'd mailed it to the Kremlin.

"Oh, no!" she replied. "I told you to drop it off at the Flower Shop on your way through the Residence."

I felt like a complete moron. How I got everything so weirdly confused I'll never know. While I'd have liked to find someone or something to blame for my mistake, the truth was that I didn't stop to make sure I knew exactly what the lady wanted.

The next morning, I told one of my older friends about my misadventure. I mentioned how worried I'd been and how stupid I felt.

"You're not really that stupid," he said. "You're just 19."

I have no idea what happened to the envelope I gave to the Secret Service agent. It is not impossible, however, that on his last night in the White House Richard Nixon received an order for a dozen gladiolas.

◆

The word from the White House rumor mill early Thursday morning was that President Nixon would resign on Friday or Saturday. One guy was weirdly adamant that it would be Saturday so that the President would get paid for the whole week. I heard one story that the President would go to the Capitol and resign in front of a joint session of Congress. Another had it that there would be a ceremony in which Nixon would sign a letter of resignation and then give Ford the presidential oath. The reality, of course, was that anything could happen at any time and that whatever the rumor mill said, the truth was probably something else. No President had ever resigned before. There were no precedents.

About 10:30, I was sent to the EOB with an armful of files and strict instructions to deliver them right away. Although I didn't run this time, I walked at my usual teenage speed which was always too fast to avoid collisions with other moving objects. I crossed the White House as quickly as I could and went straight to the second-floor stairs in the West Wing.

The stair rails and differences in elevation made it difficult to see someone coming up the stairs as you went down. I made it around the first flight without a hitch, but when I reached the second, the combination of my speed and angle suddenly put me literally nose to nose with the Vice President of the United States. In the split-second before a Secret Service agent moved me against the wall, I said something.

"Excuse me, Mr. President."

As history recounts, President Nixon had summoned Vice President Ford to the Oval Office to tell Ford that he would resign the next day. That's where Gerald Ford was going when we met in the stairwell.

Looking back at that moment, I could have said nothing or any of a million other things that weren't as inelegant as calling Ford "Mr. President" some 24 hours early. I was horrified with myself. There were a few people behind me in the staircase and, regrettably, my gaffe made its way to a higher-up who at the very least was having a really bad day. He said that he'd have me fired on Monday for insulting President Nixon. Despite being a well-practiced worry-wart, I didn't give the specter of being fired over something so ridiculous much thought. Besides that, it didn't look like there was going to be another Monday for the Nixon Administration anyway.

A little after noon, I snuck into the Press Room after hearing that Ron Zeigler was going to make an announcement. It was overcast and drizzling outside and the room seemed darker than normal, although it may have only felt that way. This time I was close to the front, a great thing except for having to stand on the tips of my toes to see anything. Suddenly, the television lights turned on and a second or two later Zeigler walked in and took his place behind the podium. He looked sad and exhausted. "At nine o'clock eastern daylight time tonight," he said, "the President of the United States will address the nation on radio and television from his Oval Office." Zeigler didn't take questions. He simply turned and walked out of the room.

The place went berserk.

Reporters were running for telephones or running outside to get in front of a camera. In their book *The Final Days,* Bob Woodward and Carl Bernstein reported that Robert Pierpoint asked Zeigler through an aide which President of the United States he was talking about. It was a very good question. Although I didn't hear Pierpoint myself, I do recall hearing several reporters ask the same question of one another. For all anyone knew, it could have been Ford he was talking about. Nixon could have already resigned and Ford could have already been sworn in. Even though the answer was Nixon, it wasn't something that you could simply assume anymore.

That meant that there was probably going to be a resignation speech.

The White House was deathly quiet the rest of that day. You might even say that the silence was deafening.

A few hours later, a memo was circulated that said that all non-essential personnel were to vacate the White House by five o'clock. There was no explanation why, but it didn't take a brain surgeon to figure out that the people at the top didn't want a bunch of rubberneckers hanging around.

I read the note, and after reading it once more for good measure, I concluded that they couldn't possibly mean me. No one ever told me that I was non-essential and, in the absence of that, I thought it was essential for me to stay. A friend from the National Security Council who felt as strongly about our essentialness as I did agreed to join me. Come hell or high water, we were not about to miss one of the biggest stories in American history as it literally played out around us. All we had to do was avoid getting caught. I loaded up on junk food from the vending machine around the corner, sat on the floor in the very back of the East Wing office with Tom Robbins' novel *Another Roadside Attraction,* and waited.

By 7:30, I'd had enough of hiding and decided to tempt fate by walking through the West Wing. I was surprised by the number of people milling around. They must have felt that they were essential, too.

As I walked past the Oval Office, I saw a couple of guys I knew moving furniture out of the room and into the corridor to accommodate the bulky TV equipment for the President's speech. They asked me to give them a hand. Along with one of the couches, I helped carry out the chair Vice President Ford sat in during his meeting with the President that morning. In retrospect, I can only imagine what had gone through Ford's mind when Nixon said, "You'll do a good job, Jerry." Ford had aspired to be Speaker of the House, not President. He assumed the Vice Presidency at Nixon's request because, at 61 and with little hope of having a Republican majority in the House anytime soon, he felt it would make a fine cap to his career. Sitting in that chair and realizing that he was only hours away from becoming the most powerful man on Earth must have been surreal.

For me, just holding the chair was surreal enough.

I also found it sort of disappointing.

I guess I expected it to have a tingle or a glow that let you know how special it was. There was nothing like that, of course. Despite the momentous events associated with it, it was just a piece of furniture, albeit a very nice one. Some years later, I chatted with a man who had worked with the moon rocks that were brought back to Earth by the crew of Apollo 11. He said he knew what I meant.

As I walked away, I saw a dark cover being stretched across the President's desk. It was supposed to reduce the glare from the TV lights. I was so intent on watching what was happening with the desk that I tripped over something on the rug. Luckily, I kept my balance. The next time I would be that up close and personal with the massive royal blue and golden-yellow rug was on a Saturday morning when President Ford's office was being redecorated. The Nixon rug had been rolled up and put in the Palm Room. There looked like there were enough wires and cables under it to operate the entire New York City phone system. Some of them must have been left over from the Oval Office taping system.

By seven o'clock or so, things were getting very real both inside and outside of the White House.

Outside on Pennsylvania Avenue, where there had to be more than a thousand people and horns were still blaring, a Mayflower moving van brought cheers and a round of applause from the crowd outside the fence as it slowly inched its way in front of the White House. Apparently, the guys in the van just wanted to see what was going on. At least there was a little levity somewhere. Inside the White House, there were people with tears in their eyes and booze bottles on their desks.

I met my buddy from the NSC at the door to the West Wing basement at about eight o'clock. Our plan was simple. With a little luck, we would walk up the stairs to the first floor and hide way in the back of the briefing room. Then, when the time seemed right, we would go to the front of the briefing room and find a place to watch the speech.

Until President Nixon took office, the press area had been a swimming pool that had originally been constructed for Franklin Roosevelt. There was a joke that if the questions got too tough, the President would make it a pool again...without any warning. On the lower level, *Washington Post* humor columnist Art Buchwald was playing cards with a group of Japanese journalists. I have no idea what Buchwald said to them, but whatever it was it had them all laughing like madmen.

At about 8:45, we made our move. The press room was crowded, hot, and so humid that you could cut the air with a knife. A lot of people were standing outside where it felt cooler. That opened the way for us to find a place to stand with a clear view of the sole TV set in the room, just behind a couple of rows of people seated in chairs and on the floor.

A live picture of the White House came on the screen.

Somebody yelled "Quiet!" to get the crowd simmered down.

It was less than thirty seconds to airtime.

My buddy turned to me and smiled.

Then he uttered a single, incendiary sentence.

"He's not going to resign."

Under other circumstances, that remark would have likely been laughed at, particularly if a reporter had said it. That night, however, at least a few members of the White House press corps noticed that our security badges didn't identify us in big block letters as Press. Mine said WHS, which stood for White House Staff. My friend's badge said NSC. That meant National Security Council.

The room exploded.

Suddenly, there was a lot of shoving. Bright, hot, blinding TV lights popped on and microphones were pushed in our faces.

We had the rapt attention of every journalist in the room. Connie Chung was even talking to me.

It took nearly to the instant President Nixon went on the air for us to convince everybody that it was nothing more than an ill-timed joke. A few reporters looked very disappointed that the already gargantuan story wasn't about to have an even bigger plot twist. Most, however, just walked away and took their irritation with them. There was one highly agitated woman whose face combined an evil sneer with half-open eyelids. She looked like she wanted to curl up for a nap and then kill something. If the President hadn't suddenly appeared on the screen, it might have been us.

President Nixon's speech lasted 15 minutes and 16 seconds. Except for a few remarks and some applause here and there, our fellow viewers were restrained and respectful. At the end, the camera cut from Nixon to the presidential seal. The seal, which was made of wood, was hung on a navy blue background and mounted on an easel in the Oval Office. It was laughably rudimentary by today's standards, but back in the day I thought it looked really cool.

Save for reporters getting transcripts of the speech from the Press Office staff, that pretty much wrapped up the evening. A lot of people, myself included, walked outside to get some fresh air. It was unusually cool for early August. From where we were standing, it was easy to see the lights in the West Sitting Hall and the Family Kitchen, which faced the West Wing and the EOB. Someone opened the kitchen curtain and looked down at the mob of reporters. I thought it might have been Mrs. Nixon. A network television correspondent pointed up at the window excitedly and told his cameraman to start rolling. The curtain closed and the figure vanished. Frankly, I didn't see the need for it. At that point, I thought the world should have just left the Nixon family the hell alone.

As I left, I heard the crowd chanting, "Jail to the Chief."

◆

I woke up entirely too early the next morning and arrived at work well before most Americans had downed their first cup of coffee. It couldn't have been later than 6:30. Pennsylvania Avenue was largely devoid of people, and the traffic amounted to nothing more than a few dozen cars and some suspicious-looking birds. I kept my eyes on the birds. Not that I was overly paranoid, but I didn't want a repeat of the bombing that sent my only suit to the dry cleaner's intensive care ward. I wasn't about to let them autograph the navy blazer I was wearing that morning, too.

Inside the White House everything was quiet and peaceful, so much so, in fact, that it was hard to believe that anything out of the ordinary had happened the night before. In my world, everything was the same except for deciding to have two large glazed doughnuts with my coffee that morning instead of one. I sat down at the desk in the East Wing office, picked up the *Post*, and turned on our prehistoric, Truman-era AM radio. Two songs I liked, "Rock the Boat" by the Hues Corporation and America's "A Horse with No Name", played one right after the other. The radio died later that day, unfortunately. When Elvis's rendition of "Burning Love" came on the air, the radio made a whining noise after the first few bars, started to smoke, and burst into flames. The lady who wore the big cross around her neck said it was a sign from God that I shouldn't be listening to rock 'n roll. It may also have been a sign that I accidentally spilled water on it and fried the circuits.

Not surprisingly, there wasn't much work to do that morning, and the lack of it gave the early-bird gossipers a chance to run amuck.

The first story I heard had President Nixon remaining in office using military force.

Nothing even remotely close to that happened, of course, but the lie scared the dickens out of more than a few people before it could be refuted. It also created two interesting spin-off rumors, both of which were made for the eternally naïve or perpetually stupid depending on your point of view. The first was a report that the President was on the phone with the White House Carpenter's Shop arranging to have barricades built in front of every entrance to the Oval Office, each large enough to accommodate giant machine guns. Simultaneously, the full fury of the U.S. Armed Forces would be turned on Canada to divert public attention.

The second rumor also involved the military. This one concerned me a little because, although unlikely, it was not inconceivable.

That tale had the Joint Chiefs of Staff meeting in secret to agree that they would delay any order from President Nixon to use military force for any reason. I remember thinking that if it was true, there couldn't possibly be worse news for the country. The Constitution would have been torn to shreds. On the other hand, I was concerned that it might not be true. Was there a plan to stop a distressed President from using the Armed Forces to keep himself in power? Obviously, nothing came of that rumor either. Still interested about it later on, I researched the issue. The answer to my question was "no". Short of the military refusing to cooperate or the Vice President and the Cabinet unanimously agreeing to remove the President under the 25th Amendment, there was no plan. Zero. Nothing.

The President was supposed to make a farewell address to the White House staff at 9:30 in the East Room. When I got there at a little after nine, there was only standing room left and little of it. Being skinny, I delicately squeezed my way to the back of the room where the television cameras were set up. I was lucky. The crowd grew so large that it spilled out of the East Room and stretched down the red-carpeted Great Hall in lines that were three or four people deep. On top of that, it was hot and the air was heavy with emotion. I heard that a few people fainted. It was understandable.

The Marine Band played Ruffles and Flourishes.

An announcer said, "Ladies and gentlemen, the President of the United States of America and Mrs. Nixon, Mr. and Mrs. David Eisenhower, and Mr. and Mrs. Edward Cox."

The East Room erupted in a thunderous standing ovation that lasted three and a half minutes. That's a long time for applause. It might well have gone on for an hour if the President hadn't started to speak.

Speaking without notes with his family by his side, he began by saying, "You're here to say goodbye to us. We don't have a good word for it in English. The best is au revoir. We'll see you again."

The President left me with a lot to think about that day.

He spoke about American leadership. Without it, he said, the world would "know nothing but war, possibly starvation, or worse in the years ahead." With it, he said, mankind "will know peace, it will know plenty." I had never thought about the world in quite such ominous terms before.

He talked about loss. "We think that…when we suffer a defeat that all is ended," the President said. "Not true. It is only a beginning, always. The young must know it; the old must know it. It must always sustain us."

He spoke about perspective. "Greatness comes not when things go well for you, but…when you are really tested…when sadness comes. Because only when you have been in the deepest valley can you ever know how magnificent it is to be on the highest mountain."

And, most important to me, he spoke about resilience with a story from the life of Teddy Roosevelt whose wife died when the couple was very young. "'When my heart's dearest died,' Nixon read from Roosevelt's diary, 'the light went out of life forever.' That was T.R. in his twenties," the President continued. "He thought the light had gone from his life, but he went on. And he not only became President but, as an ex-President, he served his country, always in the arena, tempestuous, strong, sometimes wrong, sometimes right…[and] that is an example I think all of us should remember." It was pretty clear that the President was talking about himself and what he hoped to do post-Presidency, but the lesson was not a bit less sound.

At the end, the Nixon family walked out of the East Room to another booming standing ovation that lasted even longer than the first one.

Way in the back of the East Room it was so crowded that it took a few minutes for me to even start wriggling my way through the crowd. Just like everyone else there, I wanted to get to the South Lawn to see the Nixons' helicopter off in Army One, the helicopter's call sign that day. The crowd was bottlenecked at the door, in part because people were letting members of the Cabinet and senior White House aides cut in line to get out first. Somehow, I managed to slip behind Treasury Secretary William Simon, and I stayed as close to him as I could without getting a restraining order. Once we made it out the door, I went down the stairs to the Center Hall, turned left, and went outside through the south door of the Visitors Foyer.

There were hundreds of people on the lawn that humid, foggy morning from the high-and-mighty down to people like me. I got as close to the Diplomatic Reception Room entrance as I could to see President and Mrs. Nixon and Vice President and Mrs. Ford walk to the presidential helicopter.

I applauded with the rest of the crowd when President Nixon enthusiastically waved goodbye and delivered his iconic two-handed "V for Victory" sign from the helicopter's doorway.

From the beginning of the President's speech the night before to his departure from the White House, the end of the Nixon Presidency was tasteful and dignified. As far as I was concerned, the United States had every right to be very proud of itself.

At exactly 10:00 a.m., the rotors started to turn and Army One rose majestically from the lawn into the misty air. It was as stunning and unforgettable a scene as anything Hollywood ever created.

I was standing with a couple of friends and a lady in her mid-to-late thirties whom I didn't know. She seemed very nice but wasn't very talkative. As the helicopter passed Constitution Avenue, however, she dove head first into a very unexpected soliloquy. President Nixon had been through tough times before, she said, and this was just one more crisis to endure. The President would prove everyone wrong in the end; he always did. The helicopter was going to turn around and come back to the White House.. In fact, it could happen almost any minute.

After the helicopter turned east towards Andrews Air Force Base and disappeared behind the Washington Monument, she sighed "Oh, well" and abruptly walked away. Clearly, she had a leak in her canoe. As strange as that interlude was, it weirded up a couple of notches when I learned that my friends had no idea who she was. What's more, none of us ever saw her again.

President Nixon and his family were on their way home to California aboard Air Force One when Secretary of State Henry Kissinger received the President's letter of resignation at 11:35 a.m. eastern daylight time. That was all that was required to close the book on the Nixon Administration. Although he would not take the oath of office until noon, Gerald Ford was already President under the terms of the 25th Amendment. I heard that the "Football," the black briefcase containing the necessary equipment for the President to initiate a nuclear attack, remained behind with Ford.

Incorrigible with curiosity, I went back into the White House through the Visitors Foyer and decided to walk to the West Wing to see what was going on. At about the time I reached the marble stairs to the State Floor, I saw that I was about to literally run into a huge problem. Leading a large contingent of people into the Center Hall from the Diplomatic Reception Room was Vice President Ford. In front of him were two Secret Service agents. As I reached ramming speed, I spun around and walked as fast as I could in the opposite direction. It must have looked like my pants were on fire.

As stupid as I must have appeared, I thought my reasoning was pretty good.

One sort-of collision with the Vice President on Thursday was an accident. Two sort-of collisions in 24 hours, unintended or not, started to look like a habit. When you tossed my "I have to deliver this to the President" moment on Wednesday into the mix, it would be easy for the Secret Service to assume that I was more like a volcanic-ash-spouting Mount Vesuvius type of problem than an annoying blackhead. Because that conclusion could permanently screw up my White House lifestyle, I wanted to avoid it at all costs.

I knew that I was an accident waiting to happen. I couldn't help myself.

In fact, with the help of a reckless lunch, a broken faucet, and really bad timing, it wouldn't be too long until I proved it to everyone's satisfaction.

Chapter Eight

DAVY CROCKETT

Thanks to a former Speaker of the House of Representatives, I was back in the far reaches of the East Room at 11:45 to see our new President take the oath of office.

Getting into the swearing-in ceremony had required much more maneuvering than I expected. First, rumor had it that there was an actual guest list, which I clearly would not have been on. Second, the crowd had very few people like me, which made blending in a problem. The Cabinet was there, of course, along with General Haig, other senior White House staff members, and their spouses. There were also a multitude of important Members of the House and Senate both past and present. Among them was the legendary John McCormack (D-Massachusetts), a Member of Congress since 1928 and Speaker of the House from 1962 to 1971. A highly respected champion of the New Deal, the Great Society, and other groundbreaking legislation, he came oddly close to becoming President twice in two consecutive days.

When President Kennedy was assassinated on November 22, 1963, Vice President Johnson was in an open convertible only three car lengths behind the presidential limousine. Johnson, in fact, was closer to the Texas School Book Depository when the shots were fired than JFK was. Had Johnson also been murdered, McCormack, as Speaker, would have been next in the line of presidential succession. Then, in the very early hours of November 23, 1963, a Secret Service agent guarding President Johnson's home in Northwest Washington heard mysterious footsteps on the grounds. Suddenly, a tall, shadowy figure came around a corner of the house. Just as the agent pulled his submachine gun to his shoulder, he came face to face with Lyndon Johnson, who hadn't notified his protective detail that he was going out for a walk. In the blink of an eye, the United States could have lost another President. If it had, the name on the White House mailbox would have been McCormack.

I saw the 82-year-old former Speaker walking towards the East Room and, just as I had done a few hours earlier with Secretary Simon, I simply fell in behind him. Nobody stopped me or asked a single question. As soon as Speaker McCormack had been comfortably seated by a naval aide, I high-tailed it back to the area where the cameras were.

Something went haywire with my body in between Nixon's departure and Ford's impending arrival, and I started to sweat up a storm, so much, in fact, that I had a slow drip off the end of my nose. Because I didn't have a handkerchief, I indelicately blotted it with the front of my tie. I had no choice. Standing next to me was a woman I didn't know who looked about as pleasant as toe fungus. She shot me a nasty, judgmental look and said, "Don't do that again. This is the White House, for God's sake!" in the sharpest, most condescending way possible. Even though she was right, I didn't appreciate it. "Oh, I understand!" I said as if I had just had a revelation. Then I wiped my nose with the back of my tie. That made her shudder a little. Clearly, she was not used to teenage boys.

The nonsense stopped when a man's voice came over the public-address system.

"Ladies and gentlemen," he said "the Chief Justice of the United States."

Everyone stood up. There was absolute silence.

Chief Justice Warren Burger who, with his white hair and black judicial robe looked like he had walked off of a Hollywood movie set, walked into the East Room and took his place behind one of two chairs on the platform where the Nixon family had stood earlier.

Then came, "Ladies and gentlemen, the Vice President of the United States and Mrs. Ford."

The standing ovation from the audience was loud and sustained to the point that the Fords looked a little overwhelmed by it all.

The Chief Justice asked the Vice President to raise his right hand and administered the oath of office. Mrs. Ford held a Bible on which the Vice President swore to protect and defend the Constitution of the United States, "So help me, God."

Then, without delay, the Chief Justice introduced Gerald Rudolph Ford, Jr. of Grand Rapids, Michigan with the words, "Ladies and gentlemen, the President of the United States."

The room exploded again in another standing ovation.

I swear that the air became lighter.

President Ford's first speech to the American people was candid and uncluttered. He began by addressing the "extraordinary circumstances" that had made him America's first unelected Chief Executive. "I am acutely aware that you have not elected me as your President by your ballots," he said, "and so I ask you to confirm me as your President with your prayers." He added that he was "indebted to no man, and only to one woman—my dear wife—as I begin this very difficult job." The President pledged to be open and honest. "In all my public and private acts as your President, I expect to follow my instincts of openness and candor with full confidence that honesty is always the best policy in the end."

He told America that "our long, national nightmare" was over and that "[o]ur Constitution works; our great Republic is a government of laws and not of men."

He asked for the country's prayers for President Nixon and his family.

Finally, he made a pledge. "I will not let you down," he said.

In front of the White House and across the street in Lafayette Park, people listening to the President on the radio reportedly broke into applause.

I read that on that very same day, a gentleman I was acquainted with sat in his office on Capitol Hill and wrote a letter to the man known as the "Father of the Constitution" who built the checks and balances safeguards into our system of government in 1787.

The letter read:

August 9, 1974

The Honorable James Madison
Sir:
It worked.
Sincerely,
Hugh Scott, United States Senator

I spent the rest of the day praying for something else big, noisy, and earth-shattering to happen. Although I didn't have a particular catastrophe in mind, I was sure that anything that kept the exhilaration of the past week alive would do. The excitement was addicting.

Had I been older and wiser, I might have realized that not everything in life had to raise your pulse and come with a side order of chaos to be significant. In fact, something momentous had already spread through the White House, which I hadn't noticed because it wasn't loud and brassy.

Life went on.

It was no small thing when you thought about it. As sad and distressed as many people had been that week, they had now gone back to work. They were making telephone calls, typing letters, and filling out their "to-do" lists for Monday. Had it not been for the blank walls in the West Wing where large, black-framed photos of President Nixon had hung, you might not have known that anything unusual had even happened. The same was true in the Residence and the East Wing. To the credit of the men and women of the Federal Government, the United States didn't miss a step.

There was one change, though, that made me scratch my head.

Inside the EPS Command Post in the East Wing, a photo of President Ford had been posted on a bulletin board in the center of the room. Below it was a handwritten sign with the letters P-O-T-U-S. Although the term is commonplace today, I had never seen it before and it took me a minute to figure out that it was an acronym for President of the United States. Unfortunately, I pronounced the "po" part of "POTUS" as "pot" instead of "poe" as in "poem." Thinking that it was some new expression, I threw it around a couple of times to be cool, only to be looked at like a moron. Not only did I mispronounce it, but I was wrong about it being new. It began as an abbreviation used by telegraph operators in the 1890s.

In the meantime, the Nixon family's personal furniture, wardrobes, and other belongings were being packed and prepared for shipping to what had been known as the Western White House. Julie and David Eisenhower, who lived in an apartment only a mile from the White House, had remained behind when President and Mrs. Nixon and Ed and Tricia Cox flew to California on Friday to oversee the process. As sad as it was to see the boxes, at least one funny story came out of it.

Since their father was no longer President, the Nixon daughters lost their Secret Service protection on Sunday night. On Monday, as I heard it, Julie rode up to the northwest gate of the White House on a bicycle. The EPS let her in through the northwest gate, and she pedaled up the driveway right to the front door of the mansion. When she left, she went out exactly the same way. On both trips, she rode right past groups of reporters who had been trying to interview her. They didn't recognize her, partly because in the five and a half years the Nixons were in the White House, no one had ever seen Julie Nixon Eisenhower dressed casually in jeans, a T-shirt, and sneakers, just like any daughter helping her mom and dad move.

At President Ford's invitation, the Eisenhowers joined the Ford family in the gallery of the House Chamber that night to hear the President's first address to Congress. As gracious as it was of the President to invite the Eisenhowers, it was equally gracious of the Eisenhowers to have accepted. It had to be very hard for them.

President Ford's speech was interrupted more than 25 times by applause that evening. The President promised to keep American foreign policy intact, declared his support for a strong U.S. military, and called on Congress to help him get the struggling, inflation-plagued U.S. economy "revved up and moving." He also made it clear that there would be "no illegal taping, eavesdropping, bugging, or break-ins in my administration." He ended it by saying, "I want to be a good President. I need your help. We all need God's sure guidance. With it, nothing can stop the United States of America."

Across the country, and even around the world, reviews of Ford's speech were uniformly good. People were impressed by what he said and how he said it. On the other hand, I heard one of the guys on the bus say that the speech didn't matter. In his opinion, people were so fed up with Watergate that they'd have cheered Ford for reading a recipe for Brussels sprouts.

About two years later, I went to see the movie version of *All the President's Men*. I was particularly interested in a scene that I saw being filmed near the corner of 17th Street and State Place across from the EOB. I was standing outside on the south side of West Executive Avenue, which was open to traffic in those days, waiting for my girlfriend to pick me up in my Pinto. I happened to look across the street and saw a telephone booth that had never been there before. I wandered over to see what was going on and ended up playing catch with some guys who were hanging around in a sea of cameras and lights. One of them was wearing a brown suit and tie. I didn't realize that he was Robert Redford until I watched the movie.

Before that day in the theater, the only person I actually knew who had ever appeared in a movie was my college friend who had made it to the big screen in *The Exorcist*. With that in mind, I nearly choked on my popcorn about a minute or so into the opening title sequence of *All the President's Men* when a scene of President Nixon landing on the Capitol grounds in Marine One dissolved into a shot of the floor of the House of Representatives. Stepping into the frame was a man announcing Richard Nixon's arrival. "Mr. Speaker," he said in a strong voice on the edge of a shout, "the President of the United States."

The man making the announcement was William "Fishbait" Miller of Pascagoula, Mississippi, the Doorkeeper of the House. I'd gotten to know Fishbait over multiple occasions when he stopped by the White House Visitors Office during the early months of the Ford Administration.

Because the President is a visitor when he comes to Capitol Hill, protocol requires that he be announced as he enters the House Chamber. At least once a year, Fishbait had a moment of fame on national television when he announced the President's arrival to deliver the State of the Union address. He had performed that task for every President since Harry Truman. He also did a lot more than simply manage admittance to the House. Fishbait oversaw a multimillion-dollar expense budget that included hundreds of House employees, pages, and the operations of the press galleries and cloakrooms. He was also a colorful character who was criticized more than once by Members of Congress for calling his old friend Gerald Ford "Jerry" after he assumed the Presidency.

The funny stories about Fishbait and his interactions with presidents, celebrities, and foreign heads of state were legion. One of the more famous tales took place in November 1951 when then-

Princess Elizabeth, the future Queen of England, and her husband, Prince Phillip, came to Washington on a whirlwind, two-day visit. When the royal couple arrived to tour the House Chamber, Fishbait greeted her with a casual "Howdy, Ma'am," instead of the infinitely more appropriate "Welcome, Your Royal Highness." Being polite, he decided to have Phillip brought to the speaker's platform where Princess Elizabeth was standing so that they could both wave to the excited crowd in the gallery. Adding to the State Department's living protocol nightmare, Fishbait called out to his staff with the immortal words, "Hey, pass me up the Prince."

The last time I saw him, he was on his way to visit President Ford. For some long-lost reason, he looked at me and said, "Well, young man, maybe I'll call you Mr. President one day."

My chest puffed out like a blowfish.

Then he added, "I didn't say President of what."

◆

The Fords moved into the White House on August 19, leaving behind the four-bedroom home they built at 514 Crown View Drive in Alexandria, Virginia in 1955. During the ten days between his taking office and taking up residence in the White House, it was common to see pictures of the President of the United States opening the door of his two-story suburban home at the crack of dawn and looking for the morning papers in his pajamas.

I had a friend whose parents lived in the President's neighborhood. Considering the hordes of police and federal agents protecting the Ford home around the clock, they liked to say that they either lived in the safest or the most dangerous neighborhood in America. The house, which is privately owned, was designated a National Historic Landmark in 1985. Coincidentally, it's only about a mile from T.C. Williams High School, which came to national prominence in the movie *Remember the Titans,* which told the story of the school's 1971 championship football team.

Fortunately, I didn't have to play a role in hauling any of the family's boxes. I did, however, run into a few things associated with their move that were out of the ordinary.

Sorting mail in the Messenger Service office in the West Wing one afternoon, I came across what looked like a bill from the local power company. It was addressed to Mr. Gerald Ford, 514 Crown View Drive, Alexandria, Virginia. The typed address had been scratched out. Next to it was a note in pencil that said, "Prez, White House." It was written next to a red hand stamp that read, "Return to Sender. Unknown Addressee." I guess even the U.S. Postal Service had to catch up with the news.

On another day, possibly even the same week, I was sitting in the East Wing Messenger Office when a guy about my age in a T-shirt sheepishly knocked on the wall and very politely asked me if I knew where he could get a certain type of wrench. He said that his motorcycle was outside and that he needed to fix something. Not thinking much about it, I suggested that he talk with one of the plumbers. When he said that he was new and didn't know where to find them, I took him to their shop. On the way, I told him that he was probably going to get into trouble if he didn't move the motorcycle soon.

"Really?" he said. "I don't know where to park it."

"I guess you'll have to put in the street," I said.

"Could it get towed?" he asked.

"It will if you don't feed the meter." I told him.

He looked very concerned.

I handed him over to one of the plumbers, wished him well, and walked away. I assumed that he was with the National Park Service and was working on the White House landscaping.

Of course, the polite kid didn't work for the National Park Service or any other government agency. He was Steve Ford, the President's 18-year-old son. The motorcycle was his. In later years, he became an actor and I'm reminded of this every time I see him in a movie. I sure hope that he didn't move his wheels and rummage between the White House seat cushions for change because of me. After that, I made it a point to carefully study the photo of the new First Family.

◆

Before I declared that August was unquestionably the most exciting month of my life, I should have waited for September. For that matter, I should have waited for October, too.

On Sunday morning, September 8, 1974, President Ford went on national television and told the American people that he was issuing a "full, free, and absolute pardon" to Richard Nixon for any crimes he committed against the United States from his in-auguration as President on January 20, 1969 to his resignation on August 9, 1974. That ended any chance of Nixon being indicted. Ford argued that it was in the best interests of the country to bring the Watergate matter to an end.

Not everyone agreed with the President. In mid-August, he had a 71% job approval rating according to the Gallup poll. When the poll was taken again the day after the pardon in September, the number had plummeted to 48%. Nearly 60% of the public thought that the pardon was wrong. The media was outraged, and the anger from people who had wanted to see Nixon on trial was hot and fiery. Only 25% of adults supported the pardon. The remaining 15% had no opinion. As a friend once pointed out, at least 10% of Americans believe they live in a different solar system anyway.

Not surprisingly, the topic of the pardon was a political flashpoint on campus that fall. More than a few Americans thought that there was some sort of quid pro quo arrangement in which Nixon would give the Presidency to Ford and Ford would pardon Nixon in return. The pardon also brought the departure of the President's new Press Secretary, respected *Detroit News* journalist Jerry terHorst, who resigned in protest over the decision after only a month on the job.

Many years later, I noticed that Ford's appointment of NBC News correspondent Ron Nessen as terHorst's replacement extended an already interesting line that connected American University alumni to the White House, the House Judiciary Committee, and television news. Nessen was an AU graduate. White House counsel John Dean earned a Juris Doctor from the law school. Larry Hogan, the first GOP member of the House Judiciary Committee to call for President Nixon's impeachment, received a master's degree from AU. Television journalist and *48 Hours* senior executive producer Susan Zirinsky, whose experiences at CBS in the early '80s were the basis for the 1987 movie *Broadcast News*, worked on stories about Watergate for the CBS News Washington Bureau in her senior year.

I was in that group, too, as an AU sophomore, although so far in the back of the bus that I was hanging onto the bumper. I did, however, climb the ladder high enough to become a "flag handerouter" at White House ceremonies for visiting heads of state.

My first assignment was during the visit of Israeli Prime Minister Yitzhak Rabin on September 10. I guess because handing out flags gave me some type of power over the crowd of government employees there to cheer and wave, somebody decided that I needed instructions. I had no idea that I looked that stupid. Right off the bat, I was told that I was not "handing out" the 4"x6" flags, but "presenting" them. My instructor literally took my wrist and showed me how I should turn my palm up to "present" a flag to someone. That was okay. It was even okay when I was cautioned not to hand anyone a flag upside down, presumably because they wouldn't be able to figure out to hold it by the long wooden pole. But when the topic turned to safety tips for handling the rubber bands holding the bundles of flags together, I laughed so hard that I nearly blew out a kidney. By some miracle, I kept my job. I was, however, given a stern warning not to be a "smarty pants."

I wasn't the only one having a weird day that Tuesday. As the Prime Minister's car approached the South Portico, trumpets blared, and the President and Mrs. Ford were announced.

"Ladies and gentlemen," the announcer said, "the President of the United States of America and Mrs. Nixon."

As awkward as it was, the Fords never batted an eye.

◆

The word around the Residence was that the Fords were extremely nice people. It was an understandable relief to the staffers I knew, all of whom had liked the Nixons and were sad to see them go. The story was much the same in the rest of the White House. Many Nixon political appointees were still there well into October based on the President's insistence that people weren't going to be put out on the street until they had time to find a new job. Even Rosemary Woods was still there, working on former President Nixon's papers in what had been his hideaway office in Room 180 of the EOB. It also got around that the President wouldn't let one of the butlers mop up something that Liberty, the Ford family's new golden retriever, left on the floor of the First Family's dining room. The President was quoted as saying that no one should ever have to clean up after somebody else's dog.

On September 19, the Fords graciously held a picnic for the entire White House staff on the South Lawn. I had a class that day, and the second it was over I sprinted to the bus stop, praying that I'd get there before they ran out of food. The menu, according to my pals in the kitchen, included hot dogs, baked beans, potato salad, coleslaw, and ice cream which, as far as I was concerned, covered all of the major food groups.

There couldn't have been a better day for it. The weather was warm and sunny, and the scene was as wholesomely American as it possibly could be. The Marine band was playing, the smell of hot dogs was floating in the air, and red-white-and-blue bunting decorated almost everything. The President, Mrs. Ford, and their daughter, Susan, even threw around a frisbee. Although the President had to leave after 30 minutes or so to attend a luncheon on Capitol Hill, he came back to the South Lawn about 45 minutes later to circulate in the crowd and shake more hands.

When I arrived, I followed my nose through the West Wing and out to the South Lawn through the Palm Room. No sooner did I step out than I found myself once again face to face with Gerald Ford. It was the first time I'd been that close to the President without risking an assault charge. That alone made it a special moment.

Because the meeting was very unexpected, I was forced into making a lightning-fast decision. I could either speak with the lightly perspiring President or get a hot dog and a plateful of baked beans. I'm still a little surprised at myself for choosing the President. We shook hands and had a very nice, brief chat next to a tree adjacent to the Palm Room door. He asked me my name and what I did. Ever the shy type, I asked him how he liked being President. He smiled and said that he was enjoying it.

That was about it.

I wanted to tell President Ford about something odd that had come for him in the mail, but I didn't have time. The President had people to see and things to do and so did I. After shaking hands again, we went our separate, appropriate ways. Gerald Ford went back to running the most powerful nation on Earth and I went looking for potato salad.

◆

A few days before the picnic, an inter-office envelope arrived in the Messenger Office with my name on it. That was unusual to begin with, and I ripped the envelope open out of curiosity. Had I known what was inside, I would have opened it with kid gloves.

The contents were inconceivable.

Inside was a semi-crumpled manila mailing envelope with a patchwork quilt of cancelled stamps across the top and a hand-written return address somewhere in the Midwest on the upper left-hand side. There was no insurance stamp, no return receipt, no registered mail markings, or anything else that would have created a chain of custody from sender to recipient. It was simply addressed to The President, The White House, Washington, D.C.

The mailing envelope had already been opened. I reached inside the package and took out a book that was maybe 5"x8" with a worn, thin black leather cover and the scent of an old house. It looked homemade.

There wasn't anything on the cover to identify the book, but there was a handwritten note lying on top. It simply said, "Dear Mr. President, would you please sign this?"

I opened the book to the first page. The paper was a little warped and crinkly and faded. There were hand-drawn, slightly uneven horizontal lines from top to bottom. The pages were unevenly sized and may have been hand-stitched together. It was an old autograph book. To the best of my recollection, John Quincy Adams had been the first to sign it.

I turned the pages. I blinked a few times to be sure I wasn't seeing things.

I was holding a book with the autographs of every single American president since 1825. As far as I could tell, they were even in chronological order. Interspersed here and there were the signatures of other famous figures. Vice President John C. Calhoun, General Winfield Scott, Secretary of State Henry Clay, and Senator Daniel Webster were represented. So was newspaper editor Horace Greeley, Senator Stephen A. Douglas, and General Douglas MacArthur, among many others. Some of the signatures were faded and illegible, while a few of the oldest ones were still vibrant.

I hovered over the autographs of three men I considered far larger than life.

The first belonged to David Crockett. Dynamite couldn't have dislodged me from my seat in front of the TV when NBC broadcast Disney's *Davy Crockett, King of the Wild Frontier* in the early '60s. I didn't just like Davy Crockett, I wanted to be Davy Crockett.

President Kennedy's was the second. I remembered my mother taking me with her to the voting booth on Election Day in 1960. I was five years old. I was eight when my third-grade teacher told us that he had been assassinated. He was a war hero. He rallied us to go to the moon. He saved us from nuclear war. His death turned the world upside down. His signature was the only one in blue ink.

The third was Abraham Lincoln. The President who saved the Union. The Great Emancipator. One of the most significant figures in human history.

I sat at the desk and looked at every one of the signatures for more than an hour, admittedly running my finger very gently over the ink strokes Crockett, Kennedy, and Lincoln had left behind. Why I felt such a spark about the autograph book and nothing about the chair in the Oval Office, I don't know. All I know is that the collection took my breath away. Simply knowing that these three men's hands had touched the book gave me chills.

I eventually unraveled the mystery of why the book had been forwarded to me. One of the West Wing messengers knew that I was obsessed with American history. He just thought I might like a peek at it. That was it.

As much as I loved the book, the responsibility of having it in my possession scared me to death. With mixed emotions, I put it back in the envelope and took it to one of President Ford's secretaries. She was rushed and told me to put it on top of a pile of other papers on her desk. That was the last I saw of it. By the time it would have presumably been sent to President Carter in 1977, the White House was no more than a speck in my rearview mirror.

As spectacular as the people who autographed the pages were, I've always thought that the tale of how the signatures were collected had to be the more intriguing story. The owner's faith in the U.S. Mail to deliver the book without any safeguards was astonishing in itself, not to mention his belief in the integrity of the White House personnel that handled it.

Not surprisingly, I've wondered about the fate of the book for a long time. Because I didn't have the presence of mind to write down the name of the sender in 1974, I searched old books and newspapers for anything that might have been written about the autograph book or could lead me to where or how it might have originated. If nothing else, I learned that autograph collecting was a popular hobby in the 19th century and that what set this book apart was that the signatures were in consecutive order on lined paper instead of individual album pages or collected from letters. Collecting and hunting autographs was particularly popular in Washington, and what tied most, if not all, of the signatures together was that the individuals involved all spent time in the Nation's Capital. That's even true of Davy Crockett, who served in Congress.

Although I didn't find a complete description of what I saw, I pieced together a few possibilities.

On August 24, 1899, the *Akron Beacon Journal* told the story of a Miss Florence Steele of Columbus, Ohio, who was receiving a "wedding gift of rare value...a small volume containing the autographs of many prominent men of former days, including Calhoun, Clay, John Quincy Adams, Daniel Webster, William Henry Harrison, and others." Miss Steele, who became Mrs. Edward Beck, was related to General William Tecumseh Sherman and James G. Blaine, who narrowly lost the Presidency to

Grover Cleveland in 1884. Her grandfather had been a member of William Henry Harrison's Cabinet in 1841. The Becks' honeymoon was to include a stop in Washington to get the autograph of President McKinley, who was noted as "a warm, personal friend." Edward Beck died in 1917. Florence Steele Beck died in Chicago in 1945, and the couple's only child died in Ohio in 1971. The return address for the book in 1974 was in the Midwest. Edward Beck, coincidentally, was said to be a "ready letter writer" and a "constant correspondent." Perhaps some of his correspondence included autograph requests.

The *Evening Star* in Washington, D.C. reported on October 28, 1893 that "One of the finest collections of autographs by American statesmen is owned by Mr. Arthur Simmons, who is doorkeeper for Mr. Thurber at the White House...his opportunities to meet great men have been unsurpassed. Few of them have been unwilling to give up their signatures as toll at the door." The article also mentioned a Colonel Crook, the "cashier of the White House" who had been there since Lincoln's time and was known to have a collection that included the signatures of nearly every President. The autograph book could have been passed down by another White House doorkeeper or aide to either or both men and the work continued by their descendants.

The most surprising possibility is that it might have originally been put together by a kid. On January 3, 1888, the *Washington Critic* carried an article stating that Capitol Hill pages made "quite a lot of pocket money each session in collecting autographs." The article described how pages in the Senate, the House, and the Supreme Court would swap a book back and forth to collect the signatures of all of the Senators, Congressmen, and Supreme Court Justices. Then, they would give it to one of the Senate's riding pages who were constantly going between the Capitol, the White House, and the executive departments. The riding page, as in riding a horse, would then get the autographs of the President and the Cabinet. The usual price for this service in 1888 was said to be $10 or roughly $250 today. It's certainly possible that some of the pages specialized and collected only the specific autographs a customer wanted.

In casual conversation one day, I mentioned the book to an autograph dealer and asked him what he thought it might be worth. His answer was "A lot less than you might think." He believed it would be hard to display and would require expensive restoration. That surprised me.

As far as I was concerned, it was a priceless artifact. In fact, it was magical.

◆

About a week after the picnic, Mrs. Ford went to Bethesda Naval Hospital in Maryland for a routine medical examination. Doctors discovered a suspicious lump in her right breast that had not been evident in an examination several months earlier. The next day, Friday, September 28, surgeons took a biopsy of the lump and determined that it was cancerous. They immediately performed a radical mastectomy. Fortunately, the surgery was successful. Like everyone else in the White House, I was sad that she was ill. President Ford, who was reportedly choked with emotion, flew to the hospital on Marine One through a driving rainstorm to be with his wife when she came out of surgery. I remember more than a few of the single women I worked with saying, "That's the kind of husband I want."

I liked Mrs. Ford. She was a pistol. She became a voice and a role model for millions of women across the country. Outspoken about many of the most politicized issues of the '70s, she was also friendly and said to be a little mischievous. I spoke with her perhaps a half-dozen times. Like the President, she wanted to know your name and something about you beyond the department you worked in. There was no haughtiness or any patronizing "Nice to see you," or "How are you?" baloney that came out of the mouths of some well-known people I came across. She was warm-hearted and very cool, which was inevitably among the reasons some 40,000 Americans sent cards, letters, postcards, and telegrams to the White House to wish her a speedy recovery. Among them was a note from the 90-year-old daughter of President Theodore Roosevelt, Alice Roosevelt Longworth, who wrote, "Just a line to wish you well from one who a number of years ago had the experience you just had."

It was very fitting that Mrs. Longworth wrote to Betty Ford for a variety of reasons, not the least of which was that Alice may have been the only 20th century resident of the White House who was more of a firebrand than Mrs. Ford. President Roosevelt was famously quoted as saying about teenage Alice, "I can either run the country or I can attend to Alice, but I cannot possibly do both." The beautiful First Daughter racked up betting losses, took her pet snake, Mabel, to social events, smoked cigarettes on the White House roof, and did almost everything proper young women weren't supposed to do in 1900. She was a worldwide celebrity with a wicked wit who suggested that President Calvin Coolidge looked like he had been "weaned on a pickle." An embroidered pillow in her Washington home told guests, "If you haven't got anything nice to say about anyone, come and sit here by me."

As big of a news story as Mrs. Ford's mastectomy was, the First Lady's openness about it made it into a much bigger deal with huge, positive effects. Even in 1974, cancer wasn't something that people talked about very often, much less specific issues like breast cancer. I certainly didn't know anything about it. In some circles, the topic was considered so distasteful that it was taboo. Many women over the years had kept their breast cancer a secret, and millions more died because they didn't know they had cancer until it was too late. Former child movie star Shirley Temple Black broke ground as the first nationally known figure to discuss her mastectomy in a special press conference held in her hospital room in November 1972. In the aftermath of Mrs. Ford's 1974 surgery, the American Cancer Society reported that it was overwhelmed with requests for information. Hospitals and doctors' offices reported huge increases in appointment requests.

Mrs. Ford also helped to bring drug and alcohol addiction out of the shadows when she spoke out about her own dependence on alcohol and prescription medications. She voluntarily entered treatment in 1978. Mrs. Ford co-founded the non-profit Betty Ford Center, a chemical dependency recovery facility, now known as the Hazelton Betty Ford Center. It opened in 1982 on the campus of the Eisenhower Medical Center in Rancho Mirage, California. Mrs. Ford regularly visited with patients one on one to offer empathy and moral support. She didn't retire as chairwoman of the board of directors until she was 86.

On October 11, I stood out on the South Lawn with a hundred or more other White House staffers to welcome Mrs. Ford home. As Marine One landed, people held up signs that said, "We love you" and "It was lonely around here without you." It was heartfelt. Liberty joined the Ford family while she was away and, when the

First Lady knelt to give her a hug, the dog liberally licked her face. That brought a ripple of laughter from those of us who were close enough to witness it. Being a beagle man myself, I didn't know much about golden retrievers. But I do remember thinking that Liberty looked awfully big for only eight months old.

With a new Chief Executive focused on the sea of problems facing the country, the White House was a much busier place than usual. The workload became so heavy that even I heard serious grumbling from the secretarial staff. One of the secretaries, who had known President Ford when he was in the House of Representatives, said that someone needed to tell him that they were overloaded. She said that the President would "have it stopped." Complaining to the President of the United States of America that you had too much work to do and expecting him to do something about it sounded pretty irrational to me. When I said something helpful and optimistic like "I doubt it," another secretary roared into the conversation with a forceful "Oh, no! He'll fix it!" and gave me a dirty look for doubting her.

I didn't think much more about it, but I was convinced that their elevators didn't go all the way to the top floor.

I don't know for sure what happened, but secretarial help arrived from other White House offices a few days later. When I dropped off mail one afternoon, the ladies who said the President would take care of their problems were grinning like Cheshire cats. One of them had made a little sign just for me. It said, "We told you so!" I may not have been the sharpest knife in the drawer, but I wasn't dumb enough to ignore the possibility that the most powerful man in the world had intervened. I started to regularly take them cookies.

There were other big events in October.

The Watergate cover-up trial of five top Nixon aides and *The Texas Chainsaw Massacre*, one of the most famous horror movies of all time, both opened on October 1. Some people thought they were the same thing.

The Senate Appropriations Committee reported that former President Nixon's transition to private life was costing taxpayers $7,350 a day, or the equivalent of $37,000 a day in current dollars. That did not go over well with the public. At the same time, the former President's lawyers asked Judge John Sirica to quash subpoenas ordering Nixon to testify in the Watergate cover-up trial due to illness. The former President had been hospitalized for thrombophlebitis, an inflammation of the veins in his left leg, and a blood clot. Six hours after emergency surgery to remove a blood clot in Nixon's thigh, he went into shock from internal bleeding. Although his vital signs were stable after a blood transfusion, he remained on the critical list as the month ended.

Mail started to show up for a guy named Dick Cheney, the Deputy Assistant to the President for White House Operations. Cheney, of course, later became U.S. Secretary of Defense and Vice President of the United States. I spoke with him at a reception about 20 years later and proudly mentioned that we had worked together in the White House. He said that he didn't remember me at all.

Happy Rockefeller, the wife of Vice-President-designate Nelson Rockefeller, had a double mastectomy two weeks after Mrs. Ford's surgery and spoke widely about her treatment as well. President Ford had nominated Rockefeller, the former Governor of New York, to succeed him on August 20. At the time, his confirmation was stuck in political mud. Rockefeller, the grandson of Standard Oil founder John D. Rockefeller whose wealth was estimated at nearly $400 billion in 2017 dollars, was finally confirmed in December.

I shook hands with "Rocky", as he was known, as he passed from the Oval Office to the press briefing room on the day he was nominated. Still thinking that the Vice Presidency was cool, I tried to get a job in his office. Despite making it clear that I would have run over my grandmother to be on the Vice President's staff again, it never worked out. Nonetheless, I got to know his secretary, Ann Whitman. She and Rosemary Woods were friends, although I had no idea what the connection was. Chatting with Mrs. Whitman on the phone one day, I casually asked what she had done before she went to work for Governor Rockefeller.

"Oh, I worked here," she said very matter-of-factly.

"Oh, what did you do?" I asked, equally matter-of-factly.

"I was President Eisenhower's personal secretary," she replied.

Stunned into uncharacteristic silence, I could hear the blood drain out of my face. Suddenly, however, the connection between Ann Whitman and Rosemary Woods made sense. When Ike was in the Oval Office, Miss Woods had been Vice President Nixon's secretary

"Gee, that was a long time ago," I said tactlessly.

As nice as Mrs. Whitman was, I don't think those words helped my candidacy much.

Along with everything else, the November elections were coming up. In the wake of Watergate and the Nixon pardon, high inflation, and a deep recession, the GOP was expected to lose a lot of seats in the House and Senate. That put President Ford in the eye of the storm to rally Republican voters.

It also created a lot of chatter about the President's incredible stamina among the guys I knew in their late fifties and sixties.

The President was 61. It wasn't uncommon to hear that he'd had breakfast at seven in the morning, worked all day, boarded Marine One for Andrews Air Force Base in the late afternoon, flew off to a campaign event in Air Force One, gave a speech, shook hands with well-wishers, and then flew back to Andrews, landing on the South grounds by helicopter at midnight. He might stay in the White House the following day but go back on the road the next. At 19, with the equipment nature gave me hardly out of the box, the schedule the old guys called grueling didn't sound bad to me at all. When I said that, one of them shot me the bird. Now that I'm that age, I understand why.

◆

Even though it was October and the weather was turning chilly, I continued to wear my oyster-colored poplin suit on a regular basis. My wardrobe, such as it was, had to last through as many seasons as possible. To stay warm, I often put on a sleeveless sweater under the jacket, which had barely survived the gross, disgusting White House bird bombing in August. The dry cleaner, who shot me a "you must be kidding" look when I brought it in, had done a very good job despite not liking me very much. I had a bad habit of putting food in my suit pockets at lunchtime when I was starving, in a hurry, and needed to use my hands to carry other things. Occasionally, a hot dog wrapped in aluminum foil and topped with relish, onions, and mustard would leak and leave my trouser or jacket pocket in rough condition. On top of the extra work required, I'm sure that the cleaner had to be happier than hell that I always came in with a discount coupon from the paper. No matter what dry cleaning chemicals he used, the suit always retained a slight fast food aroma. People sometimes said that they got hungry whenever I walked by.

On Saturday, October 12 I was on the run, possibly because I was the only messenger working in the East Wing that day and the West Wing was a beehive of activity. By the time lunch came around, I was famished and hustled over to the Roy Rogers Restaurant on New York Avenue to grab a roast beef sandwich, fries, and some coleslaw to go. When I got back to my desk, I took off my suit jacket, threw it on a chair, and dug into the food. As much as I hate to admit it, I often ate recklessly. That day, I was eating in gulps and washing the food down my esophagus with cascades of Pepsi.

In the mayhem, some of the juicy roast beef ended up on my left pants pocket. I went to the men's room to rinse out the stain and wash my hands, which were sticky with ketchup from the feeding frenzy. The faucet was broken. I said to hell with it, wiped my hands with toilet paper, and went back to work. Later, I was sent to pick something up in the West Wing.

As I passed through the Residence, something large and fluffy hit me near the Diplomatic Reception Room door. My jacket was uncharacteristically unbuttoned and whatever I collided with was tugging at my pants and noodling its way into my left pocket.

I don't remember who was walking Liberty at the time, but whoever it was couldn't have been more apologetic. Being a dog, Liberty had simply followed her nose to the beefy smell I was giving off. There was no harm done. I petted her. She licked my face. Then we went our separate ways. That was it.

It wasn't until I got back to the East Wing office that I realized that something was wrong. My pocket was sliced and the tear ran down the seam from the pocket to the top of my knee. None of the damage was Liberty's fault. The suit had been slowly disintegrating for at least a month. When I got home, I had no choice but to throw the pants away.

The next week, I went to the Sears store near my apartment on Wisconsin Avenue and bought new flare-bottom trousers that sort of went with the jacket. I remember that the pants nearly did me in financially. They were $6, not including tax. I told the other guys in the Messenger Office about it on Monday. Norwood laughed so hard that he nearly passed out.

On Thursday, October 17, President Ford voluntarily testified before the House Judiciary Committee's sub-committee on criminal justice in an open, televised hearing. It was said to be the first documented appearance before a committee of Congress by a sitting President in American history. The President personally assured Congress and the American people that there had been no deal involved with his pardon of President Nixon. He testified that President Nixon had considered pardoning himself and others involved in the Watergate scandal. Ford also said that he granted the pardon to the former President on the condition that he would accept it. As the basis for his decision, President Ford cited a 1915 Supreme Court decision that inferred that accepting a pardon is equivalent to admitting guilt.

The next morning, I woke up with a start, looked at the clock, and panicked. I had overslept. That was bad. Worse, I was going to have to forego breakfast to make it to the bus stop on time. Far worse than that, a large family of acne had staked a claim on my chin during the night. By the time I finally got to the White House, I didn't even get my usual late-morning glazed doughnut and cream-and-sugar-filled coffee.

None of these, of course, were towering predicaments or even small problems for that matter. They were a bunch of nothing.

Nevertheless, I felt compelled as a teenager to mire in unwarranted misery until I ate or the acne went away, whichever came first.

At about 11:30, I decided to take advantage of a lull in the work day and drag my sorry self to an early lunch. Chocolate pudding was on my mind that day, and the only place I knew that had it was the EOB cafeteria. On my way, I stopped by the Oval Office to say hello to the EPS officer stationed there and take my daily look at the nerve center of American power through the open door. The officer was a very nice man and, as much as I liked to hang around that part of the West Wing, I also liked chatting with him. That day we talked about football. He was a New York Giants fan and they were playing Washington that Sunday at RFK Stadium. We frequently bet on games for bragging rights, even though we each thought the other was criminally obnoxious in victory.

Just as I was opening the throttle on my trash-talk about New York's 1-4 record, the officer flew out of his chair. I thought he was coming to choke me.

Then, I realized that he'd seen something. He lunged toward the Oval Office door and started to close it.

To say that I was startled would have been the understatement of the year. I froze like a deer in the headlights.

Coming through the back door of the Oval Office from the south driveway was President Ford, returning from a speech he had delivered at the Labor Department. The wind was kicking up and some golden autumn leaves blew in through the doorway. The President picked up something on his desk, read it, and fired off a four-letter word.

Things were moving at high speed. Maybe five seconds had passed. Maybe six.

As the door closed, President Ford looked straight at me. He raised his hand in what looked like a motion to come in.

I had no idea what to do.

If I went in, the Secret Service might arrest me. Maybe I'd lose my job.

Then again, maybe I wouldn't. Then again, maybe the President wasn't gesturing to me at all.

I felt my throat tighten. My heart thumped in my head.

Worst case, I was pretty sure nobody would eat me.

With that, I rolled the dice. I walked into the Oval Office.

It turned out to be quite a day. But that's another story for another time.

EPILOGUE

In 1843, a Danish philosopher by the name of Soren Kierkegaard wrote that

"Life can only be understood backwards; but it must be lived forwards."

I was in high school when a particularly erudite instructor sprang that on our English class one afternoon. Having very little life to look back on then, and probably a little slow on the uptake to boot, I didn't get it at the time.

Now, I think I do.

If you want to make better decisions in the future, study the decisions you made and experiences you had in the past. Look for the themes that have made your life successful or less productive than you would like it to be.

Writing this book gave me a wonderful opportunity to look backwards myself. I saw that most of the time I've taken the road poet Robert Frost called "the one less traveled by." I've done some things in reverse, a couple upside down, and others sideways.

Here are a few things I learned:

1. Listen to your critics, but consider their motivations. Some people really want to help you in life by pointing out problems you may have not considered or suggesting alternative routes that help you avoid problems altogether. Sincere souls are usually easy to identify. They don't serve their advice with a side order of pain.

There are other critics, of course, who are simply judgmental. They're usually easy to identify too. They're insensitive. They jump to overly critical conclusions about others. They want to make you feel like roadkill.

Hold on to the sincere people and mull over what they say. Avoid the judgmental creeps like the plague.

2. When you take risks, don't depend on good luck. Life is filled with so many things that can go awry that there's even a term for it. Murphy's Law states that "whatever can go wrong, will go wrong." That's important to remember when someone suggests that you risk something, like leaving the safety of a current job for a new one.

If they're well-intentioned, what they really mean is for you to take a calculated risk. In other words, do your research and weigh your likelihoods of failure and success before you make a move.

If they don't have your interests at heart, what they mean is for you to dive in blindly and hope that everything will somehow work out. The only thing I've ever seen that's more inconsistent than good luck is getting edible food on an airplane.

3. Read a lot. This is the most obvious conclusion of all. People who read a lot know more than those who don't. They write better, think better, have better imaginations, form better opinions, and are more interesting. They're usually funnier. I'd like to say that avid readers are all taller and better-looking too, but I can't really back that up.

4. Look for the moral in every story. In mine, it's this: don't be afraid to take calculated risks, remember that they can't eat you, and walk into an Oval Office every now and then even if you're not sure you're invited. It builds character. Or makes you a character. One of those.

Made in the USA
San Bernardino, CA
24 November 2017